LUCKY JIM

LUCKY JIM

JAMES HART

FOREWORD BY CARL BERNSTEIN

CLEiS
PRESS

Published in the United States by Cleis Press, an imprint of Start Midnight, LLC, 101 Hudson Street, Thirty-Seventh Floor, Suite 3705, Jersey City, NJ 07302.

Printed in the United States.
Cover design: Scott Idleman/Blink
Cover photograph: Courtesy of Peter Simon Photography
Text design: Frank Wiedemann

First Edition.
10 9 8 7 6 5 4 3 2 1

Trade paper ISBN: 978-1-62778-214-2
E-book ISBN: 978-1-62778-215-9

Library of Congress Cataloging-in-Publication Data is available on file.

The Keys of the Kingdom by A.J. Cronin (Copyright © A.J. Cronin, 1941) Reprinted by permission of A.M. Heath & Co Ltd.

The Keys of the Kingdom by A.J. Cronin (Copyright © A.J. Cronin) Reprinted by permission of Hachette Book Group.

"Ballad of the Long-Legged Bait" By Dylan Thomas, from THE POEMS OF DYLAN THOMAS, copyright ©1943 by New Directions Publishing Corp. Reprinted by permission of New Directions Publishing Corp.

"Fern Hill" by Dylan Thomas, from THE POEMS OF DYLAN THOMAS, copyright ©1945 by The Trustees for the Copyrights of Dylan Thomas. Reprinted by permission of New Directions Publishing Corp.

Carly Simon lyrics – courtesy of Carly Simon

For Eamon

FOREWORD

To my mind, the memoir is the most problematic and unforgiving of non-fiction forms for both author and reader: To succeed it requires authenticity, unsparing honesty (but not overloaded by bathos or self-pity), near-perfect pitch, a compelling story (free of self-indulgence in conception) and, usually, a quiet sense of irony. Without those elements, tuned in harmonious balance, satisfaction eludes the tale, both for writer (as many of us have learned) and reader. My friend Jim Hart has written a remarkable and brave memoir— and he has done the most difficult work of all: used the experience of writing it to come to understand himself. In the process, the reader is the beneficiary of a beautifully wrought story of a life lived in revelation. That Jim has been a seminarian, poet, and insurance agent (and spent twenty years married to Carly Simon) contributes to the fact.

Struggle, of course, is at the heart of memoir, at least the great ones. Without it—and the ability to stare fear in the face, including the defeats and to find meaning therein—the spine of the project collapses.

For many years, I was witness to parts of Jim Hart's stunning and harrowing tale, so wonderfully told in these pages. And then one day I wasn't. He disappeared. Twelve months later, I got a phone call from Jim. He had been living a secret life. I was surprised—and then I wasn't. "A twelve-step program guru with twenty-one years of sobriety," as he writes, he had turned to crack cocaine to stop the pain—but not the revelation.

"I had been a bit of a magician in the lives of many people and yet I had lost the magic myself. I had delivered the deep belief I had in recovery to them, and they had watched me deal with my own addiction, my son's handicap, my loses, and my unusual life around fame, and now, in spite of my best efforts, I had lost the battle."

There are two other characters who define the arc of this narrative: Carly, the singer, Jim's wife for twenty years when he disappeared; and, even more so, Eamon Hart, his beloved son from a previous marriage (to another marvelous woman) born with a serious seizure disorder that resulted in profound disabilities. Jim's love for Eamon, and Eamon's for his father, is the touchstone of Jim Hart's life—and his story. And the gift of revelation.

Lucky Jim is not a clichéd or sentimental book. It looks unsparingly, doesn't blink. It's not a book of answers but rather the response to a complex man in a truly complicated life, and how he barely survived it.

This is not a father and son story, but it is. This is not a spiritual story, but it is. This is not an addiction story, but it is, not the story of parenting a disabled child, but it is, not the story of fame, but it is, not the story of gay and straight.... but it is. As Edna O'Brien has noted, Jim is a "serious and observant witness of the amazing narrative of [his own] life." It is a life that has never strayed far from goodness (though the narrator might sometimes argue otherwise) even as it has rubbed against hellish circumstance.

Happily for the reader, Jim is capable of expressing matters in both lyrical and plainspoken voice, a tough trick. Ultimately, his is a memoir about love and the nature of love.

The best memoirs take us on a journey of pursuit and struggle and passion—to find oneself. From the train ride of the opening Chapter, Jim Hart's "Lucky Jim." rivets the reader as it hurtles down the track: There is grace, crack, straight sex, gay sex, bold-face names, heartbreak, and triumph in almost impossible circumstances—the kind of life-stuff that suggests we are in for a major ride, and then delivers. Throughout, the character of the author and the indelible portraits of those he loves most—difficult and beautiful characters all—carry a rare and special tale along a breathtakingly perilous route. At its destination, we emerge much the luckier—and inspired—for having been aboard. And there is revelation.

—Carl Bernstein

CHAPTER

ONE

---◆---

I HAD TAKEN THIS trip so many times, it felt as if I should be collecting the tickets. I first rode the New York Central when they still had those elegant old trains like the Lake Shore and the Twentieth Century Limited. The train disappeared, and a moment later light swept across the Hudson. It reemerged gleaming: a silver ribbon speeding up the eastern bank of the river.

I wasn't going to make this trip at all, but Alannah, my ex-wife, insisted. She had badgered me all week until I agreed. Eamon, our son, was going to be in an equestrian event for handicapped kids in Chatham, New York, near Hudson, thirty miles southeast of Albany.

It had been ten years, and I still couldn't handle his disability and its worst symptom. It often began with a moan, followed by *Oh No!* but mostly it began in silence. Around three in the morning, the first spasm would begin, and all I could do was hold him. I prayed to God and anyone I thought I knew in a heaven that didn't exist, or I would curse at Him, screaming, *You mother fucker,* but no one ever seemed to hear. I held Eamon and told him how much I loved him. With each jerk of his body, I tried to remind myself that this was not about me. It wasn't just the seizures that were so difficult; it was everything. The last time I had him, as the door of my Stuyvesant Town apartment closed, he'd ripped off his pants to reveal that his underwear and thighs were smeared in his own shit. It took all my strength to hold him under the spray of the shower. He wasn't fond of forced cleanliness. Next came giving him an enema to avoid a repeat of the accident. Then he sat on the toilet and unloaded, and I listened as he gleefully shouted, *Poopies!* His forced laughter accompanied each splash, and I smiled for his sake, but I couldn't stand seeing him so debased.

He barely spoke. There were some nouns but hardly ever a verb, and he was ten years old. He could never tell me what he was thinking or feeling: the hardest part of caring for him. When nervous, he would place his hand below his nose and rapidly move it back and forth. The gesture evoked the state of a large injured crane moving its wing, yet unable to fly. He would never take flight, and I couldn't bear the energy expended on his behalf. In the end, he would still be severely handicapped: an injured bird ever flapping.

He always carried a toddler's toy that made realistic farmyard sounds. With a pull on the cord, a plastic arrow would spin in a circle. Various animals were depicted on the circumference, and whatever animal the arrow pointed to would make a sound: the cow would moo, the pig oink, and the sheep baa. During his visits, all Eamon wanted was to play with this toy, but he couldn't pull the string himself. If he could, I would have put him in the bedroom, closed the door and let him spin away. Instead, I was held captive weekend after weekend by endless hours of mooing, oinking, neighing, barking, meowing, and bleating. Every time I tried to rest, he would plead with me and use one of his few verbs: *spin.*

Just when I thought I would lose all control, when I thought I couldn't take another second, he would cross the room, loop his arm around my neck and say, *I love you Daddy Jim.* He would break my heart in two or three new places and allow me to go on.

Alannah picked me up at the Hudson station, and we drove through the rolling hills of Columbia County. I felt my usual apprehensions, but because I was only staying for a couple of hours, I didn't have to worry about being alone with Eamon for the entire weekend. I inhaled deeply when I saw him, to steel myself. His handicaps took precedence over everything, and I would have to abandon my construction of the world and enter his reality of tedium and mindless repetition.

By the time we arrived at the stables, he was already seated on a large black horse. He wore jodhpurs, a turtleneck, and a black-velvet riding helmet. He looked handsome and relaxed, and his problems weren't easily detected up there. As I approached, he said, *Hi Dad! Who's here?* He laughed and covered his mouth, as if a strange creature might emerge. He waited a second and then repeated, *Hi Dad! Who's here?* I looked up and shouted, *Eamon's here.*

He clapped his hands frantically, as if to say, *You should be really proud of me.* It didn't matter that a guide was leading him around the ring.

For the first time I had something I could hold onto. It felt as if most of my life with him had been spent feeding him, cleaning him, giving him enemas, or holding him while he flailed and convulsed.

The few hours passed quickly. Alannah and I were in no rush to let go of this feeling. We lingered and chatted about other things: her other children, our parents, work, and our latest loves and how they were treating us. Eamon sat with us on a tiny mound at the edge of a field, pulling clumps of grass out of the ground and throwing them in the air. With each toss, he laughed and shouted, *Look what I did!* I reached out and started pulling clumps of grass and tossed them up imitating him, *Look what I did!* We laughed and laughed and repeated it until it was time to drive back to the Hudson train station.

As I crossed the waiting room after buying my ticket, I heard *Hey Jim.* The deep bass belonged to a guy named Jake, whom I knew from Twelve Step meetings in New York. When I turned, I saw Jake and a tall, striking woman standing in the middle of the small station. I couldn't take my eyes off her, and it felt as if the other twenty or so people in the station couldn't either. They all seemed to be either staring directly at her or sneaking sideways glances. She was tall and her legs were sheathed in skintight black Lycra pedal pushers with large white polka dots. They clung to the contours of her finely muscled legs. Her rhinestone Mickey Mouse belt buckle and hightop iridescent gold sneakers made what should have looked lascivious appear whimsical.

As Jake introduced us, she turned her head toward me. She wore one finely crafted silver and gold earring that dangled halfway down the right side of her long and supple neck.

The introduction was clumsy.

Jake said, *Jim this is Carly.*

He smiled in a somewhat mischievous way. I noticed that Alannah, who was usually friendly and informal, acted a bit stiff. It took a moment for them to understand about Eamon. He seemed fairly normal, until his echoing speech pattern gave him away. He quickly repeated *Hi how ya doin'?* It made for an awkward moment until she grasped something of the situation.

As the train to New York pulled into the station, she embraced Jake, and nodded toward the three of us, *Nice to meet you.* Then she walked outside to board. I said goodbye to Alannah, Jake, and Eamon, and hurried through three or four cars looking for her. I found her in the last one, perched in a four-seater with her long legs on the opposite cushion. She was reading and already seemed thoroughly engrossed. She looked up, hesitated, and in a deep, inviting alto asked, *Would you like to sit down?*

The trees outside the train windows colored her face with sunlight and shadow, and her azure eyes changed to green, depending on the light. Her nose stretched wide, exotic and catlike. It would have been her face's most prominent feature had it not been for her mouth with its lush red lips.

She held up the book she was reading: *Catherine the Great, by Henri Troyat.*

Perfect! I had taken a two-semester course at Siena in Russian history. I thought I might impress her, but as she stared at me, I could only think of Rasputin and the myth of Catherine and the horse. I bit my tongue.

Truth is, I don't remember too much about Russian History.

It's the most romantic biography I've ever read.

She launched into a short course on Catherine and her many lovers, including the story of a lady in waiting who tested Catherine's men to see if they "measured up." She completed her précis with a description of Potemkin villages. They were façades, Hollywood sets that Potemkin erected along the Dnieper River to impress Catherine and her guests, façades with nothing behind them.

Jake says he knows you from the program.

No one, without my permission, was supposed to tell anyone else. I told her as much, and she began to apologize profusely.

Oh, Jake and I are best friends, we tell each other everything. He also said you're very eloquent and that you've helped a lot of people in recovery and he. . . .

I forgave his indiscretion as I heard the compliments. He had provided her with lots of info in the short time it had taken me to buy my ticket.

He's in the program, very eloquent, helps a lot of people, and, "he's major, major," which was the phrase she would most remember.

The train began to move.

My son has a seizure disorder: infantile myoclonic seizures.

Oh, I'm so sorry. What caused it?

No one knows. It is an idiopathic diagnosis, which means the symptom describes the affliction.

Eamon's image atop the horse, in his jodhpurs and black-velvet riding helmet, powerfully lingered. A long-stuck valve seemed to open, and I felt a rush of heat around my heart. I told the story, carefully including all the heart-wrenching details: holding him at six months old as he seized fifty times a day; holding him helplessly, knowing that each seizure inflicted more brain damage; never any answers, always just holding him, and Eamon unable to speak, walk, or even sit upright.

Was that his mother I just met?

Yes, my ex-wife Alannah.

For the first forty-five minutes, she barely got in a word. After Eamon, I went through the marriage's ending, including the description of my wife running off with a bagpiper. Then I conducted a brief tour of my alcoholism and its effect on everything. It gave me an entree into my family and my father's alcoholism and violence.

When did you start drinking?

Sixteen, in the seminary.

The seminary?

I described a mysterious world: a place of rituals, rules, and solemn vows that no longer existed, a chimera that may have saved my life. I even shared that I had a bump below my kneecap from too much kneeling. I lifted the right leg of my green Henry Lehr slacks, the only designer item I owned, and showed her my knee. *See?*

She smiled and, I thought, blushed a tiny bit.

Everything tumbled easily forward.

I sell insurance.

Really?

Yes, there are actually a lot of smart people in the insurance business, I'm also a writer. I'm trying to write a novel. William Kennedy is helping me.

A layer of complexity: throwing in Kennedy implied competence.

But I'm really a poet by nature.

Then she asked another strange question.

Except for your son, who's the person you love most in the world?

The answer was so simple that I didn't need to pause.

Alannah, no one else comes close. What she has sacrificed for me is beyond understanding. She has given her life to me in a way no one could ever have imagined.

She welled up in the middle of my response.

Oh God, I wish I had that with my ex-husband.

Children?

Two amazing children, but he will barely speak to me.

I couldn't understand that. If you had my experience with Alannah, you would know that anyone who had sacrificed so much for what was yours had to be loved. I had gone on a bit too long, so I changed course.

What do you do?

I'm a singer.

So is Alannah.

I've had some success.

So has Alannah, she just released an album.

Oh.

I could see she needed some help.

You have such unusual interests for a singer: history, literature, and even some philosophy.

She laughed, and then quickly explained.

Well, my father was in the book business.

I imagined a short man in a cloth apron covered with ink, trying to fix a printing press; I returned to something she might be proud of.

What was the name of your album?

Coming Around Again.

Nice title! I didn't actually think so; it seemed too clichéd.

What's your name? I mean your singing name.

She froze and seemed to stammer. I could see she didn't want to tell me.

Carly Simon.

Those first forty-five minutes were the only time we would ever be equals, and the balance vanished as the world moved in the opposite direction: marsh marigolds blooming backward outside the window. It ended as I heard the name that would forever haunt me. I would often wish she had never told me or had made up a new one.

I knew it was a famous name, but I didn't really know why.

Should I know any of your songs?

My biggest hit is "You're So Vain."

I knew this song, but not really. I found that I had been unable to listen to most popular music. I remembered the chorus, and I recalled standing in a bar in Troy, New York, thinking it made little sense.

I think I've heard of it.

Jerry Brown, James Taylor, Judy Collins, Linda Ronstadt, Warren Beatty, and Mick Jagger collided with each other in my mind in a confused attempt to help me figure out who this woman sitting across from me was. I didn't know, yet I knew she was a big deal. A strange instinct took over, and I wasn't going to let her talk. I wanted us to have a little bit more time with her thinking I didn't know. So I pulled the cord and let the arrow spin, oink, moo, meow, and bark. I just kept talking.

I returned to the main topics of my life and filled in some details. I told a couple of zany stories about my father, the improbable tale of the founding of the Graymoor Friars, the religious order of my seminary years, and finally my work with other alcoholics. In no time, we were passing the Otis Elevator building in Yonkers, which meant the ride would soon end. From Yonkers to Grand Central, I obsessed about how to make my move. The train pulled into Grand Central Station, and I realized I had successfully kept the conversation from reverting to her. As we stood on the platform, she looked at me with a confused expression.

You know this has been a very unusual conversation for me.

Why is that?

Usually, when I meet a man for the first time, we talk about me.

I paused. I had blown it. But when I looked up, her lips were pulled together suppressing a smile. I then uttered what may have been the best sales line of my life: *I was going to save that for the second date.*

In the main waiting room of Grand Central Station, we stood for a moment and looked up at the constellations on the ceiling. As we stared at the heavens, I felt the direction of my life changing with a speed and force that rarely happens. We stood under the dimly painted stars of the zodiac and thought we could make out Cancer and Orion, but we weren't sure. Shafts of bright light poured down through the high clerestory windows and kept illuminating us as we crossed the station. I stopped, as we were about to exit onto 42nd Street and said, *Oh, I don't have your number.*

It's Jim Crab.

What?

Jim Crab. I always form words to remember numbers by. Just dial Jim Crab.

These two simple words were about to change everything. After all the years of struggle, pain, and expectation, it was going be this random: *Jim Crab.*

CHAPTER

TWO

—————— ◆ ——————

HER FATHER HAD NOT been the squat baldheaded man I had imagined on the train, but the cofounder of the publishing empire known as Simon & Schuster. Her husband, of course, had been James Taylor, and both their songs throughout the seventies had been an open confessional revealing the strange fragility of their families and the harrowing nature of sophisticated, privileged lives. Somehow they had touched the world with a remarkable trick: that the musical insight and talent of privileged adolescents was of great value to their entire generation and beyond. Their quirky, poignant explorations of how they had felt, especially about romance, touched an enormous number of people from very different backgrounds. I didn't yet understand their narrative, but along with so many others, it was easy for me to believe that I had seen fire and rain.

I wanted whatever this call was going to bring; yet I hadn't listened to her songs carefully. If I had, I might have understood much more about the days to come.

I took a deep breath and dialed JIM CRAB. A woman answered on the first ring: *Hola.*

Oh hi, is Carly there?

Que? Nada Aqui, Nada Aqui.

OK, sorry.

I tried again and dialed another spelling: JIM KRAB

Hello.

It was a little girl's voice.

Hi, is Carly there?

Want to speak to my mommy?

No. Thanks.

I tried the next spelling GYM CRAB and immediately heard: *This is not a working number in the 212 area.*

Had she intentionally ditched me? Only one spelling remained, GYM KRAB. I had been listening to her music since Grand Central two days ago, and at last I heard her unmistakable voice. She invited me over for dinner the very next night. Jake happened to be in town, so he would be joining us.

Car horns blared like *An American in Paris*, not grating, but orchestral, and the noise of the New York evening blended with my excitement. Carly Simon's lyrics and melodies swirled within me. *Anticipation is making me late, it's keeping me wayyayyaiting. Tomorrow we might not be together. I'm no prophet and I don't know nature's wayyayyays. Nobody does it better*—hmmm. *Watch yourself gavotte.*

I bought white lilies at a bodega on the way, and I kept repeating the second half of the prayer of St. Francis: *Help me not so much to seek to be consoled as to console; to be understood as to understand.* I knew I needed to be sure to talk about her tonight, not about me. *It is by self-forgetting that one finds.*

It might have been the slow motion of the elevator, the grain of the wood, or the lobby's coffered ceiling, but something brought me back to the memory of the safest and most exciting moment of my life. I rose in the elevator on this warm May evening, but the air surrounding me felt thin and clear, sharp with the hint of an early frost. I descended from a silver bullet-shaped bus in front of the seminary building for the first time. Father Simeon greeted us, and the smell of the licorice candies on his breath cut through the crisp scent of the cedars surrounding the statue of St. John the Baptist. He greeted each of us with a warm handshake as we stepped off the bus. He shook my hand and, with a large and earnest smile, looked into my eyes and said, *Welcome home.*

I was still in this reverie as the door swung open. It felt like I had been moving above my station my entire life, and I knew I had an uncanny skill for making others feel quite comfortable as I entered theirs. It had something to do with the lessons of the Graymoor Friars, my struggles with Eamon, my journey through addiction and recovery, and my love of words. I hoped all of these things would come together tonight.

She wore tight jeans, a red silk blouse, and had bare feet and another lone dangling earring. An oversized arrangement of trumpet lilies stood before a Lalique mirror surrounded by rows of aromatic candles. An elaborate chandelier hung in the entrance foyer, and the black-and-white marble floor tiles were highly polished. I stared at the small bouquet of flowers in my hand. She took them and said, *How lovely! Thank you.*

I kept repeating my mantra: *Talk about her.*

The apartment was subtle and stunning. The flowers, scented candles, subtle lighting, and painted landscapes of Martha's Vineyard made the living room and dining room seem to appear and reappear, as though the apartment had been summoned from other times and exotic places. At one moment in the dining room, I was in Provence, and the next in the parlor, Belle Époque Paris with velvet-fringed couches and bordello lampshades. The front windows overlooked Central Park, and the southern view peered into the Dakota. The space seemed to float just above the treetops, as if the ride down the Hudson had continued through a collage of light, deception, and movement. The visual was accented by scents from candles, flowers, sachets, and bowls of potpourri placed throughout the rooms.

We walked back toward the front of the apartment, and I noticed a young boy sitting on a large stationary bike in a room off the foyer. She introduced me to Ben, her ten-year-old son. The bike was broken, and he was struggling to get the pedals to move.

I proceeded with caution. I knew from my previous stint as a stepfather to Chris and Shane that the most important thing was to be genuine—to be only who you are—that less was usually more. I asked if I might help. He said, *Yeah sure*, as if he already understood my limited mechanical abilities. I don't know what I did, but within a few minutes, the bicycle was humming along. I gained a small amount of goodwill. *Hey, thanks man.* I thought this was a good start.

Jake was soon filling in parts of my bio that he thought would appeal to her. He frequently talked about me in the third person, as if I wasn't sitting there. I would watch him do this to many people in the years to come. He pointed at me as though he was explaining an exhibit in a museum. It was a bit unnerving.

He volunteers at Covenant House. He knows a lot about literature. He thought you dated Jerry Brown, that you were Linda Ronstadt.

Carly served the dinner almost entirely by herself. She was filled with questions about my life, and occasionally she would modestly interject

something about herself, or Jake would supply her (and me) with a cue like
She knows some Kennedys . . .

I sang at Caroline's wedding.

Really?

In certain ways, I might have known some of them better than she did.
My world had changed considerably since my early days in Rochester. I was
very active in the program in New York, and I had been working with a
number of people from different backgrounds from my own: a young billionaire, men and women from very prominent New York families, highly
successful businesspeople, well-known actors and actresses, as well as a group
of people not unlike myself—guys from modest backgrounds who were trying to make our way in the big city. I never lost the message from my father
and mother that everyone was important: that power and prestige were enemies for all of us. Armed with this message and the principles of the program,
I garnered a good deal of attention for my work with other addicts.

Carly didn't linger on any stories about herself in front of Jake. She seemed
more interested in making sure that Jake and I were relaxed and comfortable.
Her wide smile and the glint in her blue-green eyes made it hard to look
anywhere else. Yet there was something hesitant in her, as though in spite
of everything, she wasn't exactly sure of herself. Her speech patterns were
unusual, as if at times she wasn't certain about the words she wanted to use.
It made her seem vulnerable and within reach. I noticed that she often held
some material of her jeans between her thumb and forefinger and rubbed it.
She did this mostly when Jake was speaking, and I wondered if she was afraid
of what he might say.

After dinner we went into the den. I heard a commotion coming from
the other end of the apartment, and I could see a young blonde-haired girl
at the opposite end of the long hallway. Carly started to scream with delight,
Dance, Sal. Dance!

Sally was hesitant. She had just arrived home from an afterschool event,
but after a little more cajoling from Carly, she leapt and spun down the long
hallway, and ended with a graceful twirl in the main foyer. She bowed, and
Carly, Jake, and I applauded. Sally was Carly's thirteen-year-old daughter:
a blossom of flowing blonde hair, long legs, and quick smiles. Her coloring
seemed mostly tawny and peach. She smiled as her mother introduced us, and
I noticed that her expression transmitted a sense of shared feminine recognition, as if to say to her mother, *I know what you're up to.*

The next day she told Carly that at first she thought I was Gene Kelly. She had just seen *Singin' in the Rain* the night before, and she thought I had been invited to dinner to surprise her. In the context of her mother and father's famous friends and acquaintances, it wasn't much of a stretch.

Jake soon excused himself and retired to the guest bedroom. Carly left me to put the children to bed, which included a long storytelling session. Before she went, she asked if I wanted to try the "brain machine." She led me into her bedroom suite where she explained how it worked. In no time, I was lying on her bed, hooked up to a strange contraption that was designed to alter brain waves that affect feeling and behavior. It had a helmet with an eye visor that flashed patterns of light that were synchronized to odd noises played through headphones. There were dials for adjusting all parts of the sensations. She worked on it for a while, until she found the settings that I found most enervating and relaxing.

Colors and sounds raced through me. I lost sense of the time and I quickly found within myself my own deepest voice. I felt in a state of unprotected innocence, and two lines of Edna St. Vincent Millay's started to repeat themselves.

God, I can push the grass apart, and lay my fingers on thy heart.

I repeated it as the colors and sounds whizzed through my brain. By the time she returned, I was grinning and nearly drooling. She was impressed by what a cooperative subject I had been. Later she would tell me that it was a very important moment in her assessment of me: that I was so open and willing to experience something so out of the ordinary without hesitation. As I stared up at her, I wondered if I might be able to *push the grass apart.*

On the way out of the bedroom, she took me on a tour of the pictures that lined the hallway between the private and the public rooms. A recent visitor had dubbed it the *Hallway of Fame.* On its walls were framed photos of Carly, her family, her friends, and many diverse famous folk: musicians, artists, writers, politicians, athletes, former boyfriends, and her one and, so far only, husband. She carefully explained each photo, and what part of her life each one represented. As I looked at the images, I realized it might be our significant differences that were drawing us together. I pictured a hallway based on the events and people of my life: Irish farmers in a field; young boys in cassocks; a very pretty Celtic wife; bagpipers; woodchucks from the Grafton Mountains; drunks from Troy, New York; George Finegan from Rochester; a large group of young, recovering alkies; and a framed picture of the largest insurance contract I had ever sold—Bear Stearns. How would our lives find common ground? What pictures might the future bring? And then, somehow, not unlike that first fall night entering the seminary, I felt myself chosen. I saw myself standing next to her. I was holding a copy of my just-published novel, with my arm encircling her waist. Another was of Carly and me standing next to Eamon in his jodhpurs and black riding helmet. And finally, Carly and I in a tender embrace as the sea sprayed around us on a small, tilting sailboat.

We settled in the living room and listened to recordings of her songs, which began an exploration of her life through her lyrics. It was after three in the morning by the time the night ended. As I was about to leave, she slipped a ring onto my finger: a copy of an Egyptian piece found at the tomb of Tutankhamen. I wore the ring from that night on. We kissed goodnight at the front door, and I went home stunned. I had jumped my place: some miraculous force had reached down and forever rearranged my position in line. The concrete and glass of the city sparkled around me in a light spring rain, and the line from the poem kept repeating within me: *I can push the grass apart.*

She had clearly been swept away by me, and unless she was just nutty, her gift of the ring seemed quite provocative. She was surely an unusual woman, but far from crazy. She had no idea about the man she was about to take on, and oddly, it didn't seem to matter to her very much. At the time I was dating three different women. Another kind of interest had begun to recently emerge. I had discovered gay phone lines, which I would sometimes call until late into the night. Again, it didn't feel definitive, just like chat. More troubling though, I had started to stop in at a movie theatre called the Bijou, which was on 14th and 3rd. It was a gay cruising space, and this felt a little more precise. It was at the beginning of the AIDS crisis, and the men looked more and more suspicious to me. I never touched anyone—I was petrified. I was frightened just to be there, but I went anyway. A few weeks before meeting Carly, I thought I should see a therapist about this part of myself. I was confused. I so thoroughly enjoyed women and yet. . . .

On my walk home, I had my first thoughts about what this life might mean for me. Not so much what I would be entering, but what I might now escape: the dreary, unrelenting middle-class obsession with making a living. I was so tired of everything about my career in insurance. I had never imagined that my exit would be like this, but I began to think it might be.

I walked all the way home from 73rd and Central Park West to Avenue C and 14th Street, and on the way, I entertained an odd fantasy about Eamon's life. Rather than the short yellow bus supplied by Rensselaer County and the various state-funded services that he participated in, I saw him in an elegant facility run by the ever-smiling and competent Sisters of St. Dominic: the ones who smelled so good in my childhood. I didn't have a concrete thought about how this would happen, just a vague vision of a villa where being severely handicapped wouldn't matter; that he would live in a place so lush and loving that it would make the suffering of the patients and their parents disappear. In some way, I immediately imagined that she might even help with this unrelenting sorrow.

The following day she invited me to a rehearsal for an HBO concert she was performing the next week at Martha's Vineyard. It would be the first live show she had done in years. She told me she had a problem with stagefright, but as I sat there that afternoon, all I saw was a supremely confident and compelling performer. I recognized her hits as though I had known them forever. As I walked into the studio in Chelsea, she was singing the last lines of "Anticipation," and her face lit up when she saw me.

Stay right here 'cause these are the good old days.

As the song ended, she screamed in a falsetto voice, *It's Jimmy Hart.* The band members waved and shouted hello.

Let's break after the next one.

I recognized the song after the first few bars.

Nobody does it better.

She stood over me staring directly into my eyes. Her gaze never left, and as the music and emotion suffused her body, she delivered every word to me. She pranced across the room as she sang, and then ended the song in front of me with the line, *Sweet James you're the best.* I thought she had improvised the line for me—that this song sung for millions had finally found its true home. It would be months before I learned that the lyric was intended for James Bond, not James Hart.

I was wearing a pair of khaki shorts, and as soon as the song ended, she jumped off the stage and got everyone's attention by yelling and pointing at me. *Look at his legs. Have you ever seen such legs?* The band and other people applauded and whistled as though they never had. I smiled and laughed, but I really didn't know how I felt. I knew I should have felt embarrassed, but as she said it, I felt like my legs had gone without their proper recognition for years.

We went back to her apartment after, and I sat at a long wooden table that filled much of the kitchen. She prepared salad and pasta for us, and I listened spellbound as she told me the story of her mother, who had brought a much younger lover into the house while Carly's father was still alive. She told me about a hidden passageway between her mother's and her lover's bedrooms, and I lost track of the story. Images of my own parents swarmed in; I could not imagine such a scene. We never lived anywhere big enough for a secret passage, but also, imagining my mother, such a scenario would have been impossible. Then there was the sexual confusion of three teenage girls being ogled by their mother's lover, in Carly's story, as their father lay dying under the same roof. Perhaps this was the origin of Carly as a Siren who lured all those unsuspecting sailors in the years to come. It might also explain why she needed to confess it all on such a large stage.

The story shocked me. Yet, as I sat there, I could feel myself push aside my own prejudices and, instead of judgment, feel compassion, even for her mother. I also wondered about the thrill of a secret passage. I remembered thinking how handy a secret passage might be. Perhaps I had built one within my own psyche that I could travel between for my own unfulfilled desires. I barely noticed as Carly cleared the table and washed the dishes. She stood in front of the sink and finished wiping them.

She stood barefoot on the cold white tiles of the kitchen floor, with her right toes perched on top of her left foot, and her long legs swung slowly, hypnotically open and shut. She occasionally touched the bottom of her left breast and gently lifted it, as if signaling a message of unconscious impor-tance. Her striking animal presence appeared to be in a negotiation with her fragile psyche and refined intellect. Her body seemed barely able to contain itself, almost as if her nervous system spread out beyond her like roots and branches seeking soil and moisture. After a few more moments, I thought I understood. I noticed it for the first time on the train when she lifted her body off the seat to see if she was sitting on her ticket. It was the degree of the angle at which the pubic bone dropped away from the stomach, and how a woman's genitalia were placed between her inner thighs. Hers formed a perfectly sensual V with just the right slant, and the force of my attraction to it captivated me. I called it "slope." If I had any notions of a fluid sexuality, it felt that her sensual force had made me as straight as any man could wish to be. It would make everything easier if I was sure. At this moment, I was very sure.

Then she asked a question I wasn't prepared for, but I thought I handled it with just the right spin.

So, when are you going to show me your apartment?

Probably never.

What do you mean?

I mean, probably never.

No really, when are you going to have me over?

Never!

I knew that no matter what else happened, I would never let her see my apartment. I instinctively knew that I had to protect her from the part of me that she could never find acceptable: the part that appeared as if it didn't care about itself, and would not be able to care for her. She thought she had a persuasive argument.

I bet I can perfectly describe how it looks.

Go ahead.

Her accuracy was impressive. She described the mattress on the floor, the socks and underwear under the dining room table, the rust stains under the radiators, the bachelor-type furnishings, right down to the Matisse print in the living room.

How did I do?

About ninety-five percent. The only thing you missed were the TV tables that I use for eating.

So, when can I see it?

Never!

She was surprised by my response. Why was I behaving as if there was a corpse in the hall closet?

If I've perfectly described it, why won't you let me see it?

There's an important difference between knowing and seeing.

She could imagine it forever, but actually seeing it could never be erased. A few days later, I wound up with a surprising ally.

My sister Lucy says that if you insist, I shouldn't push it.

Lucy?

She says I should respect your reasoning.

I'm not sure that having her see my apartment would have changed anything because none of the other obvious imbalances in our lives seemed to impress us. We both seemed to instantly comprehend that we belonged together. It also dawned on me that our relationship had been predicted, foreshadowed, and known in some unusual ways. I just hadn't yet put all the pieces together.

I remembered that sometime in mid-April, a month before I met Carly, I had gone to see a psychic. The session took place in a modest apartment on the Upper East Side. We sat at a small card table in the kitchen, and she used a deck of regular playing cards that she kept shuffling and separating into three piles.

The first thing she told me was that I had a seriously sick child, and then went on to describe a boy very much like Eamon. She then told me that whatever I did for work, I would not be doing it much longer. She saw me on an island that looked like Ireland, but it was somewhere off the coast of the United States. I was sitting in a cabin writing, and I was with a beautiful woman who adored me. I would meet her very soon while traveling.

She shuffled the cards again and separated them into three piles, and then she started turning the cards over and said, *Tell me when to stop.* I had her stop at the seven of clubs. She stared at the card for a long time, and then she started to get excited. She could barely catch her breath.

Oh my God, oh my God, my God.

What is it?

I've never seen anything like this before.

What is it?

Oh my God, it's fame!

Fame?

There's fame all over you, oh my God.

What do you mean? Is it from the book I'm writing?

Oh no, it's so much bigger than that.

I had just received a good deal of praise for a scene I had performed for an acting class I had recently enrolled in.

Am I going to be a famous actor?

No, it's much bigger than that. There's fame all over you.

Another incident was with a young sponsee of mine from the program. I was trying to help him with his problem of the moment: He was dating a string of young girls from the boroughs. I told him that if he wanted to break this pattern of unhappy relationships, he would have to start seeing real women. I became emphatic and noticed there was a large magazine advertisement on a nearby bus stop. It was a picture of a sexy looking woman, who wore one long, dangling silver earring. I said, *Do you see? This is the kind of woman you need to be dating.*

He kept trying to return to the details of his current situation, and I kept laughing and pointing back at the picture of the woman in the ad. Later I learned that it was a headshot of Carly with a caption that read ONE OF THE BORING HOUSEWIVES WHO READS McCALL'S. I had no idea; she just looked like the ideal of a sophisticated, smart, and sexy woman whom I thought could solve his problems.

The third and perhaps most startling incident occurred with Eamon. I went to visit him a few weeks after I had met Carly. He sat in the living room listening to her new album *Coming Around Again*, and as always, he knew all the words. He had a very unusual talent. Although he had great difficulty constructing sentences when speaking, he could remember and repeat any song lyric he listened to verbatim. He was singing along with great gusto, and I joined him. It was so funny to hear him sing lyrics that he couldn't possibly understand, and yet as he sang he acted as though he had full comprehension of the notion: *So romantic, So bewildering.* I figured it was a setup. As Alannah entered the room, I laughed and said, *Way to go.*

What?

The music.

She didn't understand what I was talking about.

Oh, you didn't know?

Huh?

That's been his favorite album for almost two months. He was listening to that nonstop for a month before you met her.

I sat with him and listened to him sing all the lyrics on the *Coming Around Again* album. He sang as if he understood what each song was about, and his beaming smiles indicated deep approval. Eamon couldn't make these kinds of cognitive leaps, but it certainly felt as if he had about Carly and me. The song ended, and before the next one began, Alannah moved beside me and whispered, *Freaky.*

I had rejoined the St. Ignatius Choir of my youth in Long Beach, and when I met Carly, we were rehearsing the Berlioz Requiem. It was at the well-known bass entrance of the *Tuba mirum* that I felt a physical sensation that reflected what was happening to me. I sang as loudly as I ever had in my life on the June evening of the performance. Carly couldn't make the performance, but we had already grown so close that it felt like she was sitting in the front row staring up at me.

Tuba mirum spargens sonum	*Wondrous sound the trumpet flingeth*
Per sepulchra regionum	*through earth's sepulchres it ringeth;*
Coget omnes ante thronum	*all before the throne it bringeth.*

It felt as if the entire orchestra and chorus were playing and singing within me. The brass fanfare pierced the air, and racing trumpets were followed by the pleading of the French horns, the overwhelming sound as the brass section blared salvation, and the rumbling of the tympani and the dramatic entrance of the bass voices singing *tuba mirum*—*wondrous trumpet*. It felt as if I had passed my most important particular judgment, if not my final one. I shouted my feelings of joy as I sang. I was now connected to this woman who had startled the world with her intimate public confessions. She had spent a lifetime centered on exploring her emotional life, sharing it so candidly with the rest of us, and now, the place closest to her would be known only by me. At the same time, she aligned me with a new sense of triumph. I had achieved something I had never dreamt of: I had accidentally changed everything in the twinkling of an eye, as though the trumpet had sounded. It not only summoned me on, but also acted as a salve for all the pain of the past.

CHAPTER

THREE

———————◆———————

LIGHT INVADED THE NARROW opening between the bungalows, and the movement of the shadow across the alleyway turned it into a large sundial; with just a glance, I could tell time. The pink rubber ball, *the Spaldeen*, skipped and spun in every direction. I reacted swiftly to the ball's varying speeds. At five years old, I fielded the odd bounces and difficult short hops due to my constant practice, and I was the best stoopball player on our block, Kentucky Street. I stretched to the left to field a grounder and caught sight of the lengthening shadow. It was time for dinner.

At my father's direction, the Sunday meal was always roast beef, mashed potatoes, and peas. I had trouble chewing and swallowing roast beef because of the strangulating texture of the gristle and fat. I loved the mashed potatoes and hated the peas, which I stuffed into the front pockets of my jeans, a dangerous practice. If my father caught me, or even suspected what I was doing, I would be severely beaten.

His rages were as unpredictable as the Atlantic, which roared and crashed just beyond our basement apartment—we lived on the West End of Long Beach, New York, a shanty Irish enclave in an otherwise middle-class Jewish city by the sea. I understood that his ability to control his emotions was difficult because he was quite ill with something my mother called "alcoholism." I had interior sonar though, and I was usually the first in the family to feel his storms gathering. I knew the slightest offense could set him off. Unfortunately, my brother Danny, who was three years older, had no such warning system, so he wandered into even more beatings than I did. I learned to stay away from Danny because if one of us got punished, the other got beaten as well. My father's explanation: *That's for what I didn't catch you doing!*

Now as I sat straight up in my chair, I sensed my father's strengthening undertow. As we finished saying grace, my brother extended his arm, and with a clumsy swipe, overturned the bottle of milk, spilling it all over the table. He stared directly at my father, unable to make a sound or movement. Fear coursed through his body to the tips of his Buster Brown shoes, and I watched as my father, with terrifying and silent speed, hit him with a short left. The blood spurted everywhere. My mother gasped and then silently helped Danny from his chair to the bathroom.

The vivid blue veins on the surface of my father's biceps pulsated with insistent surges that synchronized with the racing beat of my heart. In that moment, it felt as if every strand of muscle and tissue in my body might be ripped apart by the force of my fear. I kept my head down and stared at my plate, and a briny taste coated the back of my throat. I knew that any sudden motion or unclear facial expression might result in further disaster. Any perceived frown or look of confusion could cause him to launch into his ritualized inquisition: *What are you looking at?*

My father always answered his own question, which in turn made him even more furious. These solitary dialogues always ended with the same terrible phrase: *You little fuckin' cocksucker.*

When he shouted it, all the muscles in my body contracted. He pronounced the last word with ferocious diction. The first hard *k* was accompanied by a guttural chord, the second with an incredulous modulation upward, and the last with a dying fall. Every time he used the phrase, it felt as if he had discovered an infallible truth. Though I had no idea what it meant, I knew never to repeat it. I was sure it exposed my most original and unforgivable sin. Whenever he screamed that final word, the beatings would begin.

One of the rivulets of my brother's blood dripped into the gravy on my roast beef, and the green peas were already in a thick red soup. After a few more beats of silence, I scooped up a spoonful of the sodden peas and ate them as if they were not soaked in my brother's blood. I ate the entire meal, and as I took my final bite, I heard my father's heavy breathing subside. A last groan escaped from him as he rose from the table and, without another sound, he left the house. He was off to one of those secret meetings for his drinking; I sat alone, trembling.

Inside the tiny concrete space we called home, my father had absolute control. We learned important lessons from him: Never flinch, cry, run, or rat (as in never, ever tell anyone anything, no matter who asks). Outdoors always felt safer. The ocean's majesty made the rows of shoddy bungalows that lined the narrow streets look insignificant and temporary. The shore was a wilderness of dunes and beach grass, of strange creatures that crawled out of the sea: jellyfish, starfish, prehistoric horseshoe crabs, and the occasional dead sand shark. A few times, notes in bottles washed up. One contained a faded treasure map that looked remarkably authentic. Its Xs and arrows beckoned to me. I was drawn to anything that might take me away. Often when I stared toward the horizon, I would see ocean liners and fishing boats sailing to somewhere far away, and I could hear, see, almost touch the airplanes that flew overhead from every part of the globe on their final approach to Idlewild.

My mother and I woke every morning in time for six o'clock mass. I could always tell if I had wet the bed because I heard her sigh as she felt the dampness. Adding this to her daily chores made me feel both sad and ashamed. She already worked two waitressing jobs to pay the bills, and she didn't need me to add to her burdens. Even so, she felt for my plight; she had harrowing bedwetting stories of her own. Her childhood had included public humiliation at an orphanage where she had grown up in Hornell, New York, an upstate railroad town on the far end of the western tier. My bedwetting reached its peak about a year before my father bloodied my brother's nose. Toward the end of this summer, my father was out of town on a construction job in North Carolina, so after I wet my bed, I would sneak into my mother's room and climb in next to her.

On this morning, August 31, 1954, we woke up at the same moment, and she sighed as she felt beneath her. She pushed me away in exasperation, and I rolled across the bed and tumbled off the edge into three feet of water. As my mother heard the soft splash, she stared toward where I had fallen. I emerged with water streaming down my face. She ran to the window and screamed, *Oh my God*. She looked back at me and began to laugh so hard that she could barely catch her breath.

This time it wasn't me. Hurricane Carol had just hit, and because of the water already in the house, we couldn't open any of the doors to get out. The flood water was rushing in with powerful force, and we were in danger of drowning, yet my mother couldn't stop laughing, which made it all feel like a funny adventure. We wound up standing on the kitchen table as the water rose to about six feet. By the time the firemen rescued us, it had climbed to just below my chin, and my mother was still laughing as they pulled us through the basement window onto the street. (I knew she would repeat this story to others, and even though I was mortified, I was quite willing to endure my shame for her enjoyment.) She would sometimes laugh so hard that she would have to clutch her arms to hold herself in place. If something really tickled her, she swayed back and forth, and then tears would form from the intensity of her joy. I loved that anything about me could make her feel this way.

Mommy, do you think the fortune teller, you know the one on the boardwalk, do you think she can tell the future?

You mean the one in the penny arcade?

Yes, the one in the machine.

There were real gypsy fortune tellers on the boardwalk. My mother never went to see them, yet every time we were in the penny arcade, she would let the mechanical gypsy in the glass case tell her fortune. She always seemed thrilled by it, and she would wait with excitement as the gypsy woman passed her hand over the crystal ball. When she stopped, a mysterious card came out of the machine with esoteric symbols printed on the back.

Do you believe in the fortune teller?

She laughed, *Oh I don't know, I think it's just for fun.*

How can it be fun if it's not true?

It's hard to explain, but you'll understand when you get older.

Oh, okay.

I hated that explanation. Whenever I was told I would understand something when I got older, I already knew what it meant. My mother didn't want the kind of news that one of the real gypsy fortune tellers might tell her about my father. She visited the mechanical gypsy because it cost much less and told her only happy things.

Will Daddy ever be able to drink?

Oh, I hope not. Let's pray that he never does again.

Oh.

I didn't understand. If he just drank like the people in one of my favorite movies on TV, *The Thin Man*, he might become clever and charming. I thought his not drinking had something to do with why he beat my brother and me. I was filled with hope whenever my mother said he was getting better.

Did the fortune teller say anything about Daddy?

Yes, she said that he is going to be happy and healthy.

We so wanted it to be true.

My mother always found something to laugh about on our morning walks to church, often using one of the aphorisms that she thought applied to me, such as *A stitch in time saves nine* or *Children should be seen and not heard.* Or the one I always found most troublesome, *He who is good at excuses is seldom good at anything else.* With one seamless motion, she would toss her auburn hair over her shoulder and smile knowingly as she watched me try to figure out what she meant.

My brown eyes were duplicates of hers. They were part of her mysterious dark strength, and there was something in the steady spectrum of their coloring that matched her will on its march toward happiness. She had an unshakable belief that the future was going to be better than the past. I had no idea where this faith came from, but it was a buoy that sustained me. I loved to see her in her bare feet, mopping, cleaning, and often singing her favorite song: "Young at Heart."

The lyrics alleged that if you were "Young at Heart" life would be more exciting, because you were already in love, or it was about to happen. Being "Young at Heart" also assured you of a very long life. As I watched her joyously mopping, I was sure of its truth.

Clad in the luxurious and overwrought chasubles of the day, the priest looked like a great prince. He entered holding the veiled gold chalice, which he quickly placed on the altar, and then the mass began as it had in every part of the globe since 1570.

Priest: *Introibo ad altare Dei.*

(I approach the altar of God.)

Server: *Ad Deum qui laetificat juventutem meam.*

(God who gave joy to my youth.)

God who gave joy to my youth was repeated three times in the first moments. For as long as I remembered, I had longed to be an altar boy and respond in perfectly pronounced Latin, *Ad Deum qui laetificat juventutem meam.* I longed to have a joyous youth.

My mother held her missal with its multicolored ribbon bookmarks and said the rosary under her breath. We stood, knelt, and sat; the bells rang a few times, and then toward the end, there was communion.

The Sisters of Saint Dominic sat in the front pews on the left side of the main aisle and filled the church with their angelic voices. Their scrubbed and gleaming faces were framed by the drapes of their black veils and the spotless white of their starched wimples. I wondered if they washed and bathed in a special brand of sacred nun's soap; they smelled better than anyone else, even my mother. I always thought they were especially kind to her because they knew about my father.

I especially loved going to church when it snowed. My mother and I trekked through the wind-blown and snow-drifted streets laughing and stumbling. The church's large Spanish-tiled roof would be coated with snow, and outside the saints' statues were shrouded in white. We all stood in puddles of melted water by the time the priest lifted the host and the bells rang. Everyone seemed especially happy, and after mass, the younger nuns would throw snowballs at each other. I loved the sound of their muffled laughter. I wanted to join in, but I figured that required some sort of permission. I wanted the nuns to know that I was there, to invite me to play in the snow with them. I so wanted to be included, to be noticed, especially by them. They seemed to matter in such an important way, and there wasn't anything I wanted to be excluded from. Perhaps this was why my Aunt Mary, my mother's sister, gave me a nickname that mimicked my constant response to my young life's experiences: *Me too.* The snow always felt like a special event, that the flakes that had just fallen from God's hands were marked especially for my mother and me, because we had made the effort to be with him so early in the morning.

The weekend following the bloody dinner, I met my other aunt, my father's sister, for the first time. As our car approached the entrance of Graymoor, the monastery and convent grounds, my father exhaled deeply and became silent. He bowed his head, and then, not caring who was watching, smiled at his own image in the rearview mirror. The car filled with the same kind of joy that swept over me on my walk to church every morning, and now here it was within my father.

We waited for her in a park at the very bottom of the hill. The entire Hart family had made the trip: my grandmother Ella and grandfather Hugh; my father's older brother Gene and his wife Ann and and their children Little Gene and Patricia; and my father's younger brother, my Uncle Danny; and my mother, father, and brother. As the nearby chapel bell began to toll, Sister Leona, my aunt, appeared at the top of the steps. I noticed that swaths of soft white linen surrounded her face. She bowed her head for a moment as if in prayer, and as soon as she placed her feet on the grass, she ran toward us. The sun caught her wire-rimmed frames and they glistened as she got closer. She scooped me up in her arms and wrapped me in the rough woolen folds of her brown habit so that the cloth scratched my skin. She held me away from her to get a better look, and as she did, I could see the burgundy insignia on the center of her habit over her chest. As she put me down, I became entangled in the white cord and the long brown rosary hanging from it that she wore around her waist. She was still staring at me as I freed myself, and I became lost in the blue shimmer of her eyes. She turned to the family, raised her robed arms, took a deep breath, and said, *Isn't it beautiful today?*

It was the most beautiful place I had ever seen. Graymoor was located in the village of Garrison, just opposite West Point on the overgrown eastern bank of the Hudson. It was the home, or mother house, of the Franciscan Friars and Sisters of the Atonement, informally known as the Graymoor Friars and Sisters. Reminiscent of a medieval hierarchy, the friars' monastery was at the top of the hill and the sisters' convent was at the bottom.

At the entrance stood a giant wooden cross about twenty feet high that depicted Jesus as he gazed down at his mother Mary. Four life-sized angels at the bottom of the cross were blowing into long silver trumpets that tilted upward. A dense run of pines bordered us on the right, and beneath the pines was a thick mat of needles and twigs. Two small church steeples rose above the rest of the Tudor-styled buildings, and plantings of flowers and greenery overflowed onto the paths that curved through the property. An aroma of freshly baked bread from the kitchen mingled with the scent of honeysuckle, and a breeze with a nip of industrial soap seeped out from the nuns' laundry room.

Her hugs were fierce, and her embraces lingered. I had never felt anyone else in the family touch me with such physicality. I watched as she approached her father. He never made a move, as still as one of the outdoor stone stations of the cross that stood behind him. She made an enormous fuss over him, told him how handsome he looked in his white shirt and tie. Then she held his face in her hands, gazed into his eyes, and gently said the most surprising thing: *Pop, I love you and pray for you every day.*

I found her statement curious given the conversation I had just heard in the car. My father and his younger brother Danny had been talking about it on the way up. Apparently, my grandfather had attempted to drown her in the kitchen sink when she was fourteen. She had lied to him about buying some penny candy and had hid it in a secret pocket she had sewn into her coat. My father had been sitting at the kitchen table when it happened.

He held Sissy's head down in a full sink of dirty dishwater. After a minute, or so, the old lady realized he wasn't going to let her up.

My father shook his head back and forth, as if all these years later he still could still see what he was describing.

Mom grabbed an iron and clocked him over the head with it. Blood spurted everywhere. She had to hit him three or four more times before he would let go.

Uncle Danny laughed and said, *He was an animal.*

My father finished. *Sissy came out of that sink a deep shade of purple, gasping and sputtering. A month later she was off to the convent.*

And yet, I had never seen my grandfather receive such attention; Sister Leona wanted to hear all about him. She acted as if he were the most important member of the family, while no one else ever did. Somehow, because of her tenderness, he smiled. It looked like the unprepared smile of a small boy, and it seemed to push away a solid wall covering long-repressed emotions. I had never seen him look so happy. She clearly had offered him forgiveness.

My grandfather's rage had sent his sons to the hospital more than once. On one occasion, rather than withstand another assault, my father jumped out of a fourth-story window thinking that the fall would do less injury than his father's beating. And then one night, in a drunken stupor, my grandfather rolled over on his infant son Patrick and smothered him to death.

Time passed quickly as Sister Leona tried to gather news from everyone. About an hour into our visit, she said, *You'll have to excuse me. Mother General needs to see me about my new assignment. She knows you're here, so it won't be long.*

She turned to go and then motioned to me: *Jimmy, come with me.* She took me by the hand and led me through a maze of stone paths that led to the main convent building. She directed me toward the view of the Hudson in the distance. She pointed with a full, slow sweep of her arm, and the dramatic way she said, *Look*, made it feel as if she and God had designed it together.

A nun sat at a small desk just beyond the entrance. Sister Leona said, *This is Sister Athanasia; she is the portress today. Sister, this is my nephew Jimmy. You're going to stay with Sister Athanasia while I see Reverend Mother.*

Sister Athanasia was an elderly nun with an odd affliction. She couldn't keep her head up; it kept flopping over. She rested her head on her arm or placed her hand underneath her chin and acted as if this arrangement were normal. She had a small, dry, eggshell voice that terrified me, and I tried not to look at her as she spoke.

Jimmy, do you know whose feast day we celebrate today?

No, Sister.

Today is the feast of St. Augustine of Hippo. Can you say that?

Yes, Sister. Today is the feast of St. Augustine of Hippos.

She smiled.

Not Hippos, Jimmy: Hippo

Do you know what St. Augustine said?

I shook my head no.

St. Augustine said, "Love God and do what you will." Can you say that?

Yes Sister, "Love God and do what you will."

Jimmy, don't ever forget; if you love God, you will be able to do anything. Stay close to all the saints.

Yes, Sister.

St. Joseph of Cupertino could fly because he loved God so much. Can you imagine that?

I imagined it the moment she said it: a monk soaring over Metropolis with his arms extended like George Reeves as Superman. She drew me back.

Jimmy, what did St. Augustine say?

"Love God and do what you will."

Sister Leona soon reappeared, and Sister Athanasia said, *Jimmy, what did St. Augustine say?*

He said, "Love God and do what you will."

My aunt hugged me close and roared with laughter. Then she told me that she had brought me with her because she wanted the two of us to pray together in a special place. We were going to Our Lady of Angels Chapel, where the Blessed Virgin Mary had appeared to a young postulant named Sister Amelia in 1900. We walked down another winding path and passed a sign: *Cloistered, No Visitors.* She put her finger to her lips to make sure I was silent. Around the next bend, she pushed on a small wooden door that opened into a very still chapel. The air was close, and it felt as if it had been undisturbed for years, perhaps since the apparition. The bright summer sun barely entered through the narrow stained-glass windows, and the slim shafts of light were filled with flecks of dust. We knelt before a small statue, and Sister Leona told me the story.

Our Lady was dressed in a red mantle and held the baby Jesus in front of her. In her hand, she held a heart and she offered it to the young sister. So, let's pray to Our Lady of the Atonement that she will help us in the days ahead.

Sister Leona held the rosary that hung at her waist and with her fingers moving along the large brown beads, she began. She started with the Resurrection, the First Glorious Mystery. I joined her on the response to the Hail Mary.

Holy Mary, Mother of God. Pray for us sinners.

I stared into the eyes of Our Lady, and I asked her to appear. If she did, I knew the beatings would have to stop. I imagined the small statue coming alive and gently speaking to me. She did not appear, but even so, I had never felt this way before: connected to a world of much greater importance and safety. Sister Leona had chosen me, and we forged a bond that day kneeling in front of the statue of Our Lady. She had led me into the cloister because she believed I had been chosen. We finished the rosary, crossed ourselves, and left the chapel. When we rejoined the family, everyone gathered around, and she delivered the news.

I'm going to be stationed in Lincoln, New Hampshire. I'm to be the Mother Superior.

This felt like the first sign of success for the Hart family: the only daughter ran away from home to escape poverty, violence, and ignorance, joined a religious order dedicated to voluntary poverty, and became a *Mother Superior*.

The rest of the afternoon was a shanty Irish-American sing-along that included one of my favorites, Uncle Gene's rendition of "I Had but Fifty Cents." He stood in front of us and held his arms out wide with his palms up. I noticed his missing thumb, which he had lost in an ice-machine accident. The thumb's absence always stunned me. I looked at it whenever I thought he wouldn't notice. He tapped his foot, looked into the distance, and broke into song. The beat was fast, and Gene struggled to keep up with his own rhythm:

> *She said she wasn't hungry, but this is what she ate:*
> *a dozen raw, a plate of slaw, a chicken and a roast*
> *some applesass, and asparagrass and soft shell crabs on toast*
> *a box of stew, and crackers too her appetite was immense*
> *when she asked for pie, I thought I'd die, for I had but fifty cents.*

My father stood beside him clapping, and I noticed how different these two brothers, in their sweat-soaked white shirts, looked from each other: my father was wiry, muscular, and quick, black Irish to the core with a shock of dark hair, bedeviling blue-green eyes, and a mischievous smile. Gene was thick-bodied, red-haired, and freckled, with an open-faced expression of lilting wonder, one of those fellows who make the Irish so hard to dislike. They looked identical in one way—the cut of their jibs. Their bone structures, from forehead to chin, formed perfectly taut triangles, and their faces looked as though they had been created by stretching smooth canvas over solid granite. Here in this little green park at the front of the convent grounds, they were happy just being brothers.

After the singing was over, the adults sat in silence and enjoyed the late August afternoon. Sissy sat by me at the end of the bench and noticed that I was staring at the burgundy insignia on her chest.

Jimmy, it's a little complicated, but let me see if I can explain it to you. The insignia is called the Seal of Solomon or the Star of David.

She explained that the intersecting triangles represented the space where God and man come together, and the burgundy color represented Christ's blood on Calvary. Much of what she said escaped me, but her voice was soft and melodic, and it produced that safe feeling again. The triangles were also for oneness and unity, but as she continued, I faded. She laid me across her lap and gently stroked my head, and in no time I was fast asleep.

I awoke to the sound of a bell tolling in the distance. *Wake up, Jimmy, wake up. I have to go.* I awoke slowly as if out of a deep dream. Then I heard my father's gruff, angry tone: *She said to wake up, NOW!* At the sound of his voice, I jolted forward, and tumbled out of her lap onto the ground. The laughter that ensued felt as painful as any of my father's beatings. Everyone was laughing at me, even my mother, everyone except Sissy. She bent over, picked me up, and said, *Don't pay any attention to them, you're a very, very good boy.* She hugged me again and kissed me on both cheeks. She said goodbye to everyone else and then ran across the lawn and up the stone steps to get to chapel on time for vespers.

We packed into our cavernous DeSoto and made our way back to Manhattan, all crammed into the car in a rare display of peace and harmony. It felt as if the entire family had been healed by this Sunday afternoon at Graymoor, and for the rest of my childhood, I could not get enough of it. Graymoor was a place I would come to equate with Camelot, and as the very best boy in the realm, I yearned to be a true and faithful Galahad.

My opportunity finally arrived just a few weeks into my eighth-grade school year. A Graymoor friar named Father Simeon visited our house to evaluate my family. It was part of the admission process for the minor seminary. I was petrified. I was certain that I would pass his scrutiny, but I wasn't at all sure about the rest of them. My father was my biggest worry. I had never seen him be anything but respectful to a priest or nun, but I just couldn't be certain. Even though he had been sober now for a few years, his emotional reactions could not be depended on. My mother borrowed a couple of card tables from the neighbors and bought a new tablecloth. She was going to make pork chops for the dinner, which was about the fanciest meal that ever came out of her kitchen.

All the friars I had met were educated, urbane, and kind. In my worried state, I didn't focus on their kindness. I thought about my father's pronunciation and grammar for weeks before the visit; the way he said oil (earl) and toilet (turlet) embarrassed me, revealing a kind of ignorance that I couldn't bear. He might say theatre (theeayter) with a put-on pronunciation to make it sound exotic, but it made him sound woefully uneducated. I felt shame and love: a combination of familiar feelings that I often felt in my childhood. I tried to mask my enormous pride and ambition with a sincerity that was even larger. After all, God was calling me; I just needed my family not to blow it.

Father Simeon was a tall, handsome man with an easy manner, and he smelled of a strong licorice candy called Sen-Sen. His namesake in the Gospel of Luke had waited by the temple and recognized Jesus, proclaiming, *Lord, lettest thou thy servant depart in peace, for my eyes have seen thy salvation.*

Other than my father kicking my brother Danny under the table for picking up his pork chop with his hands, the evening was a success. I immediately understood my brother's situation. I don't think that any of us had ever eaten a pork chop with a knife and fork. He shouted with surprise and pain as my father connected with his shin.

Immediately, Father Simeon picked up his pork chop with his hands, and we all laughed together. It seemed that the Graymoor Friars had a way of recognizing a person that was unique in my childhood experience. You were always going to be okay with them: every part of you was more than acceptable.

Father Simeon winked at me as he was leaving to let me know it had gone well. He said all he needed was an academic transcript and recommendations from my pastor and the nuns at Saint Ignatius School.

CHAPTER
FOUR

FLYING OVER THE END of eastern Long Island, I looked down at a very different part of the Atlantic. It was worlds away from the beer concessions, boardwalks, gypsy fortunetellers, and deep-fried knishes of Long Beach. Today, Independence Day of 1987, the sun gently rippled over the water, and traces of clouds streamed above small islands and silent white beaches.

I soon stood on the tarmac as Carly wrapped herself around me. She was barefooted and wore a wampum ankle bracelet, and seemed to have sprung from the place itself: a sensual Wampanoag princess. As she held me in this first public embrace, my love became more private. I knew from the strange force of this embrace that it would need to develop deeper, secret places to balance this constant exposure.

We spent the first day in Menemsha, a seaside village: seagulls crying with the sun setting over the fishing boats softly clanging. Carly owned a clapboard cottage on a bluff facing west toward the cape. The sun left its mark: a singe of purple as it sank into the sea. The salt air seeped through the screened-in porch, and the island mist surrounded us.

She had just finished an HBO special a few weeks before and had used the harbor as the set. Remarkably, they had built the stage in the middle of it. She had called me in New York before her performance, and I was witness to her anxiety.

I can't go on, I'm having a heart attack. I'm terrified. It's too cold. Why are they making me do this? I can't. I have to cancel.

The concert was a complete success.

What was I doing here? Just a few weeks before, I was cooking grilled-cheese sandwiches in my kitchenette in Stuyvesant Town. Now I stood under the star-strewn northern summer sky holding her in my arms.

The next day we explored wandering sandy paths, silvery ponds, clay cliffs, and the island's many villages. We stood at her mother's house near Abel's hill in Chilmark and watched the wandering farmland roll away toward the sea. I began to see her deep attachment to place: This dark green island comforted her, and its stand against the cold and forbidding sea reflected her psychic wish.

She would have preferred to introduce me slowly to her Martha's Vineyard friends, but fame on the Vineyard has its own style and timing. It can be unforgiving in its exclusivity and subtle use of distance. Soft blue-green lawns and verdant hills border miles of scruffy pin oaks and marsh grass made brown by the summer sun, and fame is somehow both invisible and omnipresent.

Our first celebrity gathering was a dinner party at the home of writer William Styron—*The Styrons'* in Vineyard parlance. He and his wife Rose lived in a large rambling house that sat on a great lawn overlooking Vineyard Haven harbor. We entered a driveway with high bushes on either side, a place where Mr. Toad might appear in his motor car and with gleeful abandon, smile, point toward the house, and squeeze by us in the opposite direction. As he passed, he would doff his high hat and shout, *Good evening, Carly.*

This night I was a bit of a celebrity: the mysterious man who had captured her heart. Especially mysterious when I told them what I did for a living. The incongruity of an insurance man in her life was startling.

Fog had settled in by the time we left. A late night mist would often envelop us as we left their house in years to come: a farewell that matched its magic.

The next day I sat by the pool at her main residence, an estate located on forty acres just off lower Lambert's Cove Road. Barn swallows, cardinals, large black crows, and blue jays darted, sang, and cackled around me. A number of hummingbirds and flitting insects—dragonflies, damselflies, butterflies, and an array of mayflies or ephemeroptera, which live only a few days—buzzed past. I wondered if the mayflies were an omen that someone would soon be whispering in my ear, *Sorry, sir, your fifteen minutes are up.*

I noticed a head bobbing up and down on the other side of the stockade fence, and as the gate opened, a middle-aged man dressed in a ninja jump suit appeared. Perhaps he was sent to tell me of the error that had been made. As he came closer, I realized he was in a pair of black nylon parachute pants and a black t-shirt. He didn't have the body and demeanor for this outfit: a little old and out of shape for such hip dress, but there was something in his smile that indicated he already knew this. Since he surfaced from the underbrush beside the pool, I thought he might be the gardener or groundskeeper.

Hi, I'm Jim.

Yes, of course you are. I'm Mike, pause, *Nichols.*

I wouldn't remember much about this moment, except that I froze. I could barely speak, because I immediately suspected that if anyone would be able to see right through me, it would be Mike Nichols, a man who could tell what I was thinking before I even knew it: like George in *Who's Afraid of Virginia Woolf?* I had somehow charmed her, but how could I seduce the others?

Mike grinned anew, *Is what's her name in?*

Carly was thrilled to see him. Her feelings toward Mike seemed similar to the way she responded to Ben and her friend Jake: something familial in the warmth of her greeting. He had stopped by to make sure we were coming to a party that evening. It was at a house that had once belonged to Lillian Hellman, a boxy modern structure that overlooked Vineyard Haven Harbor. It seemed perfectly designed for Hollywood Hills rather than its rustic New England setting.

John Hersey, the author of *Hiroshima*, and his wife Barbara were already there when we arrived. In no time, I was trying out my story. It began with *I come from a New York family.* My enunciation was perfect and the tone was dignified: *A Hell's Kitchen New York family.*

John's eyes darted and quickly refocused: I might actually be more interesting than just Carly's latest date. The next arrival had the look of an Irish tinker, down on his luck but still smiling, sporting a wispy beard. He gave Carly a warm hug and turned toward me with inclusive speed, *Hi, I'm Herb Gardner.* He had written *A Thousand Clowns*, one of my favorite movies. Within minutes, Bill and Rose Styron, Mike Nichols, Mike and Mary Wallace, Art Buchwald, and Jules Feiffer were also in the room. Carly occupied a special place within this group. It had something to do with the success of a popular singer that made her relentlessly ever present in everyone's hearing and consciousness for so many years. It also had something to do with her family; being the daughter of a world-famous publisher meant that she had been hanging out with both the literary and the rich and famous since childhood. She was also in the midst of a major comeback. Her *Coming Around Again* album soon reached double platinum, with over two million sold. I had begun to change my opinion about the title song as I could feel it align with my current experience: *Who knows where or when, it's coming around again.*

Her attractiveness also had to do with emotional generosity. She was always completely interested in any conversation about fragile sensibilities, yours or hers. This was especially charming to men, to have this particular woman care about how they were feeling. As she helped expose their vulnerabilities, she was busily trying to figure out how to make them feel better. It was completely genuine and particularly compelling for the male ego. Carly was an aerial artist of the emotions, and for a few hours, others could share her trapeze.

In the cove beyond, sailboats glided and flashes of red, green, and white light spread over the water. Styron and Nichols fascinated me most. They stood apart in complementary ways; Bill always seemed to be thinking about something more important than what was taking place; and Mike, with his exquisite charm and wit, seemed to define exactly what *was* going on or, perhaps even better, what you would like to have going on.

Carly and I were seated on one of the large living room couches facing the view. Candles burned everywhere, and large sprays of flowers adorned the room. Mike sat directly opposite on another couch, and the darkening harbor stretched behind him. I could see my reflection in the sliding glass doors, and it was hard not to stare at myself. It seemed that Mike and I clicked immediately. He couldn't have been more helpful: He carried me along, laughed at what I said, and often recast it to make it funnier. The next day Mike called and told Carly what he thought.

Gifted and *handsome* is how Carly said he described me. *He said when you put your arms around me on the couch, you were the only man in the room.*

Mike Nichols made me feel that I might be able to keep up.

The shape and size of her life had so many unusual angles. On our next trip to the Vineyard we took the ferry from Woods Hole. It was in the middle of July, the height of the season. The stretch limo we had taken from New York stopped in front of the drab blue-and-white ferry terminal. She ran to the ticket window so we would make the next boat. Hundreds of people circled around amid luggage and rollicking black labs and golden retrievers. For many of the visitors, this was a vision they had only dreamt of: Carly Simon on the same ferry. She looked downward so she wouldn't have to engage with anyone. Once she got the ticket, her famous mouth, her escutcheon, as she liked to call it, sprang into action, and a warm smile embraced all the folks who stared at her. People flocked about on that first ride, not unlike the graceful seagulls that flew alongside, some closer and some farther away.

On that first ferry ride, I witnessed a scene that would be repeated in only slight variation so many times over the years: a respectful fandom that felt like it transcended celebrity. A couple felt compelled to tell Carly they first kissed to "Nobody Does It Better." A woman said she had gotten through the end of a love affair by listening to her *Torch* album.

I named her after you, a mother said, holding up her small daughter. *She's Carly.*

Carly's eyes began to water as she slipped off a bracelet and put it on the little girl's wrist. This, I discovered, was not the first nor would it be the last interaction of its kind, with a namesake walking away with a piece of expensive jewelry.

After returning to the city from the Vineyard at the end of July, I went to dinner with Father Juniper, a lifelong friend from my seminary days. We ate at a new restaurant in the East Village, appropriately called the Cloister. As we walked through the interior dining room into the courtyard, we stared at stained-glass windows that formed a wall in the main part of the restaurant. Two panels were of Saint Anthony holding the baby Jesus and, next to him, St. Francis was holding a skull, a reminder that death is imminent. Father Juniper laughed, pointed at the image, and said, *Don't forget him.*

The heat of the mid-July day lingered and my story spilled into the summer night. Father Juniper cautioned me to be careful. There was no need to rush, especially since there were children involved: *Give them time to get used to the idea.*

I read a poem that I had written for her called "MILDING." MILDING was the alphabetic code for her phone number at the Menemsha cottage, like GYM KRAB was in New York. I dialed it constantly during those first weeks, and thought it had a romantic sound. It was a sensual portrait of our lovemaking—*Do starlings giggle at your breasts upturned to the moon in a seizure of starlight?*

It may have been a bit too graphic to share with a Franciscan priest, but I didn't care, I wanted him to know what I was feeling.

Father Juniper sighed and then winced, *Is that what I think it is about?*

Yes, I think it is.

He looked away, as if he had to consult with his Seraphic Father, St. Francis, and then he said. *It's quite beautiful.*

On my walk home that night, I kept stopping to stare at the sky, creating my own heavens like the ceiling of Grand Central Station and the seminary chapel. Everything seemed blessed; the sound of the traffic was soothing, and the smells were exotic and alluring. I wandered this way for hours and relished it in a most sensuous way, all the while keeping the image of Francis holding the skull happily in my mind. Near Union Square, I populated the sky with an imaginary heaven and whiffed the faint vanilla scent of her presence. Standing in the run-down square, the smell of summer garbage reached me, and I heard the scurrying of rats. I replaced the olfactory and visual with my own words: a line from the poem I had just read to Father Juniper, *and I whispered a desire to the stutter of a wave.*

A few weeks later there was a reminder of St. Francis holding the skull, as a darker side of this life unfolded. I was back on the Vineyard, driving down the Menemsha cottage driveway. At the bottom of the short, steep hill was a disheveled man with long brown hair.

Do you know Carly?

No, why?

She lives around here somewhere.

She does?

Yes, and I have to get a message to her or she's going to die.

I might know someone who knows her.

No, it has to come from me. But you can look.

He showed me pages of frantically scribbled writing with pencil drawings of dragons, scorpions, and lambs. I recognized these as probably relating to the Book of Revelation.

If she doesn't get the message, she's going to die.

I told him I would see what I could do. I drove nearby to the Menemsha Bight, hung around the dock area for about ten minutes, and then returned, waved as I passed him again and then parked behind the house.

Carly was standing in the kitchen in a thin white-cotton nightgown. As I told her, she began to grow pale. Her eyes fluttered, and her stammer became more pronounced. This image was one I would never forget. She was lost, alone, and terrified. I held her in my arms in the tiny kitchen above the harbor; I knew that I would always be willing to help her in this way: saving a damsel in distress.

You mean he's right here.

Yes, at the bottom of the driveway.

That was thirty feet away.

Oh my God.

He says if he doesn't give you a message from God, you're going to die.

I'm going to die?

That's what he says, not likely.

We learned from the police that this man named John thought that God was speaking to him in a combination of her lyrics and passages from the Bible. Taken together, they delivered clear and direct guidance. Jesus was his savior, and Carly was the savior's mouthpiece and prophet. A passage from Revelation revealed to him that she had to return to James. John had learned that she was with someone new, and his voices insisted that she must remarry James. He had many other messages for her, but that was the most urgent one.

The police promised him that they would deliver the message, if he agreed to leave the island and go back home to Indiana. He wasn't satisfied with this arrangement, but he had little choice. He just kept repeating, *If she doesn't get the message, she's going to die.*

On the final day of John's stay, Captain Maloney called around ten in the morning.

Well, he's going to be on the one o'clock boat. You can tell her it's about to be over.

She stood at the bathroom mirror, and her reflection grew ashen as I told her.

What do you mean on the one o'clock boat? What about the message?

Are you crazy?

Crazy? You're not the one who's going to die.

I called Captain Maloney back immediately and told him that she needed to hear the message. The captain suggested a conference call from the police station. He would speak to John and see if that would meet with his approval. John was over the moon, and the call was arranged.

In a soothing tone, he quoted from Matthew 6:2: *Store your treasures in heaven.* That was the entire message. Then he asked, *Carly, could you sing for me? "The Stuff that Dreams Are Made Of," that's when the Lord started to speak to me.*

Sure John.

She sang the entire song, and when she came to the final chorus, he began to cry.

It's the stuff that dreams are made of
It's the slow and steady fire
It's the stuff that dreams are made of
It's the reason we are alive.

By the time she ended, he was sobbing, and she cried with him. Finally, he said, *The Lord loves you Carly. My dog "No Secrets" and I can go home now.*

Shortly after hearing about this event, Jackie Onassis pulled me aside.

Jim, let me ask you something. Does Carly open her own mail?

Yes, she does.

I haven't opened my own mail since the assassination—once information enters your psyche, it's impossible to make the distinction that it came from a crazy person. She must never open her own mail.

Yes, of course.

Here I was, in a few short months, speaking to Jacqueline Kennedy Onassis about how to handle my girl. So much had happened since the train ride up the Hudson.

Many of my co-workers thought that I was persisting in some odd extended joke: telling them that I was dating Carly Simon. One morning, she called and asked, *Can I see your office? Can we have lunch?*

You'll start a riot here.

That's okay—let's have some fun.

I knew she had arrived when I heard my secretary say, *Oh my God. It is you!* Also, a muffled male voice let go with *holy shit* at the far end of the hallway. There she stood, dressed in the shortest red-leather mini skirt I had ever seen. I could barely stand being me. I felt a surge of new male power. Every man should experience this at least once: to possess a woman everyone else desires. I felt that often in those first days, and it changed my sense of self, as if I mattered more on some primal level. I didn't realize until later that I had felt the same way about Alannah, on a less celebrated stage. Something in me loved showing other men that I had gotten exactly what they all wanted.

Carly and I walked down a long hallway and by this time, most of my colleagues were standing at their doors staring. I realized that I was taking a simple and somewhat unconscious revenge. They all understood that it wasn't my insurance acumen that had attracted her, but other qualities they had never really valued.

My office was on 44th and 6th Avenue; a restaurant called Cafe Un, Deux, Trois was just around the corner. Carly and I met there often that first summer, and this rather simple room became the setting for our courtship. During one of these meals, it dawned on me that she wanted to be near me every part of her day. I called Carly's friend Jake Brackman for guidance.

We are getting very serious, and you are the only person I know who knows her. What do I need to understand about her?

He needed a couple of hours to think about it. When I called him later, Jake said, *I've got it. She's the most neurotic human being I've ever known*—then he paused for a long moment— *She's the only one worth it.*

I had already been on a short plane ride with her, and I had never seen anyone quite as frightened. She also became extremely anxious riding in any car in highway traffic. Every odd noise sounded to her like a signal that her life was about to end, and it would send her into a state of sheer terror. She also suffered from numerous symptoms from panic and anxiety attacks. One of them involved racing to a cardiologist to make sure she wasn't dying. As she became more secure in her relationship with the doctor, she would reveal every part of her fragile makeup. Sometimes I could cajole her out of these states, and it gave me hope that I might be able to help her.

She was also hypersensitive to criticism, especially if it came from her mother, her sisters, her children, or her ex-husband. It could ruin her entire day. I also considered whether her attraction to me was connected too closely to her neuroses. After all, what was she doing with a mid-level insurance executive? Perhaps that was it. I seem to have lived in so many worlds that she had never experienced, and my having come from "the other side of the tracks" gave her a kind of comfort: that I would have an inner strength that could handle and even transform hers. My sobriety was a clear testament of my capability for change, and after her last marriage, sobriety was a powerful attraction for her. My ignorance about the world of popular music was a plus: I clearly wasn't a fan who had fallen in love with his idol.

It wasn't until we were on another train, on a promotional tour to Canada in August of 1987, that Carly began to understand the depth of my ignorance about popular music. She sat across from me gyrating to something she was listening to on her headset. I asked what it was and she said, *Otis.* When I said *Mr. Otis Regrets?* she laughed thinking it was a joke. As she looked at my blank stare, she realized it wasn't.

You don't know who Otis Redding is?

Well, I've heard the name, but not really.

Then she asked if I knew who Marvin Gaye, Bill Withers, or Al Green were. The vacant look on my face mirrored the strange emptiness of the tawny wheat fields we were passing. I assured her that I knew who Stevie Wonder and Ray Charles were, and that I knew they were both blind. She immediately surrendered her tape, which was a compilation of blues and gospel artists, patiently explaining about each musician and providing a brief riff on the importance of their music and their lives. *You have so much to learn.*

I had essentially fallen off a turnip truck. I wasn't a fan who had fallen in love with a star. I was a guy who had spent those formative years in a Franciscan Seminary.

CHAPTER

FIVE

THE TALL CARVED DOORS swung open from the main rotunda, and I entered the seminary chapel for the first time. It reflected the mysterious and sacred nature of my calling, and at fourteen years old, I felt both smaller and safer in a way I had never known. The coffered ceiling was intricately painted in shades of blue, and hundreds of stars were artfully stenciled in gold to light the heavens above. The construction was vaulted, hung from above and without obstruction. The heavens were bound beneath by a gleaming, silver-specked, black terrazzo floor. It was buffed to a high polish; the spotlights in the ceiling reflected and sparkled in the marble below. In the center of the black chapel floor was the large burgundy symbol that my aunt, Sister Leona, had tried to explain to me all those years before, during my first visit to Graymoor: the symbol that was sewn into her brown woolen habit, the intersecting triangles of the Star of David. In the interior of the seal was a five-point star ensconced in a burgundy heart. This brought another image to mind—the constantly beating and pulsating love of God.

The Kyrie Eleison from the Missa de Angelis (Mass of the Angels) filled the chapel, and the stone and wood of the room resounded with the plainsong sung by two hundred boys and men. A thick fog of smoke hung in the air from the initial censing of the altar, and the celebrants' gold chasubles radiated with majesty as the incense funneled and twisted in the light from the ceiling's spotlights and spiraled toward the heavens. I thought that I would never know a more sacred moment than this—it trumpeted the eternal significance of my decision, and it was being recognized by my creator in the splendor of this space. God, my father, through this astounding beauty, was sending me the message of His love, and I would never forget how it felt—like some deepest part of myself had been opened and filled beyond the brim and would continue to overflow forever.

Often when I noticed the shape of the heart in the middle of the intersecting triangles, I would think of my mother, that my fairy tale was certainly coming true, and the gleaming terrazzo floor brought me back to her magical barefooted mopping and singing all those years before. This world opened a part of me that had been waiting so anxiously for nourishment.

As powerful as all of this would be, it did not compare to the feelings I would experience due to a relationship I would form with a boy from Akron, Ohio, also named Jim. This new friendship transported me into a constantly elevated state of being. If I could feel so excited every time I was with him, I wondered what might happen to us in our future religious life together as Graymoor Friars. By the end of my freshman year, Jim and I had become inseparable. We were back from our summer vacations taking our night walk just before Compline. Our black robes fluttered and snapped as we entered the wooded part of the hillside. He reached inside his cassock, smiled, and handed me a Camel. He didn't smoke, but he scored them for me whenever he could. I lit it and inhaled deeply, and we both stared upward as I blew a cloud of thick smoke into the night air. The fall air was thin and clear with the hint of an early frost. I loved being at St. John's, and I especially loved it when we were alone together, hidden somewhere on the rambling property, like tonight on our walk before night prayer. Part of the power of our friendship was in its complete purity and innocence. We were consumed by the idea of trying to become young men who could serve God and his church. Our affection for each other was deeply rooted in the call of our vocation. We loved to talk about whether we were going to make it or not and what we would accomplish as priests. Jim was sure that the missionary life was what he wanted, and he already knew he wanted to be assigned to our missions in Brazil. He was more thoughtful than I, and he spent long hours carefully thinking about the future. He gathered as much information as possible and then studied all the angles. It was one of the reasons I knew he was going to be Father General. At this young age, he seemed to have an inner core that was sure of itself.

His smooth forehead wrinkled and his azure eyes narrowed and focused, and as he did, a slight breeze blew through his thick dark hair. He was always concerned about our studies. He especially wanted me to be thinking more about them than I did.

You know you're going to need to study harder on your foreign languages.

We had both just finished reading *War and Peace*, and Jim was captured by Pierre's moral dilemmas and Andrey's near-death experience at Austerlitz. He had a remarkable memory, and he often repeated whole passages. He grew most excited when talking about literature, and he was insistent on the importance of his reading. He would repeat an excerpt to me, and then expect me to memorize it as he had. He would slowly read a favorite section, and if he loved something he would repeat it over and over. Lately, it was most often Tolstoy.

I experienced the love which is the very essence of the soul, the love which requires no object. And I feel that blessed feeling now too. To love one's neighbors, to love one's enemies, to love everything—to love God in all his manifestations. Human love serves to love those dear to us but to love one's enemies we need divine love.

When I would complain to him about a faculty member or an upperclassman, he would laugh, and using his serious quoting-literature voice, he would say *I think you need "divine love."*

I could see and feel what was going to happen for him, just as sure as I could see and feel Queen Catherine's Creek beyond the next hill, winding and gurgling its way to Seneca Lake. He had been given all the gifts, and everyone knew it. He had the looks, the smarts, the drive, and even the proper amount of humility to lead an order of Franciscan priests. I could never tell which of his attributes I found most attractive: There was always another quality to admire. He constantly created a stronger emotional response within me. Every hour of every day, I wanted to be exactly like him. Lately, I was trying to copy his accent. A few weeks before, we had made a tape to send to his younger brother in Akron, Ohio. When I heard my voice, I knew I had to learn to speak differently. My thick, high-pitched New York accent made me sound like one of the Dead End Kids. I sounded like the son of a gun-toting hoodlum. I lacked any tone of intellectual and clerical gravitas. I vowed to be more silent so I could just listen carefully. This would be difficult because I loved to make him laugh, and I seemed to be able to do it better than anyone else. He never tired of my running commentary on the day's events. He knew I would do anything he asked, so he often played with me a bit.

This night he was silent, as though he was contemplating something serious, and I waited anxiously for what he was about to say. His commanding blue eyes widened, and he moved closer and whispered, *Want to go swimming tonight?*

He knew that my answer would be yes. If caught, we would both be expelled, but we knew it was such a daring idea that no one would ever suspect it. Jim had carefully plotted the scheme during geometry class. He had thought about which stairwell to use, which door to exit from, the best time, and the best route. He had thought about which of the deep pools in the nearby glen to swim in, the right clothes to wear, and the one towel that we would bring and bury there afterward. We knew that the greatest risk of discovery would be on our return, so there must be no evidence of what we had done. He was much more rule-conscious than I, yet he loved our nighttime mischief, and I suppose anyone who wants to be a good missionary needs an adventuresome spirit. We were much more concerned about another more serious rule, and we tried hard not to be identified by breaking it. I knew that I was his best friend, but the seminary handbook about "particular friendships" made saying it somewhat dangerous for both of us. *Students should associate with all other students and should neither form particular friendships nor cliques. They should remember that each student will gain something from each other for their own character formation.*

The entire school seemed to be in a deep slumber, and our escape into the moonless night was seamless. We raced over the bridge that spanned Queen Catherine's Creek, crossed the football field, and headed into the woods beyond. We were safe, but navigating in the dark was more difficult than we had thought. A dense forest surrounded us, so we slowly walked the half-mile to the bottom of Havana Glen. Once there, we had a long climb up the side of the gorge. The water roared as it moved swiftly between the cleft rocks and tumbled over numerous waterfalls on its way to the basin. The trail we took bordered the edge of the glen, and unlike in daytime, we could see very little below us. There was the constant noise of small animals scurrying as we climbed. We finally reached the deep, cold pool that Jim had chosen, and we sat on the stone ledge that had formed from eons of erosion. We were about twenty feet above the water, which in the darkness seemed miles below us. We sat for a few minutes in silence and listened to the loud flow of the water reverberating against the canyon walls.

Okay VC, time for a swim.

He had taken to calling me VC (Viet Cong) because of my last haircut in the seminary barbershop.

Am I going first?

Yep.

I nodded and began to undress. This was the first time I had ever been naked in front of him, and I had worried about it as soon as I had heard his plan. It filled me with dread, because at fifteen, I was still nearly hairless. I was terrified that he would think less of me once he realized that I was still pretty much a boy. I realized I needed to get the focus off my nakedness. I knew it would be safer to jump, but I needed to show him that although I was still a boy, I had more guts than anyone; so after I screamed *Geronimo*, I dove headlong into the water. As I hit the surface, my arm struck a rock formation to my left. I just grazed it, but it immediately made me nervous for him. If he jumped from where he was standing, he would land on it. I yelled up to him to wait. I swam around the pool and touched every part of it, and discovered there was about ten feet that were deep and unobstructed. I could see his dark outline above and I directed him to the safer end. I could see he was thinking about diving, but in the end, he just jumped in silence. As he surfaced, he let out a squeal and then said, *Oh my God it's cold! Oh my God!*

After my one quick attempt at dunking him, we got out. The water was freezing, and getting back to the top to retrieve our clothes was difficult. We climbed in the darkness up a very steep, almost vertical hill to get back across a waterfall to the other side. We were both blue, with teeth chattering by the time we arrived beneath the tree where we had left our clothes. We dried off with the thin white seminary towel, dressed, and ran back as fast as we could. It was a little past three when we opened the door to the underclassmen's stairwell. Jim said, *I'll meet you in the gym.* I snuck back into my dorm room and, without a sound, changed into my pajamas and bathrobe.

Once in the gym, I climbed the side stairs and into the wings of the dark stage. We had escaped detection many times behind the curtains. I waited a good fifteen minutes before I heard his slippered steps coming across the gym floor. As he got closer, I could see he was carrying a half-filled five-gallon tub of ice cream that he had stolen from the kitchen. By the time we finished, we were shivering again. He belched after his last scoop and then reached over, put his arm around my head, and put me in a headlock. I slipped out and threw him on his back. We wrestled like this all the time. We would pin each other down in every imaginable position, but tonight something else began to happen. A sensation flooded through me, not unlike the feeling I had when I could feel Our Lord or St. Francis listening to me — a kind of bliss.

He twisted my arm and pressed his body on top of mine. He clutched me in a tight half-nelson, and suddenly a new feeling spread throughout my body: a deep peace transferred from him to me. I didn't know what had happened, but then I easily slipped his hold, flipped him over, and had him begging for mercy. It was such an odd, unfamiliar feeling that I soon feigned tiredness and headed back to my dorm room.

Somehow, I knew that this had something to do with my love for him, and yet I knew it couldn't happen again.

Over the next few weeks, I became more competitive with him. He had read *Brothers Karamazov* in four days. I did it in three. I devoured fourteen pieces of Sicilian pizza in an hour-long eating contest, and Jim could only handle twelve. I wrote a novel for Father Columkille's literature class, and he struggled with a short story. Somehow our constant desire to compete with each other made us grow even closer, that the only necessary proof of our ascent toward perfection was our judgment of each other. Our competitions created a world of mutual admiration. I found myself mesmerized by the elegant insteps of his feet, and the way he pulled his thick gray-wool socks over them, or the way he carefully tied his Franciscan sash around his waist so that the lengths of the cords were perfectly matched, always precise and respectful. He marveled at how no upperclassman could intimidate me (he didn't know my father). But without question, it was the strength of my faith that held the most power over him. My faith was unabashed, while his was a bit more qualified and subtle. I remember how shocked he was when I told him that God spoke to me. He constantly asked me to repeat the story.

It was five years earlier, on Christmas of 1960, and my sister Marie had been born less than a month before. I was a soloist for the first time. I stood in the choir loft for the midnight mass dressed in a red cassock and a starched, snow-white surplice with a scarlet bow around my neck. I sang the Panis Angelicus (Bread of Heaven) and listened as the notes soared above the wooden rafters in front of me. My voice filled the church, and I could feel the world beneath pause to listen. I pronounced those words to the world: *O Res Mirabilis*, and as the last strain ended, I heard a voice deep within me, and it said, *Praise Me*. God had begun his conversation with me, and I knew it would never end.

We had just returned from Christmas vacation. I had sworn the night before that I would go skating with him that Sunday afternoon. When he came to get me, I said I was too tired. It was unusual for me to lack energy in the middle of the day, but I just couldn't get out of bed. He screamed, *You're a jerk, you promised*, and left the room. As I slept a very deep sleep, he and another boy named Denis skated their way west on Queen Catherine's Creek. If I had gone, I know what I would have seen: the smooth stroke of their skates, the sleek sound of Jim gaining speed, and the bend and curve of his body as he forged ahead. He was a very good skater.

It was a thrilling place to skate, especially in the late afternoon as evening was coming on, like gliding through a primeval wonderland. Large, crooked willows overhung the creek, and dark fallen tree branches of all sizes were frozen atop and in the ice. The slanting winter sunlight peeked through, and dark orange colors burst between the trees. The landscape moved backward, and whenever I think of that place, I see the tracks of their skates on the ice. The tributaries of the creek system led into a wide canal that fed into Seneca Lake. We were forbidden to skate on the canal, but everyone did anyway. We would go right to the southern edge of the lake, which never froze.

Just the night before, Jim had read me a passage from *Keys of the Kingdom* by A.J. Cronin. It was at the opening of the book, which we both had read multiple times. He especially loved it because it was the story of a missionary priest in China. He couldn't get over the beauty of the language. He read it over and over until I made him stop. When I awoke from my nap and my bare feet touched down on the frigid terrazzo floor, the words repeated within me.

The air was thin and clear, stringent with wood smoke and the tang of fallen apples, sharp with the hint of early frost.

The late afternoon temperature rapidly dropped, from a moment of mid-winter spring to bitter cold. The ice was thin that day from the earlier thaw, yet they sped along. I knew if they didn't hurry, they would be late for Sunday dinner. I tried to imagine exactly where they were on their way back. I could see the right and left banks of the deep tributary that were covered with snow, and disappearing quickly behind them. The trees above looked like a long, darkening nave of a Gothic cathedral; the tall, forbidding trees arched overhead and began to obscure everything but the darkness. Then, apparently, one of them hit a stick, or caught his skate, or just landed on a patch of ice that was too thin; no one ever knew, but they fell.

When they missed dinner, I knew something must be wrong, so I went searching for them. As I hurried toward the canal, I could hear Jim reciting that passage. My body was pounding, racing, pulsing, and I could hear his newly dark and dusky adolescent bass voice as I ran.

The air was thin and clear with wood smoke and the tang of fallen apples, sharp with the hint of early frost.

I was the first person to reach the spot. Their watch caps were frozen in the ice; their tracks on the white surface ended, and so did I, never really to return. I stood alone for what seemed like hours. I stared at the spot below me, knowing that they were there beneath me, and knowing there was nothing I could do. Finally, I could see scores of flashlights lighting the woods in the distance, and I heard the blare of the fire horns. I started to scream, *Over here, over here.* I stood above them unable to move.

Finally, when the boats with the grappling hooks were placed in the water, a 250-pound theology teacher lifted me from the spot. I screamed and sobbed as the car he had placed me in drove away. I begged to stay. That last eerie shot of the bright searchlights on the creek and all those men searching for their bodies made the location of their death look like a construction site rather than the sacred place of their ending.

When I arrived back at the seminary, I sat in a classroom at the end of the hall staring at the blackboard. There were dates from Friday's world history class, which had been partially erased. Each day a different student was chosen to write the appropriate dates on the board from memory. Three of the dates were still vaguely visible.

> *1050 - Astrolabe used in Europe*
> *1066 - Battle of Hastings*
> *1080 - The Bayeux Tapestry is commissioned*

For the rest of my life, I would know these three eleventh-century dates. They would emerge in their partially erased form and surface at the strangest moments. Suddenly, Father Columkille O'Shea stood in front of me, his lips trembling, and said the impossible in his Brooklyn accent.

Jim and Denis are dead. They found their bodies.

Denis was a great kid, but I would only feel Jim's death. I so wanted to hear *He's alive*, but I was told, *Jim is dead.* I could see the blue turtleneck sweater, the thick corduroys, the woolen socks that I had watched him put on so many times, and the blue-wool watch cap that he had tugged down over his head for two winters. All of my desires were unfettered in my grief. I wanted him beside me, above me, beneath me, and within me in every way possible. I wanted him with me, and I would never let go of him again, never listen to anyone who wanted him absent from me. But amid the noise of the grappling hooks scraping against the ice as they dredged in the cold water of the deep, narrow creek, I could hear the harbinger of all my sorrows to come. I could see it in the dates in chalk on the blackboard, and I could see it in the face of the young priest. Now hidden deeply beneath the frozen stream of myself, my love for this boy would be forever lost. I would never find the way to know what I really felt, but that night, I felt the certainty of my call from God slip away beneath the overhanging willows, taking the soul of my love, never to return it.

Every part of life became a vestige of a former and perfect world. Jim had gone so quickly and so far away. People kept saying that he had *gone to heaven*; not for me he hadn't. He was alive in every single hour of my day, every scent, sound, chapel service, and ballgame. He was alive in every breath that came in and out of my body; he just wasn't *here*.

The place I most powerfully felt his presence was in chapel. It was where we most loved to be, and every chapel service had been another event in our friendship. His choir stall was a bit to my left on the opposite side. We had developed a collection of signs and signals that only we understood. He would tilt his head just a little more to the left when we were about to sing the first note of our favorite hymn. Then he would smile as he did it so that we were always both smiling as we sang the first line:

Lead kindly light, amid encircling gloom,
Lead Thou me on.

As we got to the second line, all smiling ended, and we were both surrounded by the earnest power of our mission, and the overwhelming and enveloping sound of two hundred boys and men begging to be led.

The night is dark and I am far from home,
Lead Thou me on.

After Jim's death, it was impossible for me to listen to this hymn. Each time it was sung, I would begin to cry and had to rush out of chapel; and yet I kept singing it to myself, hoping that God somehow might help me. I especially focused on the final line of the first verse.

Keep thou my feet; I do not ask to see
The distant scene one step enough for me.

I considered my constant repetition of this hymn as the prayer that summoned him to me. A few weeks after his death, I had a dream that felt more like a vision or apparition. Jim walked with me around the grounds and through the seminary building. He was encircled by a golden aura, and he kept smiling and calling me *VC*. He finally held me and said, *VC, everything is perfect. I have never been happier. You must continue, continue for both of us.*

At the end of the term, I was summoned by the rector, Father DeSales Standerwick. I had spent a great deal of time with Father DeSales in the last few months. As an act of humility, he would perform the most arduous penance given each week alongside the student who had committed the gravest infraction. This was often me. In spite of Jim's final command during his apparition, I started to misbehave even more than I had before. As a result, I spent many hours with Father DeSales. I can still see the two of us breaking up rocks into gravel for a road that led from the main building to the gym. I was still an undeveloped boy and quite skinny. He was six feet tall and couldn't have weighed much over 130 pounds, and as his thin arms lifted the sledge hammer, I was often reminded of my favorite student nickname for him, *Father DeSales Standingstick.* He paused frequently to catch his breath to tell me little parables or quote long passages of poetry and literature. Yet, not once in our time together did he ever speak to me of Jim's death. I needed something or someone, but the only advice I ever received was to pray. I tried, but after the vision, prayer didn't seem to do any good. I knelt for hours in the chapel and stared at the life-sized Christ over the main altar and begged for help. Or I would stare up at the depiction of the cosmos on the chapel's coffered ceiling, lost in the swirl of the tinted shades of the blue heavens and the distant gold stars, hoping that something would happen. Usually I would leave the chapel with tears streaming down my face. After a time, I just stopped praying, and my feelings began to take the form of disobeying all the rules and doing none of my work.

I knew this was the end, and I knew what he was going to say. Of all people, I didn't want Father DeSales to be the one to say it. It would be like hearing the voice of the entire Catholic Church making a decision about me, and I knew what it was going to be: a judgment, as vivid as Michelangelo's *Last Judgment* in the Sistine Chapel, and that it would be the last and only one that would ever matter in my life. I felt myself grasping at and falling away from what I had loved most: Jim and the Graymoor Friars, and here was someone with all the necessary authority to deliver the news. If he was capable of telling Jim's parents, *Your son is dead*, then I was sure he could tell me that I was expelled.

He sat behind a large mahogany desk with his head down in a pose of contemplation. He was an ascetic, scholar, churchman, and teacher, a great teacher, but unlike St. Jerome, the great Doctor of the Church, he smoked three packs of Old Gold cigarettes a day. He carried them in his cowl; he would reach behind and pluck them out in one fluid movement. He smiled just for the briefest moment and offered me one. I made a gesture of refusal, and he said, *James, please, it's all right, have one.* He certainly knew of my daily habit. I lit the cigarette and inhaled as deeply as he did.

Well, James, his voice emitted a nasal whisper that seemed covered by incense, something sacred, and at the same time, something sinister; he always seemed to be speaking out of his nose and mouth at the same time.

You would have to be half St. Thomas Aquinas and half St. Francis of Assisi to remain here.

I paused, inhaled my bottom lip into my mouth and said,

Is that all, Father?

Yes, James.

He never said I had been expelled, but I knew I had been. In an instant, he changed his expression from one of stern responsibility to almost childlike wonder. I had seen him do it before, and I never knew how someone could shift so quickly. I thought of it then as a sign of a keen intelligence.

James, I am very fond of you. In fact, you are one of my favorite students. You have an extremely attractive spirit, which makes this even harder for me.

I wanted to make this easier for him, but just as with my father, I didn't know how. Then he told me in great detail what he had experienced the night of Denis and Jim's deaths. The worst nightmare that could happen had taken place: Students entrusted to his care had died on his watch. He told me of the horror of having to call their parents. I felt so sorry for him. I wanted to hug him in some way, but instead we just stared at each other without saying a word. Then, without warning, he jumped up from behind his desk, darted to a cabinet across the office, and in his nasal whisper said, *I've found them, I've found them.*

He then told me how he had followed Dylan Thomas to numerous poetry readings when he was a graduate student at Columbia, and how he had taped every reading. *Listen James, just listen.* He hit the play button on the large Wollensack recorder. As my soul tumbled, I heard the voice of Dylan Thomas read his poems. We sat there for hours. The sound of his words seemed to open a place within me. I knew that Jim would love this scene of DeSales and me and Dylan Thomas together. I would use poetry throughout my life as a tool to know that somewhere outside and beyond my own disappointments, there existed a way to feel.

I went through the next two weeks in a daze. I got drunk for the first time with a group of graduating seniors the day before school closed. I had two cans of Genesee Cream Ale the night before graduation. I threw up, blacked out, and had to be put to bed, and I loved it. For the first time, the switch was turned off, and it produced a silence I would come to adore. It was not unlike the feeling I had when I listened to Dylan Thomas that afternoon. The rolling incantation of his voice filled all the cracks and crevices, as did those two cans of beer.

Oh, I was young and easy in the mercy of his means.

CHAPTER
SIX

———————⋅———————

I KIND OF STOPPED functioning after Jim died, and they didn't know what to do with me, so they sent me home.

Jackie sighed gently, and then spoke in her breathy whisper.

Do you know the Kübler-Ross model?

The stages of grief?

Yes. She rattled them off: denial, anger, bargaining, depression, and acceptance.

Not long ago, someone told me about an African tribe that beat their drums and scream in anger for a whole day and night when somebody dies.

She stopped and stared away for a moment. *I was so angry about Jack, but I didn't know what to do about it.*

The memory of watching Jackie Kennedy that entire weekend in November of 1963 washed over me, and I recalled the impact of her image on my decision to become a priest. She had stood next to the flag-draped coffin, and always would, in that simple black dress and long black mantilla. Now two dozen years later, on this autumn afternoon, here she was sitting across from me in a house built by James Taylor, dressed only in a bathing suit, a sarong, and a deep tan.

Carly had left us alone while she drove "up island" to see James's sister Kate Taylor; she had bought Jackie a wampum bracelet from Kate as a birthday present back in May, and it needed a clasp repaired. This meeting wasn't exactly accidental. She clearly wanted Jackie's opinion of me, and this was her chance to get it.

They had first met when Jackie called Carly to ask her if she would sing at Caroline's wedding in July of 1986. The two women connected right away. Whatever the occasion, Carly and Jackie loved to laugh and gossip with each other, and like schoolgirls, they loved to talk about boys. They both especially adored one boy—Mike Nichols.

Now sitting at a small round table in the den-like room off the kitchen, it was all a bit much—especially when Jackie said, *Jim, you've had the most fascinating life I've ever heard of.*

I raised my eyebrows and stared. At first, I thought she was being ironic or maybe even sarcastic, or perhaps even a bit slow. What a ridiculous thing for her to say. Could she possibly mean it? Yet she stared directly at me and seemed quite sure of her observation.

I've grown up in essentially one place, one kind of society, that's what I mean. You've lived in so many—such a range.

I laughed, thinking she still might be playing with me a bit, but in the ensuing silence, it was clear that she wasn't. I had known her less than an hour, and I had revealed so many intimate details of my life, and she was still curious. I had the sense that, somewhat like a little girl, she wanted to hear from a man who was different from the others, someone whom her more worldly and experienced girlfriend had chosen from out of the pack. Jackie knew that Carly had been involved with so many notorious men of rock and roll; as well as many other men of fame and artistic achievement. Carly, a woman she believed could have almost any man, had chosen me.

Jim, why do you think you went to the seminary?

I talked about running away from my abusive father to an all-loving, all-knowing, and sane father, and about the attraction of the aesthetic: the music, the art, the flowers, the vestments, and the ritual. There was also the intelligence, education, and tender attention of the friars. I realized that the order's motto sounded like something straight out of Camelot and I repeated it to her.

Ut Omnes Unum Sint (That They All Be One)

Do you still believe in it?

I said something about how I had struggled ever since those seminary days, and how, especially after Eamon's problems, belief had become more and more difficult.

I know, after Jack, it was almost impossible, but I so wanted it to be true.

Yes, me too. I've never been happier.

I tried to touch that feeling again—to see if it could be experienced for the two of us now as we sat there.

What kind of order was it?

They were Franciscans.

I always liked Franciscans. They're different from some of the others, aren't they? They always seem so kind.

I gave her a brief history of the Society of the Atonement. Father Paul and Mother Lurana, the founders, had engaged in a love affair straight through God. Theirs was a romantic story of radical belief and passionate religious fervor.

I had noticed that women were much more taken by this story than men, and Jackie was quite intrigued. I had forgotten that her ties to the Catholic Church were very deep. After all, she had been our country's only Catholic First Lady, and she had staged the most spectacular funeral in the history of the nation — largely due to her grasp and love of the ritual and meaning of Catholicism.

It sounds so romantic.

Were they in love with each other?

Yes, no doubt.

Do you think they had a physical relationship?

I told her no one would ever know for sure, but I didn't think so.

Much better if they didn't.

I laughed, *Yes, certainly more romantic.*

Why did you leave?

I laughed again. *They threw me out.*

Unlike the nature of this first conversation, most of our time together would be light and casual. It was hard not to notice everything about Jackie, but the trick was to notice almost nothing. To make her comfortable, you had to treat her as you would anyone else, and that of course meant to carefully not pay attention to her.

Something I always noticed about her was the intense control she had of her body. I had the sense that she was often trying to hold on to it, so that it wouldn't slip its moorings and sail away from her. She often seemed to be holding it at a vertical slant. In almost all the pictures that we ever took with her, and there weren't many, she was mostly standing with her body slanting away. She seemed to be struggling for distance, especially when she knew she was being captured by the public eye. She knew that no matter how small and intimate the gathering or how famous the other folks, that she was the main event for any camera.

She rarely lingered with her touch. When we kissed or hugged, she would try to hold you away a bit, though not without affection. She was always holding herself at least a tiny bit apart. There is a picture of the two of us on her beach on Labor Day of 1987. At the last minute, she stepped away from me and stared in the opposite direction. The picture looked as though we had been shipwrecked and were looking out to sea for help.

In spite of this first moment, Jackie became quite relaxed with me. It was difficult to see her without all the filters of memory; all of us who knew her would often speak of this. Her friends wanted to let her have as normal an experience as possible. I think it is one of the great gifts that Carly gave her. Carly was more of the crazy artist than any of Jackie's other close friends, and I think this helped Jackie come to know that place within herself. Everything about her was laden in history, whereas everything about Carly was always focused on the emotional present. Carly could never fake that. If you were Carly's friend, you were going to be forced into feeling, and I think Jackie loved that in her life. She wanted to tell a girlfriend how she felt as a woman, and Carly was the perfect choice. Carly and Jackie also loved their shared mischief. I remember early on sitting in our bedroom suite with Jackie. Carly suddenly turned to her and, as though we had known each other forever, asked, *So, who would you say is the sexiest man you've ever been with?*

Jackie answered without hesitation. She answered it as though she had been eager to tell someone for a long time just so she could share the thrill of the surprising nature of her answer. Her face broke into a large smile, and her breathy voice filled with delight as she answered.

She was always interested in my opinions about men. She knew some of my history and my problems with addiction, but she also knew I was a "man's man." She could see that I formed deep friendships with other men. Also, I know she thought I was a bit of a bad boy myself, and therefore felt that I knew something about their inner workings, which she was fascinated by.

One early afternoon on the Vineyard, Carly and I were engaged in a screaming battle over some issue that I have long forgotten, and in the midst of it, Jackie called. When she asked Carly how she was, Carly, true to form, launched into a vitriolic rant about me. She kept excitedly producing more damning evidence, which I could hear from the other room. Carly's end of the discussion was peppered with well-worn phrases: *And then the son of a bitch*, and *then he said*, and *He had the fucking nerve.* Toward the end of the conversation, I heard Carly burst into spontaneous laughter, the sort you can't fake in the middle of a rage. I heard her end the conversation with *Thank you—I love you.*

Carly returned to the living room where I had been waiting, and I could see that something miraculous had happened; she was giggling.

Well, you heard me screaming?

Of course.

Well she kept saying, "Calm down, Carly, calm down."

Her saying that made me want to convince her more and she kept saying, "Calm down, Carly, calm down."

She realized this wasn't working; I kept calling you another name.

So?

She screamed, "Stop it!" I had never heard her sound like that, so I stopped. Then, she whispered, "Listen, Carly, I was married to a couple of characters myself."

Jackie had a soft spot for men who were characters. I know she found the serious, straight ones mostly too much to bear. She never seemed too impressed with men of power. Perhaps by the time I met her, she had had her fill of such men. She really seemed much more interested in people with wit and style.

One evening I was complimenting a powerful man who was a friend of hers. I said, *Isn't he amazing? All that he's done. And how many languages does he speak?*

She said, *Five, fluently.*

Really?

Yes, and he's boring in every one.

We roared with laughter at the truth of her statement.

It was just a few days before Jackie's sixty-second birthday, and I asked her, *"Is there anything that you would really like for your birthday that we might not think of?*

I'll let you know.

She called Carly the next day: *Isn't Jim a good friend of Alec Baldwin's?*

I had met him through a writer I knew and we were soon hanging out together.

Yes, they're pretty close.

Well, do you think, would it be too much to ask, Well, do you think Alec could be my date for the theatre on my birthday?

Carly called out to me to pick up the extension. Jackie and Carly were still laughing over something when I picked up the phone.

Hi Jim, I want to ask you something.

Yes.

Well, we're having dinner and then going to the theatre on my birthday.

Great.

Alec Baldwin is a friend of yours?

Yes, he is.

Well, do you think, he could be my date?

I was surprised by the openness of the request, but I acted as though there was nothing unusual about it.

I'm sure, if he can, well, let me call and ask.

Alec was the most shocked of all, but there wasn't a moment's hesitation, even though he had just met Kim Basinger, *I'm there.*

You sure?

Are you kidding? Jackie Kennedy wants to go on a date? Of course.

CHAPTER

SEVEN

THE SIENA COLLEGE FOOTBALL team had just won the first game of
the 1968 season, and we were celebrating the victory in a place called the Hat
in Albany. I found myself fully clothed on top of a young woman in the back
room of the bar. I could faintly hear a man's voice calling out.

I heard her sighs and groans, which sounded like indications of pleasure.
I emerged briefly from my blackout, and an upperclassman sat me upright
to down another shot of whiskey. I quickly returned to the sawdust-covered
floor and felt her pelvis grind against me. The man's voice was now closer
and much more strident, *James, get up! Now!* I could feel someone trying to
lift me off the girl. When I realized what he was doing, I freed myself from
his grip and returned to my sweetheart. Then I heard him again, *James, I
said now!*

Suddenly, it registered that he was someone I knew, and in a moment
of clarity, I realized he was Father Juniper, the rector of the college seminary program. As awareness flooded through me, I slowly extended the
middle finger of my right hand and said, *Fuck off.* I didn't mean to be
rude; I just needed to let him know that I was dealing with something of
greater importance. I could vaguely see him there in his Roman collar,
shaking his head in disbelief. Perhaps I finally understood an aphorism of
my father's that had always mystified me: *Be afraid of no man's face, and no
woman's ass.*

I awoke the next day, and as I stood, sawdust fell from my face and hair.
Snatches of last night slowly appeared and disappeared. I could hear the

click of a film projector, the images grainy and poorly lit. The sun was high, which meant I had missed mass, not the best move for a first-year college seminary student.

I had been readmitted to the Graymoor Friars college program after being expelled two years before, the year that Jim had died. I rejoined my class and we attended Siena, a Franciscan College outside Albany, New York. As early as the Middle Ages, these friars, the Order of Friars Minor, had houses of study in all the university cities of Europe: Paris, Oxford, Cambridge, Cologne, Bologna, and Padua. They were not newcomers to education. As one of the older friars used to say, *Not so sure about the Ivy League—still an experiment.* The Graymoor seminary was off campus and stood on a high bluff above the Hudson. It had once been part of the Van Rensselaer estate, and the massive Greek revival manor house was where the aspirants to the priesthood lived. The real reason for my decision to return was Jim. I felt that I had to follow his command at the end of my apparition: *to continue for both of us.*

I believed that the power of my love for him would see me through the most difficult of questions, for I was continuing the quest that we had begun together. I was going to become a priest no matter what I had to do. I was willing to sublimate not only my sexuality, but also my growing realization that I didn't really believe in the Jesus stuff anymore. Except for the sawdust incident, I would spend the year of 1968–69 as a celibate. I marvel now at such an achievement at the age of eighteen in the midst of the sexual revolution.

When I had shaken off all the sawdust, I opened the door to my cell-like room, and found a note taped to it in a hand that I recognized. *See me—Father Juniper.* I shuffled into the shower and tried to think of something I might say in explanation. I prayed to Jim and hummed our favorite hymn from the old days, *Lead Kindly Light.* I wanted to get this over quickly, but Father Juniper wasn't going to be back until evening, so I had the whole afternoon to quiver, shake, sweat, and pray.

He lived in a small two-room suite. I knocked. When he saw me, his facial muscles tightened, and he said, *Come in,* as if it were one word. I sat and watched him gather his thoughts. Finally his lower lip began to quiver and, in an extremely low and soft voice, he began: *Never in my life has anyone. . . .*

His voice never raised above a whisper, yet he raged and ranted on; telling me of his work, his education, his international travel, his clerical office, and finally, how in all those years, no one had ever treated him with such disrespect. It did cross my mind to go for broke and say, *Well it was about time*, but I refrained.

I let him rant until he finally ran out of steam. He just stared away and waited for me to break the silence. I didn't know what to say. I just kept repeating over and over how sorry I was. He was silent, and so in a tremulous voice, I finally said, *I suppose I should start packing.*

He looked as if he were about to nod his head yes, but then changed his mind. *I think we're going to chalk this one up to booze. But if you are going to be a priest, you'll to have to learn* how *to drink.*

Yes, Father.

Little did he know what an eager and avid student he had on his hands. And little did I know what a world-class professor I had for this course. Father Juniper was probably the best drinker I would ever meet. My criteria: drink enormous quantities, remain absolutely cogent and emotionally balanced, get up in time for morning prayers, and function perfectly well all day long. This was someone who could drink like a man, and I patterned myself in his image. We soon found our way out of the discussion about my outrageous behavior and into my opinions on everything that was going on, and within minutes, we were both holding rocks glasses containing very dry martinis.

This was the beginning of a daily drinking habit, the rector and his model seminarian eagerly teaching and eagerly learning how to drink prodigious amounts of booze. I don't think I ever missed a class because of my drinking that first year, and Father Juniper, who was a theology professor, never missed a lecture. This was especially challenging on the many nights we never slept. We often chatted straight through the night into the next day. There was little talk about theology; it was mostly about community.

We constantly reviewed how the other seminarians were doing, as though I was the assistant rector. He elevated my worth above that of the other students, and he became the only person I wanted to be near. He was the perfect example of what I wanted to be. In many ways, I felt the same way I did about Jim—except Father Juniper had made it. He had studied in Rome, he was an athlete, an intellectual, and he had both a masculine and easy way with everyone. He even had mannerisms that reminded me of Jim. One was the way they both became serious with me by calling me *James* and suddenly looking very solemn. In both cases, it always made me laugh.

I was a true naïf, and I presumed that all the other seminary students were like me, trying to be celibate. I would soon find out that some were having sex with women, some with men, and a few with each other. More enlightened views of sexuality were developing, but women were still the enemy: They stole seminarians away. There seemed to be a pervasive easy pass for all things gay, because that sin could be forgiven, and it didn't mean you couldn't be a priest. I think many of the straight students found this atmosphere uncomfortable, and it hastened their departures.

At the end of the year, Father Juniper and I walked through Washington Park in Albany where every year a tulip festival is held. We had just enough money for one martini, so we sat in a bar near the park and shared it between us. He never forgot it and wrote a long letter to me that ended with *I'll always be here to share a tulip and a martini.*

Juniper and I had one last task, my leaving the seminary. We both knew I had to go. We sat in his office, and I said it, *I think I have to leave.* Juniper smiled widely, but his eyes betrayed true sadness. He said, *Yes I think you have to go also. Why do you think you have to leave?*

I don't believe in God anymore.

You know, he said, *some of our greatest saints struggled with belief: Paul, Francis, Augustine; maybe you're just preparing for sainthood. I'm not worried about that; your faith is in your bones. I think your non-belief will change. But you have another major problem that I don't think will go away.*

What's that?

Celibacy.

I was nineteen and I had still not been with a woman. My three sexual experiences had been with men, all in drunken situations: a marine, a priest, and a poet. I thought this had occurred because of my time in the seminary and its all-male environment. I was dying to be with a woman so I could truly understand what I was missing. Here I was in 1969, two years after the summer of love, and I hadn't yet been laid. My psyche was screaming, *Me too.* This made my entire sophomore year excruciatingly difficult. I was terrified at the thought of being with a woman, so my sex life became a series of drunken sexual events with men, with one major crush on a boy whom I didn't know what to do with—I adored him.

The first time: He was sitting at the piano in the seminary recreation room. He had on the flowing robes of a Franciscan friar, and he was playing Chopin beautifully on an out-of-tune upright piano. He controlled himself, the instrument, and the mood of the room. I immediately felt that I could appreciate his talent more than anyone else, and I knew I wanted to be closer to him. The beauty of what he could create transformed him, and his entire countenance seemed to be in touch with a deeper pleasure, something beyond the rest of us. He was in the novitiate, which meant that he was a few years older. He combined physical and spiritual beauty; perhaps it was the combination of music and contemplation that did it. Novitiate was a time of intense contemplation: a final year of discernment before the taking of vows.

Everything about him seemed to glide like one note smoothly eliding into another. His long blond hair overflowed onto his cowl, and his blue eyes sparkled as he played. I could see by his second look at me, and his subsequent laugh, that he had noticed me as well. I sensed in that first moment that he was destined to live an unusually large life. Brian was gay, and it clearly delighted him, while the very thought of it drove me into dark and desperate places. So I tried not to think of it in that context, and yet I felt such a strong emotional and physical attraction.

He left religious life soon after we met. He attended the Curtis Institute of Music in Philadelphia to study piano, and one Saturday afternoon in the summer of 1970, we found ourselves in a bar near his school. We had a few martinis and, after a couple of hours, decided to go to New York. He told me about a place he was going to take me to, and his only proviso was that I had to go with him, *no questions asked.*

He decided to take the George Washington Bridge to cross the Hudson so we could see Manhattan before us. A haze from the sultry night air surrounded each lamplight on Riverside Drive and made the darkness glisten with moisture. His Volkswagen Beetle had a feel of soft luxury as we careened into the city, and our laughter echoed with abandon into the open night sky. His tiny car seemed to be the center of happiness. We parked near Lincoln Center and found The Balloon. An undercurrent of sensuality permeated this bar, and it seemed largely about men. Nureyev and the corps de ballet drank there, and Brian was excited to see it through my eyes. I thought this might be the world I should be living in, and as each lithe and perfectly contoured man walked by, I felt even closer to Brian. I knew it wasn't a lie that I probably liked women a great deal. My deception was my refusal to admit how much I liked men and, sitting there that night, I was thrilled by them. After a few more martinis, we were ready for the night's adventure. The Balloon was just the overture. He warned me not to be wary, that no matter what I thought or felt, it would be one of the most unusual nights of my life.

Moments later, I was placing my wallet and house keys in a miniature strongbox. I was given a key with an elastic band and a towel with "Continental Baths" inscribed on it. The bathhouse was located on the ground floor of the Ansonia, a landmarked Beaux Arts hotel that had been turned into an apartment building. As I moved away from the entrance, the receptionist screamed in a high-pitched voice, *Hey you, you didn't sign in.* I returned to the table and began to shake as he shoved the sign-in sheet toward me.

With this signature, I thought, *I might forever be exposed as a fag.*

Probably thanks to the large amount of gin I had ingested, I signed anyway and entered. The main room had a pool, showers, and a bar. At the other end, an unattractive and foul-mouthed girl was singing idiotic dirty songs. I couldn't see why the towel-clad boys standing in front of her liked her so much. The girl was named Bette Midler—it was her opening weekend at the Continental Baths. I tried to find a place to take all this in, but I couldn't find my bearings. A sort of shimmering vapor separated me from the other boys. I knew I wasn't like them; I just couldn't be.

Brian soon disappeared into the Baths' labyrinthine maze. My heart broke as he walked away. I tried to follow, but I lost him. There were long corridors with small cell-like rooms without ceilings. The pungent aroma of amyl nitrate permeated the space, and I was surrounded by heavy breathing, moaning, and the insistent sighs and yelps of men on their way to orgasm. I couldn't get accustomed to the sounds and rhythms, and I roamed aimlessly, stunned by what was going on around me. Some of it was behind closed doors, and some was out in the open. As it turned toward morning, I longed to express something of myself in this strange world. I walked by a room where ten or so very good-looking young men had formed a circle and were stroking each other. I thought this was an activity I could participate in, nothing definitive. It lasted only a few minutes; I was too excited for it to last longer. I went home confused, but not unhappy. I felt that I was *just a bit of* a homo, as exemplified by my *restrained* activity.

I don't know how I processed all of this at the time, except that my father had an expression that no one seems to use anymore. Whenever I was late for something that didn't send him into a rage, he would ask, as though it were possible, *What took you so long? Did you go by way of Canarsie?*

Canarsie in this expression represented a place beyond the pale: a location near the ends of the earth. It turns out that Canarsie is only 18.9 miles from Long Beach, and yet it seemed so far away that you could only get there or return from there with immense effort.

My sexual confusion and many other parts of my life were also right under my nose, yet so far away. Here I was at a gay bathhouse trying to figure out how to be straight: an odd place to discover my love for women. I guess as my father might say I was going *by way of Canarsie.*

My father had certainly gone by a circuitous route from Hell's Kitchen in the 1920s through his recovery from alcoholism and his emergence as a truly remarkable father as he continued to stay sober. My relationship with him had also traveled a rather circuitous route, and one incident stands out as emblematic of how he transformed his relationship with me. He had changed from those early, wildly abusive days into a father who kept seeking to find ways to love me. Our attempts at getting closer throughout our lives would make the trip to Canarsie seem worthwhile.

He had a deep feeling for people who had it tough. He didn't have anything against people who had it easy; he just wasn't very interested in them. He had a special, large, and infectious smile for folks like himself. My father's smile was stunning, because it transformed the sheet of granite that served as his face into a mug with a leprechaun's sudden delight. He had certainly come up the hard way. Yet as he grew older, his harshness kept softening, and more and more it was about how he could get closer to his life and the things he loved, though he had taken many circuitous routes. He had definitely gone *by way of Canarsie.*

The incident that began to change my relationship with my father in a palpable way was during Christmas vacation in my first year at college, which would make it December of 1968. I went with him to the train station to pick up a guy named Lucky who was going to be speaking at my father's group of recovering alcoholics. My father kept talking about what an amazing story this guy Lucky had. He had been in prison for murder, and now he was a happy and sober member of my father's fellowship. At this point in my life, I was drinking a number of very dry martinis on the rocks as often as I could. I was drinking every day with Father Juniper and, due to his excellent instruction, I had learned how to hold my liquor quite well. So the idea that this murderer didn't drink anymore didn't seem like much of an accomplishment to me. After all, I drank about as much as anyone I knew, and I was becoming a Franciscan priest. Drinking didn't make me want to start shooting people.

The whole logic of this recovery business seemed to be built on rather shaky ground. My father himself used to say that he had been institutionalized more than fifty-five times before he was thirty-five. I never quite understood what "more than fifty-five times" meant. Did it mean fifty-seven times or nine hundred times? I would slowly learn over the years that he had been a career criminal, pretty much until he got sober at thirty-five.

I was very impressed with Lucky's physical presentation. A very large baldheaded black man with two gold earrings stepped off the train. Lucky was about six-four and probably weighed in at about 280. He was an impressive sight. My father and Lucky immediately kissed one another and then embraced tenderly. It was hardly a perfunctory hug, but rather the long and tender touch of people in love. I was shocked. What did this mean? It clearly wasn't about lurking sexuality, rather quite the opposite. It was about two extremely tough men not being afraid to express something powerful toward each other in public.

I was quite disturbed by the tableau, and when my father arrived home at the end of the day after dropping Lucky back at the train station, I attacked.

You know, I don't get it. You kiss and hug this big black murderer whom you barely know, and you've never hugged or kissed me my entire life.

My father was stunned by this, but not at all in a defensive way: He was stunned happy. He crossed the living room and said, *Well that will change right now.*

He held me in his arms tightly, and kissed me tenderly on the lips. For the rest of our lives, he would greet me that way every time we met. It would take us a long time to figure out our relationship with one another, but we did finally get there.

I guess I felt that my sexual identity was going to be discovered in much the same way: that I would have to go *by way of Canarsie.*

CHAPTER

EIGHT

———————◆———————

THE HOUSE THAT ALANNAH'S father left us was a copy of an Italian villa in Northern Italy. The mansion had a colonnaded portico, tapestry wall coverings, eighteen-foot ceilings, a formal dining room, and many fireplaces. It was perched on a promontory on the side of a large and lush valley filled with oak, beech, birch, maple, pine, and assorted cedars. A long circular driveway came down the side of the mountain. The view of the house from above would have made a great magical snow-globe of winter, except there would have been a few cracks, including no central heating during our first winter. It got so cold that some inside walls in the unheated part of the house became coated with icicles and frost, like the dacha in Dr. Zhivago. We were located just above the village of Petersburg in the foothills of the Berkshires just east of Troy, New York, far away from the well-heeled, neatly manicured villages farther south and east like Stockbridge and Lenox. A number of our neighbors still hunted everyday for their daily food, which included deer, possum, and squirrel.

I was working in Albany for a health insurance company, Group Health Incorporated (GHI), which specialized in selling group health benefits to unions. I happily submitted to sacrifice myself to the task. I'd met Alannah on the first day of my enrollment in graduate school in theatre at the State University at Albany in 1972. I thought I was going to embark on a career as a theatre director, but this blonde beauty with her whimsical and elusive Celtic spirit captured my heart. She was also the tender and sensitive mother of two young boys. By falling in love with her, I had finally turned in my black cassock and abandoned the murky world of somewhat-celibate men for her clarity and light.

The first time Alannah and I made love, something strange occurred. Touching her made me tremble; it was uncontrollable. I trembled and shook so violently that she would have to hold me until it stopped. This went on for the first months of our lovemaking. I took this to mean that I could not control my feelings for her, that our marriage must be our true destiny. I believed she had touched the core of my sexual and spiritual being: I was not only clearly meant for women, but specifically for this woman.

The course of our true love had been tricky; she had a way with men, and there was always another circling about. For a few months, a seminary friend of mine stole her away. He was a painter and I was a poet, and she couldn't make up her mind which art form and practitioner she was going to embrace. She finally decided on the poet, a decision that resulted in the poet becoming a businessman.

Many people from this time would become lifelong friends: artists, writers, actors, musicians, dancers, teachers, and bagpipe players. One of the writers was the soon-to-be renowned Albany novelist William Kennedy. A group of us drank together every Thursday night in a bar called the Marketplace in Albany, beginning our weekends with excessive boozing, singing, and endless talk about books and writing.

In many ways, it was idyllic, yet there were certainly problems lurking. Something was splitting within me as surely as a copper pipe might crack in extreme cold. I kept soldering and patching the leak with as much alcohol, good cheer, and hard work as I could manage, but I couldn't find a way to really fix it. Something was wrong with me, something unexpressed and hidden, which Alannah recognized long before I did.

On a bright spring morning in 1976, Alannah and I sat on the long sloping lawn, and she told me she was pregnant. We both knew the night it had happened; we were sure of it. We had been captivated by our lovemaking and spoke of it the next day. I was stunned by what she told me next.

James, I think we're in trouble. I'm worried about us having a child.

What? I mean we've had some troubles, but with time. . . .

You're drinking all the time. You're never home.

I'm in sales; it's just part of my job.

It's deeper than that. There's something wrong with us.

I know, but I think it's the pressure, supporting all of this is hard.

James, I know, but I think you resent it. I don't think you want to do it anymore.

No, I love you. I don't mind.

Listen, anyone would resent it. I get it, but we shouldn't pretend. We need to face the truth.

I didn't know if I minded. I just couldn't do everything and drink the way I needed to. I dug deep and offered her an unfair but difficult argument.

Look, haven't I supported you and the children?

Yes, oh don't go there.

Have you ever loved anyone as you love me?

No, but that doesn't mean. . . .

Imagine what a child born of our love will be like, just imagine.

The conversation went on like this for the rest of the afternoon and by the end, I had convinced her that this child would be the great miracle between us. I knew that I would change; I was sure of it. It turned out that I was right about the profound change that was about to occur, but it wasn't one I could have predicted.

It was the Fourth of July, 1977—we sat on the beach in the late morning sun. I had a hangover that made all my muscles feel both taut and spastic. Only a drink would stop the shakes; I was already sweating heavily. We were visiting my parents, so I had tried to wait as long as I could to start drinking, but I knew I wouldn't be able to hold out much longer. A little relief occurred when the moisture forming on my eyebrows dripped down and soothed my dry eyes. The day was still and stifling even by the water, and as I looked out toward the horizon, I could see that the waves were small and soundless, as if the ocean had been fixed by the sun into a surreal stillness.

Eamon, my six-month-old son, sat next to me gurgling and making animated, jerky arm movements as if he was trying to control a runaway orchestra. I tried to find something about him that could keep my interest a little longer, but I felt no real connection. I felt much closer to my eight-and-ten-year-old stepsons Chris and Shane than to my own son. It was as if he were a foundling left on my doorstep. I couldn't figure out what I was supposed to do with him.

It was past noon and in a few minutes, I would excuse myself to go to the bathroom, but instead I would head to one of the beer concessions on the boardwalk. I thought about the delicious effect of the first few cans of beer, but as I stood up to make my exit, I realized I might appease Alannah if I played with Eamon for a moment. I crouched in front of him and started reciting an old family nursery rhyme, which was accompanied by running your fingers up the baby's torso.

> *Mousy, mousy climb the stairs*
> *see if Eamon says his prayers,*
> *if he doesn't say them right*
> *mousy, mousy take a bite.*

I pinched him and shook him gently by his fleshy leg. Often he found this amusing and would smile and drool, or even coo a bit. Today, he just stared glassy-eyed into the distance.

As I was about to leave, I looked down at him one last time to make my concern seem more sincere. As I stared at him, something odd began to happen: his fists clenched and his head dropped and then jerked slightly upward. There was no sound. He just convulsed over and over, as if an unseen force, a vengeful puppeteer, were pulling and releasing him. Within seconds, we realized that he was having some sort of seizure, so we carried him off the beach and out of the scorching sun. I kept saying that my sister had once had a febrile seizure and that this was probably the same thing.

We ran the few blocks to my parents' apartment and called my childhood pediatrician who was, oddly, in his office on the holiday doing some paperwork. We walked the short distance to his office as Eamon continued to seize and spasm. My hangover, combined with what was happening, meant that the muscles in my body were twitching, and I feared I might convulse along with him at any moment.

The pediatrician just stared down at Eamon. He didn't pull out his stethoscope, otoscope, or laryngoscope; he just watched him contort and spasm. For the doctor, this was a strange coincidence, because he had just returned from a medical conference where he attended a lecture on this kind of seizure. He finally said he was almost certain Eamon was having *infantile myoclonic seizures*, and that quick diagnosis and treatment were crucial. He meant very quick, because he told us to drive immediately to the Nassau University Medical Center where a pediatric neurologist would meet us.

We drove from Long Beach to East Meadow where the hospital was located. The first part of the drive on the Meadowbrook Parkway winds through the marshland that surrounds Jones Beach on the north side, a few miles east of Long Beach. Macadam, supermarkets, fast-food restaurants and Fourth-of-July traffic disappeared, and we entered a wonderland of pristine nature: a place with its own enduring logic and beauty. I stopped talking and stared out at green islets surrounded by blue-gray water and noticed two mallards in flight. When I returned my gaze back to Eamon, he was still seizing. For the first time in years, I prayed in some way. I prayed that something so obvious would not be true. I trembled at the thought that only something outside the natural order would be able to restore him to health; I had no idea if I would be able to summon that force to him. In that moment, staring out at the wetland so pulsing with life, I knew that I was in danger of losing mine. I knew that without my son, or perhaps worse, with a shattered son, my entire creation was in danger.

We soon reentered the frenzy of suburban life and within minutes were on an elevator to the pediatric wing of a large medical center. The size of the facility and the presence of a helicopter pad confirmed this was serious. For the first time, it dawned on me that Eamon might die. There would be many days ahead when I would wonder if that wouldn't have been for the best.

Was it a sin of the father or a sin of the mother? Or perhaps was it the revenge of our Irish heritage and its generations of drunkenness and insanity? I thought of my father's drunkenness, never my own, but I did think of my sexual activities. Perhaps I had caught some rare sexual disease that had infected me with seizure-causing microbes that I had passed down to my son. Later I told a doctor about my suspicions, and he asked me if I had ever had any venereal diseases. I told him no, and he gave me the most logical answer; Aristotle had said it years before, and I had learned it in the seminary: *Nemo dat quod non habet.* (You cannot give what you do not have.)

The young doctors who welcomed us kept telling us how lucky we were because Dr. Borofsky was on her way, and she was not only the head of pediatrics at the hospital, but also a world-renowned expert in childhood seizure disorders. She had left a family picnic somewhere nearby and was rushing to meet us. This gave me a little bit of hope, but I think I already knew the news could not be good.

Dr. Leatrice Borofsky's arrival changed the atmosphere from a sleepy holiday hospital unit to red alert. Suddenly, interns, nurses, technicians, and residents were scurrying everywhere. As she examined Eamon, she barked at everyone, including Alannah and me. Her Russian accent and clipped enunciation made her even scarier, but my chief memory of her that afternoon is of her bushy eyebrows and loud barking. She wanted to know everything that had happened to Eamon and everything about our families. Her questions were delivered in rapid-fire sentences, and she expected the answers at the same speed. She asked one particular question more than once: *Are you sure you two are not related?*

She diagnosed Eamon quickly and confirmed that it was *infantile myoclonic seizure disorder.* Myoclonia occurs in adults as they are falling asleep; as we are about to drift off, there is a mild startle reflex called a hypnic jerk. This is a type of seizure that the adult brain is able to withstand. Unfortunately, a six-month-old's brain is still in formation and cannot yet protect itself; so instead of a very limited jerk, it becomes a serious disorder that is in certain cases nearly impossible to control. The most serious damage is done in the first days of onset.

Dr. Borofsky ordered injections of ACTH (adrenocorticotropic hormone). She explained that it wasn't known why this drug worked, but that it was appropriate at this stage. She then told us something that got my attention: ACTH would hopefully prevent Eamon from going into something called *status epilepticus.* This chilling Latin phrase had no exact meaning, but Borofsky said that this took place when seizures were of such a long duration that they resulted in death. She was hopeful this wouldn't happen with Eamon, but she wouldn't know right away. She also told us, without any emotional intonation, that Eamon would be severely mentally retarded. Each spasm was inflicting significant brain damage.

The Latin phrase returned me to the classroom at St. John's where I was awaiting the news of Jim's death. I could see the dates on the blackboard again: *1066 - Battle of Hastings,* the most important date in English history; and I knew that this day would be the most important in *Eamon's life - July 4th, 1977.* If there was a Bayeux Tapestry commissioned of the *Battle of Eamon,* it would stretch over many years, and Alannah would be pictured holding him in her arms, and I would be seen fleeing to look for reinforcements. Was I in the battle or fleeing from cowardice? I was adrift with no plan. I had lost the friend I had loved as a boy, and now I was struggling not to abandon the boy I was supposed to love most now. After this, I would never be conquered. I would never lay myself open to feelings that I could not withstand. Alannah had a different, powerful, and immediate reaction, and because of it, she saved Eamon's life.

I lasted until around five o'clock, and then told Alannah I was so hungry

I had to get something to eat. I noticed a bar/restaurant across from the hospital. As I entered, I heard Sinatra's voice, which I always found corny yet soothing. He was belting out "My Way." I sat at the bar and ordered a double Jameson on the rocks. There was no way I was going to be able to lift it with the shakes I had, so I sipped the whole drink through the tiny opening in the cocktail stirrer. The quick effect of the Irish whiskey allowed me to hold the next two without any problem.

Alannah stayed at the hospital that night, and I went home to sleep and drink a bit more. The Fourth-of-July fireworks exploded all around me. People were celebrating their independence as my son was losing his, forever. From this day on, Eamon would always be dependent, and he would never know what an independent life felt like. Alannah and I would clutch each other and sob and stare away as we tried to comprehend what was happening to us, and to him. We had no idea what we were going to do, and no one around us knew what to say. The only person who had any advice at all was my father; it was odd, but somewhat helpful.

All I can tell you is that I couldn't do what you are going to have to do. I couldn't, but I think you and Alannah will be able to.

In a sure and certain way, we were on our own. I tried hard to be all the help I could be to Alannah, but I was too dazed to be much good to anyone. His brain damage was occurring as we stood at his bed staring and talking to him. There was nothing anyone could do to stop it.

Alannah was the brave one; instead of retracting into the ozone with me, she prepared to fight. At the outset, I was ready to surrender. Through Eamon's illness, Alannah's character began to find a new formation. She held Eamon ever closer to her: With each seizure, her love somehow deepened.

The pediatric floor of a major hospital is one of the saddest places on the planet. Infants dying of cancer, heart ailments, brain tumors, and all sorts of bizarre afflictions: One boy bleated like a sheep throughout the night. Everything was all wrong here, the *Institute of Everything Gone Terribly Wrong*.

One morning, Borofsky came in for a quick visit and saw me sitting in Eamon's room, staring vacantly into space with my mouth agape. She barked in her thick Russian accent and said, *Come on; you're coming with me now.*

I accompanied her and her young entourage on daily rounds. Most of the patients on this wing had little chance of recovery. They were here to die. Young, blameless children in all sorts of pain and discomfort spending their last few days on earth hooked up to tubes and monitors and machines, and as she walked me back to Eamon's room she quietly said, *You are a lucky man, Mr. Hart. You are going to be able to leave here with your son, you will have him and be able to find a way to love him, and he will be able to love you.*

Then she abandoned her soft, gentle tone.

So stop feeling sorry for yourself. People are depending on you. The next time I see you, you better have a big smile on your face.

I whispered a yes, and without another word, she turned and hurried out of the room. I looked down at Eamon, who was still seizing, and for the first time, I realized I was crying for him. For the first time, I was crying for the life he was going to have to live, not for myself.

We returned to the deep blues and greens of our strange corner of the Berkshires, a different world than the one we had left. We kept watch as Eamon continued to deteriorate. His seizures never abated, and it was clear that his physical and mental development were being profoundly affected. It wasn't just what we were watching but what we were losing that made it so difficult. Whenever I heard the lyrics for "Morning Has Broken," which was popular at the time, I thought of what had suddenly broken for us, what was so full of promise and so impossible to surrender. We had dramatically lost our way within the beauty of our new creation. Nothing sprang fresh, and nothing would ever seem new again. I understood this and no one could convince me otherwise.

At the beginning, our friends and families kept searching for a solution in spite of what many of them knew. There were strange cures, better hospitals, special prayers, and one strange diet after another. We were willing to try almost anything that might work, but the seizures never stopped. Through the years, Eamon's seizures might pause for a few weeks, or a few months, but they always returned. When he first came home, we gave him injections. I had practiced for days on an orange and thought I had become adept, but I was able to do it only once. Each time after that, I shook so hard I couldn't do it. Alannah became proficient, as though she had always been an RN.

I kept working and drinking. These two activities gave me a sense of competence. We needed money more than ever, and I could drink about as well as anyone I knew. Sometime in the fall of 1977, my ongoing skirmish with the shakes escalated. I was initiating my own neurological difficulty. If you haven't had alcoholic tremors, it's hard to understand how difficult they are to combat. I should have injected myself with Eamon's ACTH.

I believed I had the right to turn off all the lights and enter into as much unconsciousness as I needed. You could find me almost any day or night in bars of all different descriptions throughout the Capital District. At some point, usually later in the evening, you would find out about my very ill son. When questioned about how I was handling it all, I would deliver a well-rehearsed speech about how I had an innate faith about it all, and how my love for my son was so deep that somehow we would triumph over this problem. I never connected the fact that I was handling this by drinking around the clock.

I was shocked in October of 1978 when Alannah announced that she had fallen in love with a young musician whom she had met a year earlier. He played several instruments well, but his main instrument was the bagpipe.

I lost my wife to a bagpiper named Mark.

I still thought that the love Alannah and I shared would conquer all, even this. I argued that the three of us could somehow do it together—that we didn't need to end our marriage. I tried to control my emotions of anger and sorrow, so they would more easily see the rightness of my argument. I thought I loved her enough to share her with another man, but it was too much to ask of them; they wanted a new life together, and they needed me gone to start it. Yet Alannah and I would always be intertwined, connected deeply by our son's challenges.

I left "the mansion" in the Berkshires and went to live in a faux basement apartment, the extension of a boiler room, in downtown Troy. Oddly, I felt great relief, for now I could abandon all the responsibilities—my son, my ex-wife, myself—and drown my sorrows on those old cobblestone streets by the Hudson River.

A woolen scarf, a piece of tweed, church bell towers ringing, cars skidding on snow and ice on narrow streets, dingy basement bars, a haze of pot, and the flow of the river always rushing by; sex in an alley next to *The Famous Lunch*, where they served miniature hot dogs with chili and onion toppings; this was Troy. Fistfights, tall stories, shuttered whorehouses, and my heartbreak; they all collided that snowy winter. I washed my shirts by hand across the street from the world-famous Troy Music Hall. I placed my wet socks on the hot ceiling pipes, and I slept on a mattress on the floor. It took me a while to realize that the strange tickling I felt during sleep was caused by large water rats scurrying over me.

I moved to "Ilium" from my tumbledown country villa in the Berkshires. I moved or rather had been moved from the boys I helped raise, Chris and

Shane; from my ailing son; from the country town I had thrived in; and from the woman I was still madly in love with. Strangely, Mark seemed to have no problem dealing with Eamon, as if he had been born to it. If there were a god, he had searched creation for this man and made him responsible for my son.

I managed to hang on by grit and lots of booze, and I soon found friends who were tailor-made: the daily communicants of Troy's drinking life. There were even a few who drank more than I did. By the time I had downed the first very dry martini of my separation, I knew I could survive here. I could drink as I needed, and given Eamon's troubles and the choices of my soon-to-be ex-wife, everyone would understand my need for heavy anesthesia.

Troy was a democratic drinking town; no social distinctions mattered. The members of this inebriated family would exclude you only if you were too much of a pain in the ass, didn't buy drinks for others, were overtly cruel, or terminally dull. Hilarity and entertainment skills were highly valued, and the real test was your ability to drink and drug and, except in the case of death and bankruptcy, to remain of good cheer. My new life centered on three bars, all within easy walking distance. If you squinted a bit or were looking out through a snowstorm, which were frequent, Troy could still take on the look of a prosperous Victorian city. This old city sat between the headwaters of the Hudson and the Troy Hills to the east. It felt as though I was nestled in a place of safety; a place where forgetfulness and merriment could abound, far away from the pain and regret of the Berkshires.

The curious social structure of Troy's drinkers had rather vague boundaries about certain issues. For example, sleeping with someone else's man or woman wasn't automatically seen as a felony. It was often considered a misdemeanor. When everybody is drunk all the time, morals become a little more flexible. There were fistfights, and on occasion, a gun was pulled, but mostly it was about singing and sex and drinking. Trojans loved to sing. If it didn't heal us, at least it joined us in a way of being in the world that was without argument, a way that was pure sound.

I am sure alcohol saved my life. Every time I thought of my love for Alannah, which was almost all the time, I took another drink, or thought about how and when I could get my next one. The exquisite pain of helplessly watching my son in his daily struggle was nothing compared to the loss of my wife. I had bet my entire emotional life on her love, and I couldn't comprehend how she could move on. I was still quite young, but I felt vanquished. I needed another self, someone to fall back on. I would often hear Dylan Thomas's voice rolling off the old Wollensack from that day long ago in the seminary, and the last lines of "Fern Hill" followed me, along with his rolling Welsh baritone.

Oh as I was young and easy in the mercy of his means.
Time held me green and dying.

CHAPTER
NINE

———————————◆———————————

THERE WAS A HEAVY fog that was finally clearing. I had just dropped off three of my bosses from the Metropolitan Life Insurance Company at the airport so they could catch their flight back to New York. We had spent a couple of days visiting and entertaining the company's clients in Buffalo. I had recently been hired to run their upstate office in Rochester, and I had relocated there. Although I had been pretty much drunk now for weeks, no one seemed to notice.

As I watched the planes take off and land, my own haze cleared up, and I made a final decision.

I had to stop drinking.

One of the unavoidable signposts of my problem had appeared on a recent Saturday morning. After a typical Friday night out back in Troy, my best drinking buddy Ned volunteered an opinion.

Jim, you've got to stop drinking.

What do you mean?

Watching you drink is like watching someone spit shit through a bugle. It's an amazing feat, but no one wants to watch it.

I didn't know how I would stop, or even if I could. Booze had control over me. I was drinking around the clock, and I needed it to function at all. When I tried to stop, my body would shake and sweat. At any sober moment, the reality of being alive was going to overtake me and make the business of living and breathing untenable. I needed to repress, no, actually eradicate so much of my life.

I flew back to Rochester that evening and considered my alternatives. In the end, I knew of only one way that worked, and that was the dreary organization that had been the bane of my childhood. I just couldn't believe that my life had come to this, but it had.

At exactly eight o'clock on June 4th, 1981, I walked into my first recovery meeting on St. Paul Street in Rochester, New York. The meeting was held in a seedy storefront with the *Volunteers of America* on one side and a row of empty stores on the other. It had an unmistakable look and feel of "Bringin' in the Sheaves." As I walked into the dimly lit, sweltering room, I realized that I was conspicuously overdressed, and my blue pinstripe suit seemed to be a clear statement that I was not one of them. They certainly didn't act particularly warm and friendly; the mood seemed depressed and sullen.

I have no memory of anything that anybody said, but I do remember looking up at the Twelve Steps, which hung on the wall, and thinking they were preposterous.

How could people believe this crap? God cares about whether you drink or not? He didn't seem to care very much about the millions of Southeast Asians who had recently been killed. He didn't seem to care about whether Eamon seized himself into retardation, but these people believed that God was busily on the lookout for them, the street people of Rochester, New York, watching over their not drinking.

They had a direct line to God, they said, because they had *put the plug in the jug*. I immediately judged this as delusional and was about to leave when I noticed that with only one exception, everyone in the room appeared to be sober.

I immediately dismissed all the steps that mentioned God or used a code for God like "higher power." The only step that caught my attention, and that I thought I would be ready to do, was the Fourth Step: *Make a searching and fearless moral inventory of ourselves.* I believed at that moment that I was truly searching and fearless—which might've had something to do with the fact that I was drunk.

At some point I raised my hand and was called upon. I gave a brief speech about how this program could save their lives, and how it had saved the lives of people I loved. Toward the end of my rambling remarks, I mentioned that it had taken a couple of drinks to get me there. The mood of the room shifted. It changed from somewhat wary to hostile, so I wrapped up with another couple of sentences and sat down. The meeting ended soon after, and we stood, held hands, and said the Our Father, the Protestant version. Another flag went up.

Afterward, I stayed in the back of the room near the door, and people passed me; some nodded hello, and others just ignored me. Finally, a young couple came by. The woman looked at me, smiled, and then turned to her boyfriend and, in a thick German accent said, *Help him George, he needs help.* George swung her to his other side, bent down very near to my face, and said, *Fuck him, let him die.*

This was my warm welcome. I was furious. My father was sober twenty-eight years in 1981; I felt I should be entitled to some special treatment. After all, it sometimes felt to me that my father had started the whole thing. Those mornings with all the drunks at the table, singing duets with Bill W., the founder, and all those endless years of listening to this recovery crap, and this was my greeting?

A middle-aged woman with a platinum-blonde dye job and layers of poorly applied makeup approached me. She called me "Sweetie" in a way that only a working girl can. It was a kindness that melted my anger for a moment. She told me that there was a ten o'clock meeting a few blocks away, and that I should go there. It's impossible to say what I would have done if these two exchanges hadn't taken place, but in retrospect, I think I needed them both to propel me to that next meeting.

In not unusual Twelve-Step fellowship fashion, George, of *Fuck him, let him die*, became my best friend and saved my life. George was a couple of years younger than I, but he had certainly been to the dance. He was an unemployed cab driver who dressed in jeans, a plaid shirt, and a green combat jacket, no matter what the weather. Also, his father had been sober for quite a while before his death, so he understood *the fucked-up-son-of-a-recovering-alcoholic-father syndrome.*

George and my father saved my life. They were going to do it through an organization that I had disliked for a very long time. I was stunned by my father's reaction when I first told him I was going to the program. I heard the phone drop on the other end, and as though he had been informed he had just won the lottery, he screamed, "Oh my God, thank you God." When he recovered his wits, he told me that he and my mother had prayed constantly for this moment for years. I had no idea that they thought I had a problem with alcohol. He had never said a word to me. His firm conviction was that he was the last person I would ever have listened to about my problem. Now

I would be listening to him all the time in my quest to stay sober. I also called George many times a day, and he had the same answer, no matter what my problem. He always began the same way.

Are you listening to me?

Yes, George.

Are you listening? Yes!

It's all dog shit, don't think, don't drink, and go to a meeting, especially don't think.

If I tried to offer an objection, he would interrupt me with a repeat of the same advice. He said this to me over and over and over, and somehow it always got my attention, and for at least a few minutes of my day, I would experience some peace. Of course, his advice contained only a half-truth, but it was the half I desperately needed.

In other ways, George and I were so dissimilar that our relationship was rarely a competition. There really wasn't anything we wanted from each other, except the companionship of a trusted pal who has your best interests at heart. We made an odd pair: George was all of five-six, and I'm almost six-four. I was most often suited and shaved, and he was usually in his green combat jacket with a two- or three-day growth. We became inseparable.

Unfortunately, although it is good advice in early sobriety, *It's all dog shit* doesn't quite cut it if one is looking to live some kind of full and responsible life. When a drunk sobers up, all the conditions and feelings return that made you want to drink in the first place. I still couldn't face most of those.

What I clearly had a passion for was working with newcomers to the program and, as I did, I began to understand a good deal about my father, and that feeling of tenderness that would come over him when he was helping another drunk. It was a powerful feeling to go from being in the depths of drinking yourself to death, within a few weeks, to helping others survive.

The people I got sober with in downtown Rochester were quite a crew. Many of them had jail time under their belts, and some had considerable prison time. Attica was less than an hour away, so many of the ex-cons drifted toward Rochester. A couple of my new running buddies had committed murder and had just recently been freed. There were hookers, snake-oil salesmen, hustlers, petty criminals, sober drug dealers, a guy who lived under a bridge, a retired dishwasher, and me. Given the lives that they were happily holding onto thanks to sobriety, I began to believe I might be able to hold on as well.

I didn't possess a higher power myself, but I was helped by their rock-solid belief that their lives were better sober. I began to learn that there had to be more than cash and prizes as rewards because these people weren't going to get many, and they knew it. Somehow, I trusted them because their recovery seemed to be in their bones, not just in their heads.

After a few months of these inner-city meetings, I suggested to my father that I might try out a suburban meeting. His reaction was so instantaneous and impassioned that I paid attention.

No, no, no, keep going to those downtown meetings. Don't go to the suburbs until I tell you it's okay.

I took his advice, and it was almost a year before I made my way to one of the Rochester suburbs. Later I asked him why he had insisted.

I was so scared you would go out there and meet people like yourself: educated, successful people that you would compare yourself to. I figured you might talk yourself out of sobriety. I knew the people downtown weren't interested in your bullshit. They were only interested in loving you and helping you stay sober.

CHAPTER

TEN

LISTEN, KID, THAT'S A lot of pressure

Bill Herrick, an old pal from the Albany days sat across from me. Bill had a house on the beach in Gayhead. We had spent the day together, first at Bill's house and then at a long lunch in Vineyard Haven. Bill was a novelist and former actual American communist. He had been wounded in the Spanish Civil War: a soldier in the Lincoln Battalion of the International Brigade. He had written a terrific novel about it called *Hermanos*.

We were brothers of a sort. Bill had grown up in the rough Jewish world of the Lower East Side, and he equated some parts of my father's experience with his own. I had met him in Albany through Bill Kennedy years before. He was tough minded about life and curious about my new situation, and how I was going to handle it. He had read a first draft of my novel, which he thought had promise but needed a lot of work.

How are you gonna do all of this?

You mean the book?

For Christ's sake, I mean all of it. You have some life on your hands. She's a huge star, estate on the Vineyard, house in New York, two children, a novel, and, well, let's just say she's a fucking icon. I mean she's sexy as hell, but I hear she's pretty fragile.

Well, we're madly in love, so what does it matter?

Oh listen, I liked her right away, but how can you do all this?

Well, I'm working hard on the book.

Look kid, you know I like you a lot, but writing a novel doesn't happen because you need it. It happens with a ton of work and a fickle thing called luck.

Well, I'm counting on folks like you and Kennedy to help me out.

It's a big gamble. You're whole future built on a book?

I know. I know.

Do you? Come on, a few months ago you were selling insurance, and now you're a novelist? It's a lot of pressure, especially living with her. Well, you know I wish you well, and Kennedy and I will help any way we can.

Thanks, I know.

Have you met her ex yet?

No. We're going to meet next week.

Well, that should be interesting.

I picked up the lunch tab quickly, as though money would never be a problem for me again. Bill noted the gesture and sighed.

After lunch, we walked down Main Street to the *Bunch of Grapes* bookstore, and in a brief conversation, I convinced Ann Nelson, the owner, that she had to order Bill's books that were in print. She ordered them on the spot. After all, I was Carly's new man, and we brought all sorts of folks into the store. Bill was thrilled, and he immediately thought I should consider a new career.

Man, you're good at that. You should be an agent.

Yes, but just for my friends.

All right, kid. Good luck with everything.

Late one night in the fall of 1987, barely three months after we had met, I proposed to Carly. We were in the darkened dining room of her New York apartment. Dressed in only my jockey shorts, I knelt in front of her, and I knew I couldn't stop. She stared into the distance for a few seconds, and then returned to me with the warmest of smiles.

Yes. Yes, of course.

We began living together in New York and the Vineyard. I quit my insurance job and never looked back. Carly and I both agreed that my working for an insurance company would not serve our new lives. She would support me for a couple of years so that I could work on my novel full time. I would also help raise her children, so meeting their father seemed both important and natural. I grew even more curious once I met James's mother in the Martha's Vineyard bookstore. She peered through a small book-sized space in the biography section.

Hi Jim, I know who you are.

Hi Trudy, yes, I know who you are. Nice to meet you.

Jim, I was wondering something. How does it feel?

How does what feel?

How does it feel to be marrying my son's ex-wife, raising my son's children, living in the house he built, and to look so much like him?

In thirty-seven years, no one had ever said I looked like James Taylor, but since I had met Carly, many people told me there was a similarity, and now *his mother* was saying it.

I'm attracted to tall, dark, handsome, balding men, she had said, when I put the *are you really over him?* question to her. *Is that so weird?*

It was late afternoon when he parked his minuscule Ford Fiesta in front of the house. He didn't immediately come to the door; instead, he roamed outside, looking over the place as if it were still somehow his. He seemed to be meditating next to the apple trees by the roughhewn fence that formed the border of the horse pasture.

James finally made it to the kitchen door. He was holding two apples he had picked from the trees bordering the horse pasture, trees he had planted. He placed them on the kitchen counter, smiled and said, *What beauties.* It was as if he was about to preach a silent, mimed parable entitled *The Miracle of the Two Luscious Apples* but then changed his mind. James moved around the marble counter in the center of the kitchen and shook my hand. He had a well-practiced, polite smile. We moved into the den off the kitchen, a small, comfortable space I came to call the "crook." It had a hobbit-like feel to it, and the low wooden ceilings of the room made us seem even larger.

James was in every part of the house. On a recent afternoon, I had reached up onto one of the wooden beams and found a set of rusted drug works that may have been left from his old heroin days. So much of him would always linger here.

It was hard to concentrate; I was startled at the similarity of our appearance. It seemed that James also noticed and tried to mask his surprise by tilting his head to one side. He was in control of this exchange, and yet his manner seemed humble and inclusive. It wasn't until much later that I realized how upsetting this situation might be for him.

I had spent days thinking about it, and I had filled seven or eight pages of a yellow legal pad with points for our discussion. Because of my nervousness, I conducted a long monologue while staring down at the text. When I finished, there was a long silence, and I finally looked over at James.

Jim, that was very smart.

Thanks, I spent a lot of time on it.

Jim, he started with slow deliberation, *I think our main job is to get them to eighteen alive?*

We both laughed. As James laughed, I noticed a similarity in our manner. Like me, he had pliant, conspiratorial facial muscles that broke easily into mischievous laughter. James's charm was carefully measured, more still and refined than mine. I focused on making others more comfortable and entertained, while James kept people a long and, perhaps longing, distance away. As I looked over, I noticed his biceps. They had the same sort of blue veins running down them as my father's. They were large and pulsating, and announced a sure strength. It was a masculinity with few curves, etched and angular, and needing no further explanation. On the other hand, I negotiated to be just slightly more male. I came from a much more violent place than James did, I thought, but I wasn't at all sure that I was tougher.

James asked about Eamon, and when I started to respond expansively, he shifted in a way that told me he had already moved on.

Jim, nice to meet you.

We shook hands again; James grabbed the two apples from the kitchen counter and went out through the kitchen door. This was the longest we would ever be together. I had no idea that James's animus toward her ran so deep. In that moment, though, James had lowered the bar regarding the kids by giving me such an easy answer, but he also offered another kind of warning.

The thing that worries me most is what happens to the children of famous people, if they don't find their own lives. I hope that doesn't happen to Ben and Sally.

Three horses, two lambs, and a belled goat named Juliette grazed in the fields beyond the wide front lawn of our main property. I sometimes stared into their eyes from the window of the cabin, as I searched for a better word for my novel. They were a motley group that didn't belong together, yet they provided each other with protection and comfort. I especially liked Juliette. She was ungainly, awkward, and had the distant gaze of an outsider, yet she was the most carefree in spite of the bell. I thought of the animals as part of the backdrop, and I didn't expect to build much of a relationship with them, but Carly was different. She would often feed them from her hands, and usually, at least once a day, she would come out and sing to them. She always sang the same song—"My Bonnie Lies over the Ocean." I never learned the significance of this tune, but somehow she felt this was what you sang to farm animals. They would stop what they were doing and listen to her like rapt fans, as though they understood that she was extremely talented.

I was different from the other parents. James Taylor and Carly Simon were famous, and Kathryn Walker, James's wife, was a successful and prominent New York actress. They all knew fame and success in their own right. I seemed to be living some sort of gender-reversed Cinderella story and, oddly, the glass slipper seemed to be a perfect fit. Perhaps we all should have been more concerned about how quickly and easily I fell in line. I drove Carly's 1967 cobalt-blue Mercedes SL convertible around the Vineyard as though I was to the manor born. I wonder how others saw me those first few months, as I became part of the Vineyard scene. With each new cashmere sweater I pulled over my head, I could almost feel myself changing. I had the ability to adapt seamlessly to this new, luxurious life.

I involved myself in recovery meetings on the Vineyard right away, but I had to be careful about what I said. I couldn't be very candid about what was going on in my life, especially if it was about my wife or the children. The locals, the year-round residents in recovery, were struggling mostly with putting food on the table, and they didn't need to hear about my difficulties adapting to privilege.

Since my novel was largely based on my father and my family, I often heard their voices. As my grandmother might say, *that idiot thinks he's the cock of the walk*, or my father's statement of absolute fact that he said so often and with great conviction: *There are no shortcuts, everything has a price, everything.* I felt that I had proven him wrong, but I did occasionally wonder about the price. I expected the most difficult place would be within my new family.

I remembered an image from a college literature course. I hadn't thought about it for years, but one evening as we sat around the dining room table, it came to me. I found a copy of the novel, and as I read it, I could still hear the voice of my favorite professor David Hodgdon. His excited and strained tenor communicated the brilliance of the opening image of Henry James's novel *What Maisie Knew*, about a child of divorce being raised by two sets of frivolous parents.

She (Maisie) was taken in the confidence of passions on which she fixed just the stare she might have had for images bounding across the wall in the slide of a magic-lantern. Her little world was phantasmagoric—strange shadows dancing on a sheet. It was as if the whole performance had been given for her—a mite of a half-scared infant in a great dim theatre. She was in short introduced to life with a liberality in which the selfishness of others found its account, and there was nothing to avert the sacrifice but the modesty of her youth.

I had a strong feeling that I wasn't yet one of the selfish adults. I knew I wanted to protect Ben and Sally, but I wasn't sure from exactly what or whom, perhaps something to do with a world that would take advantage of them because of their fame. But I also wanted to protect them from the fame within their family that might steal crucial parts of their developing selves. Perhaps it should have been a larger concern of my own—what might be taken from me by this world. James Taylor's words resonated, and I began to feel similar to the position that the children were in: that fame was all around us, yet it had nothing to do with anything we had achieved on our own.

If James had worried about his own children, I wondered what he thought of me as the spouse of this famous woman. Caesar had said it at the beginning of the Gallic Wars: men closest to luxury become soft and womanish. Yet it was some of these feminine qualities that Carly loved most about me. I had a great supply of patience for her struggles with capricious emotions. At first, I did wonder what expensive pairs of designer silk underwear might do to my masculinity, as well as my being financially dependent on the woman who bought them for me. Would it make me less of a man?

I now had the added and odd responsibility of protecting James's reputation as a father. He had an enormous public persona, and I was privately involved in trying to protect and nurture the two most important things in his life. I believed I needed to protect him in any way I could, especially with his children. Interestingly, over the years, I was constantly asked by friends and strangers, *Was James a good father? He does a pretty good job* was about as critical as I would ever get. I tried to never say anything negative, no matter how I felt in the moment. As I grew closer to Ben and Sally, some of my feelings extended to James. After all, there were so many good qualities in both of them that I couldn't help but think of their father in a good light. I spent no time with him over the next twenty years, but James would often be on the other end of the phone saying hello and asking how I was doing. I felt a kind of oppression from James's fame, but this was certainly in the area of things I could not change, so I tried to understand how to be in love with a famous woman, with a famous ex-husband and famous children. I was certainly the only ordinary entity in the entire extended family.

Carly surely felt that James was indelibly hers—she shared children with him—and together they had been the famous golden couple of their generation. In spite of the charged atmosphere, I hoped that James and I might come together as "just guys" to create a counterbalance, but that never was to happen. And yet, he was a constant presence in my life and, as with Carly, there was hardly ever an elevator, shopping center, airport, or car radio that wasn't playing one of his songs. After a while when people asked how I was doing, I would solemnly say, *Well, I've seen fire and I've seen rain.*

One early morning, Carly put her arm around me as we woke and said, *I need to ask you something.* The imploring tone of her voice implied that this was going to be an important conversation.

I need to know, would you love me if I weren't Carly Simon?

I wasn't sure if I would ever be able to answer that question properly, but I knew the right answer for this moment.

Of course not. Who would that be? I can only be in love with you. I'm stuck with Carly Simon, and I couldn't be happier.

In my most paranoid moments, I would wonder if she had fallen in love with me because I reminded her of him. One of James's recordings came to mind: *Something in the Way She (He) Moves.*

Apparently, at least to his mother, I looked like James. Did I move like him as well? My fear was not unlike Carly's. I might never be loved just for myself, but rather for an image of something I could never be. It was impossible to separate Carly from Carly Simon, the star. I wondered if she would be able to love Jim Hart without my reminding her of James. It certainly made my life and love much more complicated. And yet, despite these issues, I had never felt so secure and cared for.

It also felt that my life was far less trivial than it had been, yet this might be a fatal delusion. I seemed to be meeting every famous person still alive, and many of them seemed genuinely interested in me. In addition, I returned to writing my novel and lots of new poetry, and I was in love with a woman I believed to be the most extraordinary creature. Yet this might be the place where my life would become deeply unimportant—where I would never be more than an asterisk to more significant lives.

Not only was James's public persona and music everywhere, but I had no idea how much of the Taylor family I would have to absorb, although so little of it would ever have to do with James himself. That first fall, there were Taylors everywhere and, to make matters more confusing, I liked them all. They were kind, fun, and wonderfully unaffected; there were uncles and aunts and cousins of Ben and Sally, Carly's ex-sister- and brothers-in-law, and their idiosyncratic and interesting grandmother Trudy. Kate Taylor, James's sister, was very close to Carly, and she and her husband Charlie Witham were constant visitors that first year on the Vineyard.

There was Alex, James's older brother. His talent was considerable, but drugs and alcohol had captured him.

He wants to speak with you.

It was late, past midnight; he often called around this time. I took the phone from Carly.

Goddammit Jim, I mean, I love you guys. You and Carly, aw shit, Jim. It doesn't get better than you guys.

Alex was very effusive when he was drunk or high; often he was both.

I mean goddammit, Jim, you guys are the best. Ya know there are a lot of assholes. I mean, I have some in my family.

This was a topic I was definitely very interested in—but I tried to steer clear of this sort of conversation. It might become too incestuous.

I mean, I love James, but I mean sometimes he . . .

Alex I get it. Sometimes I'm not so perfect myself.

Ha, that's right. Goddammit, Jim—that's why I love ya.

How are you tonight?

Jim, I mean, Jim. I'm high as a kite. I mean, aw well, I mean, Jim, come on—give me a ride to the end of this sentence.

I would have given Alex a ride anywhere. He was the kind of drunk I loved: charming, funny, and yearning for unconsciousness. He had no discernible regard for conventional life and values, and yet he could be as seductive and charming as anyone I knew. He was often looking for money from Carly when he made these calls. It never was for very much: a few hundred dollars seemed the usual amount.

Goddammit, Jim, I wish I could be sober like you. I really admire your sobriety. When I get back maybe we could go to a meeting together.

Unfortunately, that only happened once. Alex would struggle with his alcoholism for the next five years. It did dawn on me that perhaps this was a way that I could convince James of my worth in all of this—by helping his older brother get well. But it never happened. Though I sure wish it had. Alex died on James's forty-fifth birthday.

In addition to being surrounded by Taylors, I was beginning to be surrounded by Carly's neuroses. It turned out that I had found many of them endearing, and they actually created a place where we could feel quite equal. Extreme terror tends to level worldly distinctions. She was a collection of unwarranted anxiety, surprising bravery, and a compelling openness about her many foibles and fears.

She begged to get off the plane before we left the ground. We were flying on a now-defunct airline: MGM Grand Air, a refurbished 727 with art-deco staterooms and other posh amenities. Carly thought that these surroundings might help with her fears. She deemed *hurtling through the sky in a metal tube* highly dangerous, and each noise and disturbance was a sign of imminent doom. The private compartments made her feel even less safe than a regular plane as she feared the focus might not be on the engine and the skill of the pilots, but rather on the interior decorations. We had drugged her as heavily as we thought safe, but she was still jumping out of her skin. Her fingernails dug into me, and she alternately moaned, screamed, and cried. At times, her body became completely rigid and she stared vacantly into space. She shook as though she was about to have a seizure.

Bill Murray and Bruce Jenner, who happened to be on the flight, both took a shot at trying to alleviate her fear. Bill told her a number of jokes and Bruce followed with a thorough explanation of the statistical safety of airplanes, and then a detailed description of the workings of human anatomy during panic. He held her wrist and took her pulse aloud. As he said *1, 2, 3,* she stared intently into his eyes and as long as he counted, she seemed better. But just as he finished, the plane took a sudden bank, and that was it. She returned to her state of utter panic.

About forty-five minutes before our landing at LAX, a passenger who had been seated in the back of the plane walked past us. As soon as Carly saw him, her head lifted and she sprang up with a resplendent smile. She instantly knew that the rest of the flight would be fine. The passenger was Max von Sydow. Carly grabbed his hand and pulled him toward her. *Oh, thank you so much.* Carly looked at me and said, *It's Jesus. We can't crash!* Von Sydow had played Jesus in *The Greatest Story Ever Told.* We laughed together, and part of the laughter was because her certainty was so powerful. Max

Von Sydow had made everything okay: like Jesus, he had performed the important miracle; he had saved her. That he had no idea who Carly was made it even more certain.

I was thrilled to be exploring Carly's many worlds. They were filled with drama and fascinating emotional highs and lows. Yet we both wondered how I would live my life within hers.

We both suspected that preserving mine would require a miracle, because I didn't possess a place for us to live within. Many people warned us of the difficult choice we were making, but no one provided us with a reasonable alternative. We could have decided to abandon her world and live in mine: to raise her children in my one-bedroom Stuyvesant Town apartment and launch a new life together using my small savings. We joked about this at the time, but neither of us thought it a real possibility. In retrospect, I guess it was an option, but how does anyone make that kind of decision without a deeply held and shared radical belief, like Jim and I once had. The only part of my life that was intrinsic and that could never be altered or shed was my son.

Eamon, who was now ten, arrived for his first visit to Martha's Vineyard on a summer afternoon in August of 1987. He stepped off a small private plane piloted by his stepbrother Christopher. The first thing I noticed about Eamon was that his eyes were covered with a watery film, and he seemed unable to focus properly. He was tired, which always frightened me, because that state would often precede a seizure. Yet he was thrilled to see me, as though I was reward enough for his perilous journey. Like Carly, he never felt secure in the air.

On the short drive to the house, I kept telling him over and over whom he was going to meet: Carly, Ben, and Sally. After repeating it five or six times, he could still only remember two of their names at the same time. Whenever I picked him up over the coming years, he would ask about one of them right away, and then an hour later, he would ask about the next, and sometimes as much as a day later, about the third. He got around to all of them, but with long delays.

He opened the screen door with a crash and startled Carly as she sat at the kitchen counter.

Who's here? I said.

He clapped his hands together as though he was about to do something quite magical. *Carly Simon!*

He ran to her and hugged her awkwardly. I watched as the two human beings I loved and cared for most held each other in their first embrace. Eamon was nervous, and he did something that was an indication, placing his hand under his chin and waving it frantically back and forth, as though he were using a special code to a secret club. He then looked at her intently and asked, *What time is it?*

Carly looked at the clock over the kitchen sink and said, *3:07.*

Eamon continued to stare at her and asked again, *What time is it?*

She answered again, *3:07.*

This went on a number of times, and Carly thought he might be satisfied with her answer as time moved ahead and she said, *3:08.*

Eamon stared at her one more time and asked, *What time is it?*

In this brief exchange, she saw for the first time the kind of profound challenge that Eamon presented. For the past ten years, I had lived within this dynamic, and something about her discovery of it broke my heart again. Her seeing it for the first time made me so sad and somehow ashamed. She grabbed him and hugged him close to her. I knew she wanted to help, but she was also keenly aware that he was beyond her ability to fix him.

As she held him, she looked over at me with a pained and sorrowful expression.

My God, what a sweet child he is.

Eamon wiggled out of her arms, and as he walked away with his back to her, he said, *I love you Carly.*

I could feel it wasn't working, even though everyone was being so kind to him. The nature of his handicaps stunned them. Ben and Sally greeted him sweetly, but my fantasy that they would somehow be able to enter his world and take him on was not going to happen. Ben patiently played basketball with him and then swam with him, but I could see that Ben and Sally were too busy with their own young lives. Making their new, severely handicapped brother a priority was not going to happen.

Carly gave it much more effort. She sang with him, fed him, and tried to entertain him. She even made up a quick little song for him that would make him roar with laughter. It was quite simple, but the end of the song would result in grabbing a part of his body and squeezing it.

Baby, Baby, Baby, take a trip on Eamon's knee, stomach, chest, or whatever body part she happened to choose. She so clearly wanted to help in some special way, but as with most other people, including me, it was a frustrating process with very little satisfaction. I understood during this first visit that I was now left with the responsibilities of my old life—Eamon and Alannah— and those of my new one. I had no idea how this could possibly all work. I just prayed we would find a way.

He was quite antsy on this first visit, so I put him in a car to calm him down. A CD of Carly's was playing and Eamon sang along and smiled and said, *Carly Simon*. Somehow the sound of her voice was more soothing than her actual presence. He was able to invoke a Carly while listening to her recorded music. As soon as her CD started to play, he would enter a rapturous state. He knew the lyrics to every song, and although he sang them with Carly in person on this first visit, it never quite had the same power as listening to her recordings. It made him laugh, as though this live Carly was an odd imitation of the voice he heard through a speaker. They started to play a game that would continue forever. She would sing a line of one of her lyrics and Eamon would finish it for her. This was great fun for Eamon, and it made me love her even more.

The next day, we explored the island together. I thought that time alone with me might be helpful. Eamon and I arrived in Oak Bluffs in mid-afternoon. Oak Bluffs is the most commercial and touristy of the towns on Martha's Vineyard. Still, it is more charming than tawdry. It has a tabernacle in the middle of the town surrounded by miniature gingerbread Victorian cottages.

The *Flying Horses*, one of the oldest operating carousels in the country, was near the center of the village at the bottom of Circuit Avenue. It is rather precious with its small antique wooden horses. I put him on the ride, but as he came around again to face me, I could see that I had made a mistake. His facial muscles were rubbery and distended, his eyes were filled with panic, and he seemed to be holding on for dear life. As he caught my eye, he tried to smile, but he looked like he was spinning in a circle he couldn't control. He was constantly spinning everything he saw: lampshades, coins, water glasses, salt shakers, dishes, bowls, silverware, but his own spinning did not give him any pleasure.

I'm not sure if it was his odd appearance or the strange, laminated expressions on the horses' faces, but as he rode around on the carousel, I began to feel that I might also be spinning out of control. What had seemed like such a good idea now seemed frantic and dangerous. The calliope music grew eerie and ominous, like a score from a Hitchcock film. I grabbed him off the ride and held him close to me. I held him tightly and told him that I loved him. He wriggled in my arms trying to escape, but I wouldn't let go, and I ran with him toward the ocean. We jumped in and he started to spray me with water and laughed as he got hit with waves from behind. Somehow in this moment in the ocean together, I knew that I was now alone with my son. The random force of the rolling waves reminded me that I had no idea how I was going to deal with his problems. And then, as he often did, Eamon relived a recent experience after it occurred. He held his hands as if he were holding the reins and screamed over the noise of the next crashing wave, *Flying Horses.*

A couple of years after Carly's *My Romance* album was released, Eamon had a procedure performed that we hoped might achieve some control of his seizures. It was minor surgery similar to the insertion of a pacemaker. It had been successful in helping some patients with intractable epileptic seizures like his. The added complication, given his many issues, was that he had to be put under general anesthesia. We hated this idea, but given all the facts of Eamon's case, it was the only way the surgeon would perform the procedure.

After the surgery, a very strange thing happened: Eamon refused to come out from the anesthesia. He just stared into space for hours, right into the next day. Clearly, there was something beyond the physical taking place. It was as though he was trying to punish us for having done such a thing to him. It seemed that he drifted even farther away every time Alannah spoke to him, as if he was consciously punishing her with his unconscious self. His psyche was normally so fragile, that we began to be concerned that we had done some irreparable damage. Alannah was starting to become frantic. He stared glassy-eyed off into the distance and refused to speak. It looked as if he was fully awake but refused to return. Alannah had left the room for a moment, and I began to sing "My Romance." As if he couldn't possibly resist, as I got to the blue lagoon line, his still-boy-soprano voice filled the room with me, and he laughed as if it had all been a big put-on. Eamon said, *Carly Simon* and smiled. He said it as though he shared a most important secret with her, a secret that only the two of them would ever know.

———————◆———————

IT WAS NOVEMBER 6TH, 1987, and as we approached Mike Nichols's house, I noticed that Patrick O'Neal, the well-known Irish-American actor of an earlier generation, was standing out front. Patrick had been a traveling companion in recovery, and I knew him quite well. His easy smile and gentle manner made the moment easier. He was a man who had struggled mightily with his own demons within the world of fame.

The occasion was a birthday party for Mike at his townhouse on the Upper East Side. A row of stretch limos lined the street. I had already spotted Harrison Ford, Paul Simon, and Sigourney Weaver ahead of us. I soon met Dustin Hoffman, E.L. Doctorow, Elaine May, and Richard Avedon in the front hallway. Jules Feiffer introduced me to Candice Bergen, who said to Steve Martin, *Do you know Jim Hart?* Rose and Bill Styron greeted us in the hallway.

It was a glamorous party, and the toasts for Mike went on for what seemed like an hour. They were all prearranged. It started with Harrison Ford.

When I first met Mike, I thought he was the funniest man I had ever known. After a few months, I thought, no, he's the smartest man I've ever known. And now a few years later, I know he's just the kindest man I've ever known.

Numerous other toasts were given, filled with thoughtfulness and wit. The final toast was reserved for Elaine May, Mike's famous comedy partner of the fifties and sixties. She stood, lifted her glass, and delivered her toast in a shy and halting manner.

When I first met Mike, I thought he was the funniest man I had ever known. After a few months, I thought, no, he's the smartest man I've ever known. And now a few years later, I know he's just the kindest man I've ever known. She paused dramatically. *And I can't believe Harrison came here with the same toast.*

The party roared in approval. She somehow knew that with just the right pacing and timing, she could bring down the house.

I soon found Patrick standing by himself near the front of the town house. He looked as uncomfortable as I felt, more like a farmer from Leitrim than an urbane, handsome Irishman: There seemed to be something humble within him. He smiled weakly and glanced around.

I'm really glad you're here. I hate these fucking things. Who do these people think they are? I can't stand most of them, but Mike's okay. I like you, kid. You're the real thing. Don't be taken in by these people. I'm telling you, I know.

I didn't know what to say. Patrick had been in the world of New York and Hollywood fame for years.

What would your father think of all this?

Patrick had heard my father speak at a meeting a few years before, and my father had made quite an impression. Patrick always asked after him and loved to hear stories about him.

I don't know. He's never heard of most of these people.

No, I'm sure.

My grandmother used to make fun of my grandfather. She would say that she came from a two-cow place, and that "he had nothin', and would never have nothin', because his father before him never had nothin', and his father before that," and that he had come from "a one-cow place."

Patrick laughed loudly. I was touched by how much Patrick didn't feel he belonged, and how much he didn't want to belong. My feeling was a bit different. I definitely wanted to be a part of this. In those early months, I became convinced that I had been made to handle all of this.

My father would probably say something like, "You look like Astor's pet pup."

Boy, I like your old man.

A good deal of healing had taken place between my father and me by then, and an important event had taken place just the previous Christmas. I told Patrick the story.

I was home in my apartment last Christmas. It was about three or four in the afternoon and I was still in my bathrobe. I was writing about my father's family, and then I was just writing about my father, and then I was suddenly in a fiery rage. I couldn't believe something that he had done to me, something that made me so angry that I just picked up the phone and dialed my parents' number. He answered on the second ring.

I said, *Listen I need to talk to you.*

Merry Christmas.

Yeah, Merry Christmas. I've just been writing about you, and I need to tell you, you need to make amends. I mean you need to tell me something. I mean what you did to me . . . you need to . . . I suddenly found myself screaming into the phone, *I mean you really need to tell me something.*

You're right. I do need to tell you something. There was a long pause. *In fact, it's something I've been meaning to tell you for a long time.* There was another long pause. *What I've been meaning to tell you is "Go fuck yourself."*

I could barely speak. I was sputtering into the telephone. What, you said, how dare, what do you. . . . He interrupted me.

You have to stop this. Please listen to me.

I'm listening.

If you're going to have a happy life, you're going to have to forgive me. I've had to forgive myself for what I did to your mother and your brother and you, and I have. There are other things in my life that I thought I would never find a way to forgive myself for, but I have found forgiveness, even for them.

My rage subsided for a moment, as I considered what some of those things might have been.

And let me tell you, he said, *it's worse than you think.*

What do you mean?

Well, the thing I'm telling you, that you have to do, I stole from you with my abuse. I was the person who was supposed to give you the ability to forgive, and I stole it with my violence.

I was stunned by this insight. He had pinpointed a part of my deepest confusion.

To forgive me, you're going to have to learn it from strangers, but I know you can and will. You have to forgive me, not for me, but for you...

A look of wonder spread over Patrick's face. His clear blue eyes and the wide-open expanse of his face reflected his amazement.

Wow.

Yeah, from a raving lunatic to one of the smartest and kindest guys I've ever met. I just wish it had been sooner.

Jim, you're so lucky to have him.

I know.

* * *

Just six months after we met, on December 23rd, 1987, I heard her respond to a question from an Episcopal priest that I still couldn't fathom. *Do you take James Michael Hart . . .*

I do, she whispered. Her wedding gown looked fashioned for a fairy tale princess, and I wore an Issey Miyake tuxedo with elegant samurai-like, ballooning pants and a stiff white bib. I only lacked a tachi sword, the symbol of a masculine warrior, and missing from Carly's gown was the warmth of a long Russian sable.

I listened in rapture, as she and her two sisters Lucy and Joanna sang an arrangement of "The Lord Bless You and Keep You." Snow was falling from the slate-colored sky, and the narrow streets of the old Vineyard whaling village were covered with a light dusting swept in from the sea. The small storm gave the ceremony a touch from beyond.

As we left the church, we let the flakes melt on our tongues, like schoolchildren. The snow, which had begun as we exchanged our vows, left a white blanket on the Mercedes convertible in front of the church. This was our wedding limo that had a *Just Married* sign on the back and tin cans tied to the bumper. Carly had bought this car for James years ago.

We almost didn't make it to the altar. There were jitters all around and a last-minute fight over a prenup. I felt strongly that I shouldn't agree to it. The balanced judgments of accountants and cynical touch of attorneys interrupted the wild abandon of *for better or worse* and *'til death do us part* that I needed to drown out the ways in which I felt Carly's life, financial and otherwise, swamped mine. I had the good sense to give in, rationalizing that we would be together forever, that we had transcended judgments.

We had decided not to invite our families to the wedding: A small, private ceremony was the way to go. I was happy not to have to integrate my family into this event, so I was glad that Carly thought it would be best for her as well. A week before the wedding, the Simon family rebelled and informed Carly that there was no way they were going to miss her wedding. Instead of my family, I hastily invited a few recovery buddies, and Carly invited some of her Vineyard friends, who included James's sister Kate and her husband and their children. Carly considered Kate as one of her own sisters, so it didn't seem strange to her, yet the absence of my own sister and brother haunted me. The clear and chilling message that took me a long time to get was that my family wasn't that important.

★ ★ ★

My parents and I were in an adjoining room behind the glass window, and Carly sat in the sound room with the announcer of a pop-music radio station in Charleston, South Carolina, in the early winter of 1988. Carly had planned a radio tour for Savannah, Georgia, and Charlestown, that would make it easy for my parents to meet us. They would drive down from Wilmington, North Carolina, where they had retired. So we had all gone to the radio station together. We were married but she hadn't yet met my parents. In the first sweet act of her relationship with them, Carly said to the announcer: *You know the first thing I would like to do is dedicate a song from my album to my new father- and mother-in-law, Larry and Betty Hart. I just met them today for the very first time.* She told the DJ that it was the fifth cut on the album. The studio was filled with her beautiful rendition of "As Time Goes By." We all beamed with laughter and smiles and were united by the magic of that song. My father kept shaking his head and smiling, and then he began to sing along, and Carly and my father serenaded each other along with her voice over the sound system. He emphasized the refrain and blew a kiss to her through the glass.

Somehow in the course of our day, we had promised three different restaurants that we would stop in and say hello. They all wanted the distinction of being able to say, "Carly Simon ate here." That night we traveled from restaurant to restaurant in what seemed like an old memory of bar-hopping.

At the last restaurant, Carly said, *Larry, how are you doing?*

My father leaned back after taking his final bite of creamy cheesecake, and his face came alive with an endearingly mischievous smile. Instead of addressing Carly, he turned to my mother and said, *Betty, she wants to know how I'm doing? How am I doing? I just had my third free dessert.*

In this gesture, I could see his magic. He tilted his head back and closed his eyes. He captured this experience as though it was his, as though he could feel in this breath everything from Hell's Kitchen in the 1920s to Charleston, South Carolina, in 1988. He seemed to hold all of the feelings of his life within him, that even his famous new daughter-in-law was his possession. His journey, *by way of Canarsie*, was the experience of true value. In the creamy taste of his last dessert, he understood and relived the wonder of his life. He grasped it like no one else. I understood now why he was always the most compelling person in the room. After a pause with his eyes shut, he leaned across the table, held Carly's hands in his and said, *Darling, this is really living.*

When we got back to the hotel room that night. Carly immediately said, *You never prepared me for your father.*

Well, I tried to describe him for you.

No, you never told me what a star he is. I don't think I've met anyone quite like him. There's such a powerful aura about him.

CHAPTER
TWELVE

THREE DAYS AFTER THE ceremony, on December 26th, we took a tiny plane to Nantucket and had a brief honeymoon in a romantic snowstorm. On our return, I stared at a full-page picture of the two of us in the latest issue of *People* magazine. We stood under a bare winter bower that looked like the entrance to a winding brick road. Carly held her skirt out full for the shot and smiled directly at the camera, and I looked down at her in adoration. My life was no longer private; it was now *officially* public.

Although I was certainly aware of Carly's profile in the world and the company I was now keeping, things actually seemed fairly normal until my two worlds collided at a noon recovery meeting on the Vineyard that same week. I had "shared" about how happy I was about falling in love and getting married. I explained that I wanted to share this with the group because it was all due to being sober. Suddenly one of the locals sitting beside me became unhinged and started screaming, *Jesus fucking Christ, if I had just married Carly fucking Simon, I'd be fucking delirious. For Chrissakes.*

It had all happened so quickly, like an accident. We took our real honeymoon six months later on a transatlantic voyage on the QE2 to Southampton.

The maître d' had sat us in front of a large floor-to-ceiling window that looked out the port side of the ship. The Princess Grill was a fancy yet a slightly less formal dining room than the Queen's Grill, and we had been told by the Cunard people that the Princess Grill would be more to our liking and less crowded. The ceiling was entirely silver and the booths were red leather. On top of the four pillars bordering each corner of the room were four tall sculptures representing earth, wind, water, and fire, made entirely out of coral and seashells.

It was June 25th, 1988, Carly's forty-third birthday. We had just left, and I was still vibrating from watching what I had seen so many times in movies and newsreels as a child. We sailed between the Statue of Liberty and the soaring, iridescent skyline of Manhattan as the ship pulled out of New York Harbor. As we sat waiting, all the lights dimmed and then suddenly went out. The wait staff lit a number of candles and brought them to our table. As we sat waiting for dinner to be served, the ship came to a shuddering stop. The captain's voice came over the loudspeakers to announce that there was a minor electrical problem. They were working on it, but it would be a few more hours before we would be moving again.

I stared out of the vast floor-to-ceiling window and suddenly realized that the QE 2 had stopped directly in front of Long Beach. Through the darkness, I stared out at the scene of my childhood. We were so close to the West End of Long Beach that I could actually make out Kentucky Street, my old neighborhood. At first I laughed and pointed this out to Carly. As I continued to stare out at the small lit windows, the house I had grown up in appeared, and I began to cry. I could not get over the distance I had traveled from this tiny bungalow, and my crying soon became deep and urgent sobbing. Carly moved her chair closer so she could hold me. She said nothing; she just gently embraced me. How had I arrived at this place? The deep cracks of shame from violence, poverty, and ignorance seemed to lift from the narrow street of my childhood, washed away on this night by the ocean, hopefully never to return.

For me, boarding the QE 2 and traveling first-class with a world-famous star was the fulfillment of some never-imagined dream. The richness of this moment carried me away. The ship's problem was soon solved, and we sailed on.

It was an especially rough crossing that kept Carly in bed for much of it with vicious migraines. I mostly walked the decks and stared at the rolling gray waves. At some point, I realized that this was where my father had misspent much of his youth: on the foreboding North Atlantic. I thought of the risks he had taken to feel better, and it amazed me once again. I thought of the demonic control alcohol had on my family.

Many of my father's stories of the sea had always seemed fantastical, and they seemed even less believable as I got older. I remembered as a child how my father's program buddies would egg him on about them. Those men all seemed ancient and, except for my father, they wore faded white dress shirts and suit pants held up by suspenders. My father's sponsor Chris was often there. He had only one leg; he had lost it in World War I. They often asked my father to tell the Anzio story. It was so exotic-sounding that I had never repeated it, but one long summer afternoon, I told it to a group of insurance buddies sitting around a cafeteria table in the home office. One of them happened to be an ex-Navy fighter pilot in World War II, and he was aghast as he listened. He said it was true, and that he couldn't get over hearing about it all these years later. He said it was a scandal at the time, that my father's antics had potentially endangered the entire Allied invasion.

The story goes that my father swam into Anzio the night before the Allied invasion with a tall sailor from Texas in order to get some booze. My father's question to the Texan before they left was a good one: *Can you swim?* Apparently he couldn't, at least not well enough, for on the way back, the Texan started to drown. My father had told him before they left that he had better be able to swim because he wasn't about to save him. Good to his word, my father kept swimming back toward the ship alone. To rescue the Texan, they broke the invasion blackout and, as a result, the Texan spent the rest of the war in Leavenworth.

Of course, my father's good luck, and his swimming ability, meant that I would arrive in the future and now experience my own remarkable voyage across the sea. I felt close to him, perhaps because I now believed that I too could take exotic risks and cast my lot on the right side of life's accidents. As I looked over the rolling waves of the North Atlantic, I had yet a new appreciation for his question to the tall Texas sailor: *Can you swim?*

CHAPTER

THIRTEEN

———————◆———————

RON VAWTER, AN OLD college friend, stood in front of me on the corner of Waverly and 6th Avenue. He seemed to glide sideways, somehow
catching me unaware, and kissed me on the cheek. We hugged each other for
a long time. When I finally looked at him at arm's length, Ron seemed etched
out of the crisp autumn afternoon. His dusky voice and sly smile underlined
the initial image. He had often created a strange clamor within me. He was
a subversive, a kind of secret agent. So much of his work as an artist with the
Wooster Group was a kind of subversion: a way to get at the truth of things.
I both loved and was terrified by this part of Ron. His cadence and stride
immediately captured me, and he called me by a name that no one else ever
did. In his most soothing voice, he said, *Jimmyboy.*

It was the last week in March of 1988, and we hadn't seen each other for
some time. We had spent a great deal of time together in the West Village in
the early seventies. We shrugged and walked together on this short, whimsical street toward the red brick of the Northern Dispensary. We turned left
onto Christopher at the end of the block near Sheridan Square. Ron's life as a
performer had begun to take off in so many ways, and I had been busy with
Carly. Ron said, *Let's have a drink at Boots and Saddles,* a gay leather bar on
Christopher Street. *There's a cute bartender who's a friend of mine.*

You know I don't drink anymore.

Right, do you mind if I do?

No, not at all, let's go.

Ron ordered a "Jack" on the rocks and lit a cigarette. He loved to smoke, and we had smoked and been drunk together so often. I wished I could have joined him for a few, but I knew I couldn't.

Jimmyboy, Carly Simon?

I know, it's odd, isn't it?

I guess. You'll tell me all about it—everything.

What's happening with you?

Well, my commercial career is finally taking off. I've made some films recently—small but good roles.

That's wonderful.

It's quite bittersweet.

Why?

I have just been diagnosed. I have the AIDS virus.

Oh Ronnie.

We hugged each other in the dim light of Boots and Saddles on Christopher Street. The cute bartender looked on approvingly. I kept touching Ron, and we just kept moving closer and closer to each other. I wanted to kiss Ron down to his bones and tell him with one physical gesture how much I loved him.

We were alone here for most of the afternoon. Just the two of us trying to share what had happened in our lives. We wanted to be alone just to feel and taste and see each word and gesture. Ron had a number of whiskeys but didn't seem drunk at all.

We rushed through so many people and memories—all the nights at various gay bars and all the guys I had slept with before Alannah and I were married—many of whom Ron helped me pick up. I especially remembered a couple of nights at a gay bar in Brooklyn and a flirtation with a sexy young man named Noodles. We danced through the night in a haze of booze, pot, and amyl nitrate. Every time I took a hit of amyl nitrate, I moved closer toward him. Noodles was dressed in skin-tight white bell bottoms and his legs were, muscular, lithe, and sleek, and as the drug took over, I so wanted him, and when the short effect of the drug wore off, I wanted him so much less. This sensual push and pull went on all night, and I felt that sleeping with Noodles would have forced me to declare something forever. I was always drunk or high on something in those days in the gay world, so nothing felt definitive, but this moment was different, as if Noodles could overturn everything within me. Something about his total commitment to his sexuality would have meant that I would have to commit also, and I knew I couldn't, just couldn't. Yet the image of Noodle's swerving body and wide smile stayed with me forever.

I would see Ron again fairly soon. Happily, he was an acquaintance of Edna O'Brien, who had become a great friend to Carly and me. Carly had been introduced to Edna through Jackie, and they had formed a fast friendship. Edna had written a play about Maud Gonne and William Butler Yeats, and we thought Ron might be of help. Of course, given Ron and the Wooster Group's emphasis, Yeats would have to be somehow deconstructed, and a crossdresser would probably play Maud Gonne. It didn't matter to Edna; she had a sharp and trained eye, and she recognized Ron as the real deal, a true artist, and admired his work. The last production I saw of Ron's was a one-man tour de force called *Jack Smith/Roy Cohn*: one of the most terrifying and moving theatrical pieces I had ever seen. Ron played two men who had died of AIDS while Ron himself was dying of AIDS.

I knew Ron and Carly would like each other; they were both zany sorts of artists, and that quality was intertwined in their work and personalities. I worried that Ron in a mischievous mood might reveal some of my gay secrets to Carly, but I was willing to risk it. I wanted the people I loved to know each other more than I wanted my secrets protected. I was never exactly comfortable when the two of them were together. I presumed that somehow the truth would come out, but it never did. We all got busy with other things and then Ron got sick.

I sat one afternoon with Edna, Ron, and Carly at a restaurant in Soho. As I looked at the three of them, I felt excluded. These three had already achieved a great deal of success as artists. I knew I was just like them; I just hadn't yet put myself to the test. There was something in the three of them that I lacked: a kind of bold and vigorous assertion of self. I felt they all cared for me deeply, and yet I lacked what I felt they had assembled—an array of tricks. My alcoholism and Eamon, and my detours in supporting both, had interrupted me. Yet in other ways, I felt more mature than all of them. I thought they were all capable of harming themselves and others in a way that I never could: They lived much more in the sway of their emotions. I felt sounder, as though nothing would ever overturn me.

I was struck by how much Edna and Ron knew about me in certain ways that Carly never would. Edna knew all about being an Irish Catholic from a poor and violent background, and Ron knew the other stuff. These were two parts of me that Carly would never really know, and they were at the core of what I had wrapped in a kind of secrecy to protect myself. It was a bit like the distinction I had made about my apartment: the difference between knowing and seeing. I guessed my father's questions were apropos: *Had I gone by way of Canarsie? And could I swim?* I thought I was answering both of them resoundingly, except there was one question missing: *Could I arrive as myself?*

My calls to a sex line ominously named "The Dungeon" would indicate yet another circuitous path. It was a gay S&M telephone line that appeared in ads in the *Village Voice*. We had set up a writing office for me in a room that Carly had on the roof at 135 Central Park West. It was a remarkable space—soaring above the park in a pyramid-like structure that had tiny, high windows. Sometimes when I would get bored, I would call the S&M sex line and chat with guys about what they wanted to do to me. They all seemed to have growling bass voices with very particular and bizarre instructions:

You are a worthless worm. You will be my slave.

I will?

*Who gave **it** permission to speak?*

No one.

*That's right. **It** will only speak when I tell **it** to.*

Ok.

That is not how you address your Master. You will start every sentence with Thank You, SIR.

I will? Oh, thank you, SIR.

I never remember being sexually excited by any of it. I was just fascinated that people had such unusual desires and were willing to express them to others so candidly. We had so many phone lines that it never dawned on me that someone in Carly's accountant's office would be checking the bill and report back to her that calls were being placed to The Dungeon.

She lived with suspicion. She had been trained in a house of lies as a child, and her many relationships with celebrities, artists, alcoholics, and drug addicts had sharpened her sense that she was never getting the truth. I knew that she would trace the calls to their source, so the only thing for me to do was to admit what I had done. I was terribly ashamed on so many levels, and I made an immediate appeal in my confession.

Please, whatever you do—don't make me talk about this ever again. It will never happen again, I promise you, and please let's not discuss it. It's too embarrassing.

I sobbed throughout this admission, certain that this would be the end of our brief marriage. I am not sure whether Carly actually understood that it was a gay S&M line. After a day of thinking about it, she said she would never mention it again, and in fact she never did. The last thing she said was, *I think it must have something to do with the seminary. You must be a very bad boy. Do you think you need to be punished?*

We didn't revisit this, ever.

CHAPTER

FOURTEEN

———————◆———————

CARLY APPEARED AT THE door of my writer's cabin on a sun-filled spring day. She was writing lyrics for a song for Mike Nichols's new movie *Working Girl*. She heard it as a kind of urban anthem, but she was stuck and thought I might be able to help. The opening of the great secular dream, James Joyce's *Finnegan's Wake*, came to mind. I opened the book and stared at the first sentence.

The first word jumped off the page, and I had it: *riverrun to river run*. I could hear the river flowing into a song, answering the dreams of everyone in the great city of New York. I considered the hortatory subjunctive, *Let us*. Many hymns exhort a congregation to action, but I heard the sound of a command. The river, like us, needed to be unleashed: to be allowed—*Let*.

I found a copy of the collected works of Whitman, and I circled images in a kind of frenzy. The lyric seemed to write itself: waking dreamers, silver cities, morning lights, running fog, the edge, sons and daughters, great and small, even Jerusalem. I threw them all together and produced the first draft. I thought it was good, but what did I know about song-writing?

Carly kept reading it over and over without saying a word. I had written words to a somewhat formal hymn. She then turned it into a popular song, with a deeper emotional appeal. She did this with just a few phrases: *bluer than the eyes of your lover, trembling, shaking, Oh my heart is aching*.

Then she searched for melody and rhythm. She strummed the guitar, played phrases on the piano, hummed a lot, and grew quiet, and then in a few days emerged with the song. Her ability to work within the swirling forces of inspiration and the savage nature of her critical judgment were humbling to observe. At the end of this ongoing dialogue, she created a song that would touch millions of people—strangers. She had a mysterious access to the beating, vital emotions of all sorts of disparate folk. Although she was from a famous and privileged world, she connected to worlds of which she had no firsthand experience.

As I sat in the Ziegfeld Theatre at the premier of *Working Girl*, I watched with amazement as my words accompanied Carly's music in the dramatic opening scene, as the camera panned across the water from Staten Island to downtown Manhattan.

"Let the River Run" would be the first song ever to win a Grammy, a Golden Globe, and an Oscar.

I sat in the Shrine Auditorium at the 61st Academy Awards and heard her say, *I want to thank my husband Jim Hart for the best words in the song.*

A vibration coursed through me as millions of people heard my name for the first time. I wondered what all the people who knew me were thinking when the camera briefly focused on me.

After the ceremony, our limo driver was unable to find us, and we wound up sitting on the curb. She held the Oscar in her hands and rested it on the curb edge. As we saw ourselves in this scene, we began to laugh hysterically, for it seemed a perfectly timed message about achievement in general and fame in particular. I reached into my tuxedo jacket pocket and pulled out the earrings that Melanie Griffith and Carly had borrowed from Harry Winston.

Imagine, four million dollar's worth of jewelry in my pocket, and we don't have a ride.

We were in no particular rush. We had won so big, and now we were happily in the moment. Carly finally stuck out her thumb. Someone recognized her and gave us a ride into town.

Carly didn't always feel so happy and sure of herself. She could become very insecure. Her psyche worked in some unusual ways. Once she became convinced of something, it became almost impossible for her to change her mind. I referred to it as her sonar. Once she picked up a ping on her screen, she had real trouble believing that it could be false, or that it would ever go away.

During our second year together, she became convinced that the women in the writing class I was taking at the 63rd Street YMCA were madly in love with me. She became so sure that she hired a private detective to trail me. She even created an alias, "Snake."

She was so sure that all the women were madly in love with me because they *had* to be. I assured her that she was wrong and that, even if they were, what would it matter? She read all of their writing, and the more she read, the more persuaded she became that not only were they in love with me, but that I must be returning their affections.

One night as I left the classroom, I heard a woman's voice in the hallway. She was greeting all the students in a heavy Spanish accent. As I passed, I caught a glimpse of her bright red hair, spike heels, and red lipstick. She had a short black veil hanging from her hat covering the top half of her face. In a thickly accented voice, she said, *Good Evening!* I turned and stared straight at her. It took me a moment to realize that it was Carly dressed as a Latina hooker. She had come to the YMCA on West 63rd street to see the women who were in love with me and confirm for herself the authenticity of the detective's reports (which were so boring that she finally stopped having me followed).

I was the first person up that Saturday. It was around nine. I was wandering around the kitchen in a pair of white-linen pajamas. I hadn't worn pajamas since I was a little boy, but I could see that they were a bit more elegant than my underwear and might be more pleasing to someone who had to sleep with me. The phone on the kitchen wall rang, and I picked it up.

Hello.

Jim? Hi, it's John, pause, *Kennedy.*

I immediately knew which John it was, but it was polite of him to give me the whole name.

Hey, John. How are you?

Pretty bad.

What's the matter?

Oh, not that you would, but have you seen the Post *this morning?*

No, I haven't been out yet.

Well, I'm on the front page. It says, "The Hunk Flunks."

Oh shit, I'm so sorry.

Yeah, it's bad enough to flunk the bar exam again, but to have it on the front page. I just need to hide. I can't go tonight. I'm too depressed.

John, I'm so sorry. Of course. Just take care of yourself. If we can help, let us know.

Thanks.

I could only imagine what it must feel like to go through this kind of public ignominy. I went into the bedroom to tell Carly that John wouldn't be going to the Stones concert with us tonight. I had only just recently learned the difference between the Rolling Stones and the Grateful Dead. I had always conflated the two into the same band.

Carly woke up and sprang into action. She paged through her large blue Filofax and called John back.

It's Carly.

She hardly gave him time to explain.

Who cares? Listen John, you can't do this. No, you're coming tonight.

She let him go on a bit more.

John, I know about this stuff. Listen to me. You are going to come tonight and we are going to have a great time. You love the Stones right? Exactly. You have to be here at six on the dot. Don't be late. You're welcome.

She hung up and started to put her sleeping mask back on.

He's coming?

Yes, he has to come. Otherwise, they win.

I felt her elegant and specific force in this exchange. For so many reasons, she was one of the few people who could have done this for him. He needed a favorite and powerful aunt, and in this moment she was happy to be that for him.

I sat in the limo across from John, next to Allen Ginsberg and his seventeen-year-old boyfriend. Allen kept taking pictures of the three of us. It was quite obsessive and a little creepy, but he seemed unable to stop. He kept chattering away as he clicked his camera and moved to set up yet another shot. He was like our own special paparazzo. John and I just kept laughing. Allen's boyfriend was a very slim, fair, and innocent-looking young boy. He looked much younger than seventeen. If he had said he that he was fourteen, I wouldn't have questioned it. He had no beard, and his body seemed somewhat underdeveloped for someone his age. Allen introduced us.

Oh my God, you're with her every day?

Well, yes.

She's my favorite person in the world.

Mine too, and I laughed.

No, she saved my life. I've been listening to her since I was a child.

Really.

Yes, I know all her lyrics.

Then he revealed that he had her CD with him as well as a photo.

Do you think she would mind if . . .

I'm sure she wouldn't mind.

He looked at John and Allen and said, *I hope you guys don't mind. I'm just so nervous. I can't believe I'm about to meet her.*

He treated John and Allen as if they must have the same feelings that he did about meeting Carly, and he seemed unable to perceive that they did not.

He was nearly squealing by the time she got into the limo and sat across from him.

Oh my God, Carly. Oh my God.

The boy stared at her the whole way, as if he was in the final rapture.

You know that you are dating the man who wrote "Howl"? I tried interrupting him.

He was not impressed. He just rolled his eyes and laughed and went back to adoring Carly. Then Carly said to Allen, *My husband Jim is a wonderful poet.*

Allen kind of grunted, shook his head, and took another picture.

When did you know you wanted to be a poet? I asked the great poet.

He put his camera down for a moment and for the first time was engaged.

I never wanted to be a poet.

No?

No! I wanted to be a bank teller.

A bank teller?

Yes, I became convinced when I was about sixteen that if I could just hold money all day that I would be okay.

I see, so did you become a bank teller?

No, no one would hire me.

Why? Back then there was a bank on every corner filled with tellers.

I was such a fuckin' fruit, they wouldn't hire me. I had to become a poet.

When we arrived at Shea Stadium, we were ushered into a room with a few hundred other people. The place was jammed with a boisterous and excited crowd all waiting outside the Stones' dressing room. I was trying to figure how they were all going to meet the Stones when I realized that I was alone with Ginsberg and his boyfriend. John, Ben, and Carly had gone in to see the man who had almost broken up her last marriage, and here I was in a room with Allen Ginsberg and his teenage boyfriend.

I was sure this was intentional and I seethed throughout the entire concert, thinking how ridiculous Jagger looked strutting around the stage; how
the music was so loud I couldn't really hear it, even though I was wearing the
earplugs Ginsberg had given me; and how no one here had any sense or taste.

How can the world think this shit is any good?

On the way back we had two limos, and John and I were the only passengers in one of them. We were allowed to follow the Stones back into
Manhattan. John was quite happy and seemed to have forgotten his problems
with the bar exam. I continued to seethe.

As I entered our apartment and saw Carly, I couldn't stop myself. Rage
filled me as I began screaming awful things at my wife. Ben eventually
emerged from his room and said he was going to call 911 if I didn't stop. I
could see from the fear in his eyes that he wasn't kidding.

I turned to Carly and saw how terrified she looked. I started to sob. She
instantly came to me and held me.

I'm so sorry, but it wasn't my fault.

Please stop, don't.

I had seen something about our lives that could not be undone—I was
certain. I would never be enough to capture the part of her that Mick and
James and so many others had already captured.

We finally got into bed together, and she held me tightly.

*Don't you understand? I could have had those people if I wanted them. I didn't
want them. I wanted you.*

I remembered something as we fell asleep. I told her about how I had met
Allen Ginsberg in 1973. I went to the memorial reading held at the 92nd
Street Y for Pablo Neruda. It was a great event with all sorts of prominent
poets in attendance. Allen read during it. I decided to walk home down Lexington Avenue. It was a beautiful early fall night, and I was still moved by the
service and the resonating sound of Neruda's poetry. As I walked downtown,
I realized that there was someone trailing me on the other side of the street.
I kept looking over and finally I realized it was Allen Ginsberg, and that he
was gesturing to me to join him on the other side.

You were at the service, weren't you?

Yes.

I thought so.

Allen and I walked for blocks. It was only all these years later that I realized what he must have been interested in. At twenty-three, I still pretty

much looked seventeen. I had told Carly my own little story of someone famous who had been after me. As I lay next to her that night and listened to her sincere apologies, I wondered if I had been seducing celebrity as long as she had.

———————◆———————

CHAPTER FIFTEEN

'TIS ANOTHER CONTINENT.

Edna gasped as she took in the view. The ocean surrounded the land on two sides, and a few hundred feet below was a large freshwater pond that was a spectacular part of the property. An osprey dove toward the water dipping into its gradient blues and iridescent spangles. Edna twirled for a moment like Julie Andrews at the opening of *The Sound of Music*.

No, 'tis Shakespeare!

For months we had thought about this new Vineyard property and, in what seemed like an impulse, Carly bought it. We were going to forge a new life together and, after two years of living in houses haunted by the ghostly presence of James Taylor, we were going to move to a new place, to create a life without an oppressive past.

The specter of James would always be too large, and there was nothing we could do about the songs on the radio, his concerts, his albums, and his place in the culture, but at least we would no longer have to live in the space that he had built. And yet I was still a usurper, and I soon realized that I didn't have enough strength to overturn the old order—the kids rebelled. They thought of the house that their father had built as their home, and they didn't want to leave it. I argued forcefully that the children should not be making this kind of decision about our future, but Carly could not be dissuaded. She said she couldn't do it to them and, after endless planning and dreaming of our new life to come, she sold the property.

In my memory, there was often the hint of frost. The fireplace in the "crook" would be roaring, and there was a tang of fallen apples in the air. Carly would then enter into a kind of a trance. She would begin to make her simple pasta sauce and, like a great maestro, she would enter the zone, the place that she went to whenever she created anything. Suddenly it was as though she was being channeled by some other spirit—the one that was inventive, brave, and not afraid of risk. The garlic was cut at once with precision and abandon, and then she would scoop out whole tomatoes from a Hunts can. They had to be Hunts. It was in this scooping out and squeezing of each tomato into the pot that the magic of the sauce took place. She held each tomato as though it was the one that was going to make the difference; she would squeeze, caress, and cajole the juice out of every tomato.

This second Vineyard winter, which was our third year together, took its toll.

Luckily, our moods didn't often conflict, but when they collided, breathing and being with each other could be difficult. Occasionally, I could match her sorrow, and when I did, she almost always summoned the strength to put her own feelings aside and attend to me. On one particular snow-covered, marooned afternoon, she came up with an odd solution.

Come on; let's go for a spin.

What?

Just put on your jacket and get in the car.

I reluctantly climbed into the red Volvo station wagon.

Just drive around the property.

OK.

She popped a CD into the car stereo and began to play a Smokey Robinson song, "Cruisin'."

We circled the perimeter of the estate for more than an hour and she kept playing it over and over. We were bounded by the gray sky and the remnants of a snowstorm, but after a few minutes, we had begun singing along.

We couldn't believe that such a simple device actually worked, but it did. We kept touching one another as we sang: caressing and cuddling as we drove around the edge of the property, "Cruisin' together." We were giddy by the time we arrived back at the house. She had saved us from ourselves, as she often did. She was so often searching for ways to bring us closer. The phone was ringing as we came through the kitchen door. I reached it first.

Hello?
Is Carly there?
Who's calling?
It's Smokey Robinson.

CHAPTER

SIXTEEN

———————— • ————————

MY MAZDA RX7 SPUN across both lanes of the Mass Pike. I thought I
had slowed down enough, but the ice on the descent was too slick. Two full-
size sedans were spinning down the hill in front of me and came very close
to colliding with each other. They wound up safely stopped on either side of
the highway.

I came to a full stop out of the skid and stalled in the passing lane per-
pendicular to the flow of traffic. The driver's side was facing the oncoming
traffic, and I saw the approaching grill of an eighteen-wheeler about twenty
to thirty yards away. The driver was a large woman with long dark hair that
flowed from beneath a baseball cap.

I stared at the oncoming truck and said, *Goodbye*—a form of instant res-
ignation about my coming death. I didn't struggle; I judged my life to have
been complete. There was no time for a rationale, just a knowing flash that I
had made something of it all.

The car had been my fortieth birthday present from Carly. Ben had
woken me that morning and told me I had to come downstairs. As we got
to the street, he tossed me a set of keys. Sitting in front of the building on
Central Park West was a black RX 7 convertible with a red ribbon around
it. Less than a year later, my present hurtled me into this final spin. I had just
completed a first draft of my novel and was bringing it to Bill Kennedy in
Albany. As the grill of the truck approached, I was glad that I had gotten that
far. There would at least be something to read.

The truck hit me and I assumed that my journey to death had begun, that

I would soon be somewhere other, other than just beyond a sign that read *Highest Point on the Massachusetts Turnpike.* The truck hit the frame of my car, and instead of crushing it or rolling over it, it struck like one billiard ball striking another, and I slid down the road sideways,

The truck driver and I got out of our vehicles at the same time and ran toward each other. She grabbed me by both arms and held me. She was struggling to breathe.

You're alive, Oh my God, oh my God, you can't be alive. It's a miracle. You can't be alive. I hit you straight on.

I used a phone in one of the cars stopped behind me and called Carly. She answered on the first ring.

I'm on the Mass Pike and I've just been in an accident. Yes, hit by a truck. No, it's amazing. I'm completely unhurt.

I sat with the driver Debbie back in her truck. She was breathing so heavily that I thought she might have a heart attack. After a few minutes, the troopers arrived and began to close the road. When the ambulance arrived, everyone agreed that Debbie was the one at risk, so they took her to the nearest hospital. They tried to persuade me to go, but I assured them that nothing had happened, that I was absolutely without a scratch. I waited for the tow truck to take my car and me to the next exit.

I was dropped at a gas station with a Rent-a-Wreck outlet. Another couple had just rented the car before me, and they started to chat. I was in a rather euphoric state and began to talk to them about the miraculous nature of my life: connecting the seminary to sobriety, straight through to meeting Carly on the train, right to this accident. This older *American Gothic*-looking couple actually knew who Carly was, and they were impressed that her husband was sitting beside them in a rural gas station. They glanced at one another when I began to talk about being sober. It turned out that their son had a drug problem, and he had just entered a treatment program the night before in California. They wondered if I would be willing to speak with him, and I happily gave them my number.

I was anxious to get to Albany for dinner with Bill and Dana Kennedy. After what had happened, I wanted to get the manuscript of *A Bag of Tricks* into Bill's hands. This felt like a story I might be telling at literary parties for years to come: my near fatal accident on the way to deliver my manuscript.

I had gotten the idea and title for the book, *Bag of Tricks*, from a kid in the seminary. His name was Russ. He was a senior when I was a freshman at St.

John's in 1964. He was an oddity in the Catholic seminary of the time—a smart, hip black kid from Harlem. He was also extremely and unconsciously sensual. All the students wore black cassocks with a white Franciscan cord around the waist, and Russ's sensuality extended even to the cord. He wore it with the style of a jazz musician, slung in a way that the bottom of the two cords crossed just beneath his dick. It was as though he was having a sensual experience with each step. He was quite mature for eighteen, and he seemed worldlier than some of the younger, newly ordained priests. His masculinity was completely authentic. He could have been my father's black son—elegant and yet completely and utterly masculine—like a boxer trained by Balanchine. Very few men combined this quality: my father and Russ certainly did. A couple of the priests had some of it, and a few of the older students. Many of the other kids seemed to be either trying too hard or hiding something.

Russ had a rich baritone voice and often led the choir. Standing in the middle of the chapel on the burgundy terrazzo inlay of the intersecting triangles of the Star of David, he directed us. He united the sacred and the profane with each gesture: the very essence of cool. Russ had recently observed me in action with some of the tougher kids from the sophomore class. There was an intense hazing process that was constantly in place, especially for smart-ass kids like me. My hazing seemed to last almost the entire two years, because I was always mouthing off to someone. Russ had witnessed some sophomores beating me up, and as soon as they had let go, I mouthed off again. None of these kids understood the kind of beatings I had withstood from my father without so much as a tear; there was just no way they were going to intimidate me physically. Many of them were mystified by the amount of pain I could tolerate and keep smiling. Russ had been impressed.

A few days later on a Saturday afternoon, Russ stood outside his dormitory and saw me heading for the stairwell.

Hey kid!

Hey.

I didn't know if he was about to punish me for something, or if he was going to make me do something for him—one of the favorite occupations of upperclassmen.

I saw you the other day.

Yeah?

Yeah, you weren't afraid of them. You from New York?

Yeah.

We New York boys aren't afraid of much.

There was a long silence. Upperclassmen often employed it as a method of control, and Russ was a master. He knew that I was not about to leave his presence. He was the most masculine and worldly guy in the senior class, so that made him most important. Also, he was black and therefore different from the rest of them and more mysterious. I wanted to be Russ's favorite underclassman immediately. In the midst of the silence, he gestured for me to enter his dorm room and sit on the bottom bunk bed. He walked toward a small closet. He opened it and rustled beneath his extra cassocks and then asked a strange question.

Do you have a bag of tricks?

A what?

A bag of tricks?

He lifted a large brown paper bag from the bottom of the closet, and walked with it over to the bunk bed.

You have to have a bag of tricks. Everyone has to have a bag of tricks. He held the brown bag up high for a moment, as if it was about to be incensed by a thurible.

Here!

He turned the bag upside down on the green Army blanket covering the bottom bunk. Out fell all sorts of items: a pint of whiskey, three or four packs of cigarettes, condoms, matches, a small flashlight, a *Playboy* magazine, a rolled-up wad of bills, and a copy of *Catcher in the Rye*. Russ picked up the red paperback with the orange print on the cover.

Read this, but don't get caught. It's contraband.

OK.

I trembled at the thought of being misled, and I was terrified of being thrown out, but I was much more afraid of displeasing him. It felt like I was embracing some mysterious, sensual path and turning my back on God. I put the book inside my cassock and down the front of my pants.

Everything on the bed was contraband. How could he have all of these items and keep them in a brown paper bag inside his locker? I didn't understand how he avoided getting caught—there were regular inspections by the prefects of discipline. He quickly put everything back into the bag and then jumped onto the top bunk. He removed one of the ceiling tiles and placed the bag up in the ceiling.

Okay, now get out of here.

Yes, Russ.

I quickly turned to go, and he said:

Hey, kid! Don't forget, get yourself a bag of tricks.

I told Bill and Dana about the ride over, and as supper was being prepared, I had a quick nap on their sofa. Bill had taken my manuscript into the next room, and suddenly I felt him standing over me.

Jesus Christ, this is unbelievable.

He was ashen. I couldn't figure out what he was saying.

This is unbelievable. Do you know the opening sentence of your book?

It took me a second to remember it, but as I did it stunned me. We stared speechlessly at each other.

"I died on January 9th, 1966."

Jim, my friend from the seminary, was the posthumous narrator of the first chapter of the book.

That's twenty-five years to the day, and you should have died today. Unbelievable.

SEVENTEEN

ALAS, TOO MUCH IRISH Catholic guilt and soul-searching for my taste. But I do think he's good.

I learned that *alas* was a favorite word in rejection letters from publishers. I received a lot of them, but Michael Korda's hurt the most because he was the editor-in-chief at Simon & Schuster. Carly's father had given Korda his first job.

But in late spring of 1992, after my agent Pam Bernstein called to tell me she was leaving the business, the most important agent at William Morris, Owen Laster—whose other writers included Robert Penn Warren, Ralph Ellison, Gore Vidal, Norman Mailer, Margaret Mitchell—agreed to take me on. On top of that, Al Silverman, the publisher at Viking and a friend of Bill Kennedy, had agreed to read the book. And a few weeks before, a new friend, Stephen Kennedy Smith Jr., had introduced me to Dr. Robert Coles, the renowned Harvard professor, psychiatrist, and author, who invited me to be a section man (teaching assistant) for his course called *The Literature of Social Reflection*. Carly's friends started to introduce me as a professor at Harvard, and who was I to correct them?

Then, after nine months of silence on the book front, Al Silverman got back to me—he thought it needed another rewrite. This innocent opinion felt like a rebuke—yet another book party, album release, film or Broadway opening, celebrating yet another new friend's success, not to mention my wife's endless achievements—I was at the center of the world of commercial artistic success, and I couldn't get one small book published.

How's the book going?

Jackie broached the subject awkwardly as we sat alone by the pool.

I'm almost done with another draft, I think.

It's so hard isn't it?

Jackie was searching to find a way say something to me, and it made her uncomfortable. She took a deep breath and launched back into the conversation.

Do you think you should be doing just the book?

What do you mean?

Well, do you think it's enough?

Huh?

I got it. Even though she was a book editor, I assumed that Carly had put her up to it. It was just so unlike Jackie to get involved in other people's uncertain artistic pursuits.

Books are so unpredictable.

Yes, you of all people should know.

There was a long silence, and then she took a bit of a different tack.

Do you know of my cousin, Louis Auchincloss?

The writer? Yes, never read anything—not my kind of material.

He's quite prolific, I think over fifty books.

Have you read them?

No, well a couple when I was younger. Well, he's also been a very successful lawyer.

How nice for him.

She could feel where this conversation was going, but I assumed she must have promised Carly she would see it through. Carly later insisted she never had.

You know, he would often leave a legal meeting and finish a paragraph on his way to the next one.

Jackie kept talking, making her case about my need for another sort of life. I didn't hear much more of what she said—I had summed it up this way: the most famous person in the world was telling me I was a loser, and the person I loved most had put her up to it.

Jackie, can I ask you how many novels you've written?

She didn't answer; she just stared away.

That's what I thought.

I left the pool and walked into the house. I felt so bad on so many levels. How could I have spoken to Jackie that way? She was so clearly trying to be helpful and I had been so incredibly rude. And yet, possessed by my rage, I passed Carly and went up to my bedroom, where I packed my bag and called the airport to make a reservation on the next flight from Martha's Vineyard to New York.

When Carly returned to New York a few weeks later, we went to various psychiatrists and marriage counselors, and with each appointment, we seemed to grow more despondent. The end of hope for a psychiatric solution occurred when we found ourselves walking down opposite sides of Madison Avenue after our most recent appointment. We were both sobbing hysterically.

When an attempt at something called "Chinese Couples Therapy," where an older, more experienced couple helps the spotlight couple, became a heated game of two-on-two—Carly and the other husband versus me and the other wife—she was sure that I had to leave.

I moved into a one-bedroom apartment on West 97th Street. It reminded me of my grandparents' tenement apartment on Amsterdam Avenue, where I had watched the Greyhound buses glide beneath the window as a child. Only this one was much smaller.

I was broke and the smell of the ammonia-washed hallways, the empty crack baggies in front of the building, and the scattered hypodermics on the sidewalk in the morning were evidence of how far I had fallen. The thin walls of my new apartment were a rent-regulated tan, and my life seemed to go from vivid color to frightening drab, all in one instant. I remembered a Depression-era song my father used to sing.

Rich man takes the taxi,
poor man takes the train.
My old man walks the tracks,
and he gets there just the same.

As I cooked a grilled cheese sandwich, thinking about how I was going to pay the rent, I felt something rise up from my toes into my temples and I started to laugh hysterically. Suddenly, I saw the last five years of my life for what they seemed to be—a comical fairytale coming to an abrupt end.

As I looked down at the cheese melting over the browning bread, I had never felt more sober.

Some weeks into our separation, Edna O'Brien called to invite me to be her date at a dinner party at Steven Kennedy Smith Sr.'s on the Upper East Side. It was just a date between friends, but Carly processed it quite differently. She later said that one of her biggest fears was that I would wind up with someone more famous and more beautiful than she, and this date with Edna seemed to signal the beginning. This thought drove Carly crazy, and her fear produced a space for us to tentatively get back together. She had been writing her opera, *Romulus Hunt,* a roman à clef, about her, James, and the kids. I was thankful that I was living separately during most of those weeks as she focused on what I considered to be one of the major unspoken problems in our marriage. We soon knew we couldn't bear being apart, and we decided to start living together again. To do my part, I took a symbolic job refurbishing apartments. I was burning and scraping paint off walls eight hours a day for ten dollars an hour. I arrived home filthy, sweaty, and covered with dust, and each day I walked in the door, I could see Carly grow happier. In some odd way, my willingness to make ten dollars an hour scraping paint began to persuade her that we could remain together, that indeed I had some of the integrity that she had counted on. Nothing seemed to touch her like my willingness to perform physical labor on our behalf: to have sinew covered with dirt and sweat, to be her "John Henry."

She used this reference all the time. As the folk story goes, John Henry agreed to race a steam engine pile driver for land that would be given to the winner. A "steel-driving man" with a singular determination, John Henry makes a fitting hero. But the ending of the tale never seemed to figure into Carly's thinking. John Henry beats the steam engine, but dies doing it.

Lillian, my old secretary from Metropolitan Life called when she heard I was starting a company and offered her services for free. *Don't worry, you're good for it; you'll succeed.*

I had met a guy in Upper West Side recovery, and we started an advertising rep firm. It was theoretical until we located the Institute of Management Accountants, the client that started our company. We had no office, no money, and no staff, and no idea what an association of 100,000 management accountants might need. As it turned out, we had considerable persuasiveness, goodwill, and enough energy and talent to launch the business. We had almost no knowledge of the industry, but with my partner's experience in advertising, my sales and marketing background, and my credit cards, within a year, we had what looked like a success, and Lillian had been paid. The luck of our timing didn't hurt. Our business took advantage of the financial software industry's explosion in the boom days of the nineties, and we were good at what we did. This venture took an enormous amount of energy and time, and gave Carly and me much more time apart than we'd had before. We remained supportive, if somewhat confused, about what kind of relationship we were building. Yet we knew we were deeply bound by our love for one another, and this endless willingness to try new solutions seemed to be the proof, though we never seemed able to really get to the truth of what troubled us. In a certain way, we dealt only with the practical problems in our relationship, like how to live in three different places at once, and the reality that I needed to support myself from now on. I was the CEO of a growing marketing and advertising company, succeeding in a career that didn't matter to either of us. Meanwhile, Carly was releasing albums, publishing children's books, scoring movies, working on an opera, and continuing the balancing act of being the famous Carly Simon, a loving spouse and mother.

I continued to feed what Carly called my "artistic soul" by starting a new novel. One of the philosophy professors at Siena had been a confessor at Nuremberg. I had always been fascinated by this idea. The actual priest seemed decidedly uninteresting, but I imagined what he might be like as a fictional character, someone who had to forgive the Nazis for the most unforgivable acts a human being could commit. I imagined a story of fascinating ethical questions combined with the dramatic drive of international espionage. The experience of Nuremberg haunted him forever and drove him out of the priesthood. The priest could not forgive himself for what he had been forced to forgive since, theologically, no one, no matter how guilty or wicked, may not confidently hope for forgiveness. There is only one sin that cannot be granted absolution—the sin against the Holy Spirit: the belief that what you have done is beyond forgiveness, one of the great, paradoxical doctrines of Catholic theology.

Don't move your feet.

Jackie didn't quite understand.

Just move your body.

As she watched, I planted my feet firmly and let the music course through me. Jackie slowly understood, and she began to move with tentative, jerky motions. I closed my eyes and relaxed into the pulse of the music. I felt the Vineyard summer night as I moved beneath the full moon, instructing Jackie

Onassis on how to dance. When I opened my eyes she was gyrating in front of me. The beat had taken her, and she had let go. As I caught her eyes, she smiled and then shook her head, and in her deep, breathy whisper, she said, *I've never done this before.*

Of course, I had never done this before either. Just that afternoon I had learned how to do "Mess Around" from Polly Landess. It's a simple way to dance. You plant your feet and don't move them at all, and let the music course through you. Polly was a dancer and choreographer. We had done theatre together when I was a graduate student at Albany State, and we had only recently reconnected. So much of my life was filled with things I had never done before. It all seemed an improvisation, always somewhere over my head, and yet oddly I kept reaching higher and for more. That night Jackie and I both inhabited our bodies, and for once her iconography disappeared. I couldn't remember when I had ever seen Jackie so joyous, as if she had finally found some way to connect to a self that had been lost long ago. Maurice Tempelsman (Jackie's boyfriend) and Jackie called the next day to say how much fun they'd had, and Maurice told me that he'd found Jackie doing "Mess Around" in front of the mirror when he woke up.

The moon had cooperated, as if it had been lassoed over our property for the event we had named in its honor: *The Moon Party*. It seemed that everyone would be coming. Jackie had been very excited about it, and she and Carly had come up with the idea that everyone should wear white. Some parties just build their own vibe, a life of their own before they happen, and this was one of them. The Cronkites, the Styrons, the Pfeiffers, Mike and Mary Wallace, Art Buchwald, Peter Feibleman, Patricia Neal, Jake, and his new wife Mindy, and Jackie, were there among many other local artists and Vineyard characters.

I was the emcee, and Carly was going to sing to end the evening. Everyone was asked to prepare something that involved the moon: to read a poem, sing a song, or act a skit, and most of the people did just that. There was a small stage at one end of the barn with the moon and stars painted over it. The song Carly chose was "Paper Moon."

It was clear that we had survived our struggles, and now we could return to the business of marriage: taking care of each other. It felt that this party was an announcement to everyone that our life was going to work. We had recommitted to each other under the splendor of the full moon. After the party, we walked arm and arm back to the house. As we neared the kitchen door, we noticed a large green form attached to the screen. As we got closer, we saw that it was a luna moth: the largest and most beautiful I had ever seen. The tops of its wings were edged in a purplish-blue color, and it didn't move as we approached. Only after we closed the door and turned off the light did it escape into the darkness.

EIGHTEEN

THE PRESIDENT WAS HOLDING Chelsea's hand as he entered, and he held her next to him most of the afternoon. It was an endearing image, the most powerful man in the world tenderly protecting his daughter, and it served to soften everything about the visit. My nervousness lessened as I looked at them. Hillary entered right behind, and her very genuine smile also helped. Earlier in the morning, I had taken a tour of the property with the Secret Service. The property seemed to be glistening and unfolding for the presidential arrival, and by the late August afternoon, it had turned into a perfect summer day—not a cloud in the sky. The large lawn rolled away from the main house and formed a small valley between the house and the opposite hill. In the middle stood a willow that threw a vast, serrated shade across the lawn—as though it had been planted years ago just for this event. It had a relaxed curve, yet its sweep spoke to privilege: it gilded the sunlight as it passed through it creating more elegant and gentle golds and yellows.

No, this is a low-level security detail.

I had just asked the agent about how hard it was to protect President Clinton on Martha's Vineyard. The Secret Service agent was walking with me around the perimeter of the estate.

How long have you been doing this?

Almost twenty years.

So, who's your favorite President?

I'm not allowed to answer that. I can tell you that the Clintons are remarkable—

really human. They know who my kids are, what grades they're in, my wife—all that stuff, really warm people.

As we examined my writing shack, only steps from the house, he said, *We'll put the football here.* The mechanism that could destroy the world in a nuclear Armageddon was sitting on the desk where I had written my novel. I was stunned by the fictional possibilities; I barely heard him when he said, *We'll put the snipers right behind that little hill over there. You won't see them from the house.*

I was overwhelmed as I realized that the possibility of global mayhem and destruction would be located on the very spot where I wrote. I wondered what it would be like if something cataclysmic were to happen while they spent the afternoon with us.

I had been secretly obsessed about the personal security check. They needed everyone's social security number to do a background check on all of them.

I thought about the Continental Baths.

The President gave Carly a big Arkansas "hello" and stepped across the small country kitchen to embrace her. He then turned to shake my hand, and he lingered for a moment.

Jim, I think we're going to get to know one another. So I need to know one thing. What rock were you hiding under? You didn't know who she was?

There had been a book recently published that contained the story of how Carly and I had met, and how I didn't know who she was at the train station. No doubt someone on their staff had read it.

You'd have to know Troy, New York.

As I answered, Clinton looked somewhat confused and quickly disengaged from following my point. Jackie's words from her phone call just before the Clintons arrived echoed in my mind.

They were about two hours late, and as we waited, Carly kept calling Jackie to ask what she should do. Call them? Make a fresh meal? How should we address him? On the last call, Jackie had finally had enough and with mock exasperation said, *Oh, Carly, for Christ's sake, he's just another President.*

The next day, Kay Graham asked me if I thought the Clintons had enough *gravitas*—she didn't think so. I explained to her that they were probably too young to feel weighty enough for someone of her generation. I repeated Bill Styron's evaluation of him, that Clinton's understanding of Faulkner was astonishing. Kay didn't seem very impressed with that fact. I immediately had felt that what they were missing was not *gravitas*, but *mysterium*. They carried with them the secular notion that politics was the answer to most of our problems. It reminded me of the feeling I had way back in second grade when I spent two months in public school: that secular life was without magic. Bill Clinton's relationship to politics began with the now-famous public handshake he exchanged with President Kennedy when he was a young teenager at the White House. My relationship to politics had been sealed all those years ago when I heard the words of the final requiem prayer at President Kennedy's funeral: *May the angels lead him into paradise.* We came from very different places.

Throughout the long afternoon, I kept repeating Jackie's statement to myself to feel less nervous. It helped to be reminded that he was after all *just another President*, even though he was the only President who had ever sat across from me at our dining-room table. The longer we sat there chatting about so many things, the more I liked both of them. I certainly hadn't been sold on him at the beginning. During the Democratic primary, I had convinced Carly that Jerry Brown was the guy we should support, and Carly did something she hardly ever did—she sang at a couple of Jerry Brown's rallies. I believed a radical change was needed, and the Clintons seemed to represent the same old party politics. And then there was Clinton's personality. The first time I saw him on television, I remembered thinking *I know him. He's the kid in high school who does the same shit as me, and never gets caught.*

I became convinced of my assessment when Senators John Kerry and Chris Dodd made a special visit the summer before telling us that we had to back Clinton, that he was the best-prepared politician to be President. This made me even more suspicious. Why were they trying to strong-arm us, or rather Carly, into backing Clinton? Why did it matter to them? It turns out that it mattered because Clinton needed to appeal to middle-aged moms who were burdened by their jobs, finances, and families. In subsequent elections, those women would be identified as the "soccer moms." Many of Carly's most devoted fans fell into this demographic. It also turned out that the last night of the national campaign, the final rally for Clinton, was going to be in New Jersey; and if Clinton won New Jersey, which looked very tight, he would win the election. Essentially, New Jersey was going to be decided by Carly's fans. Clinton knew that all celebrities and dignitaries were important, but that Carly might make the most difference in this huge media market with this important group. Carly had no intention of leaving our cozy

Central Park West apartment that night, but Clinton himself called and pleaded with her. He pretty much put the history of the country on her shoulders.

Carly, darlin', if you come, I'll win.

We found ourselves at the Meadowlands that night, standing on the stage in the first row of a bleacher packed with scores of other celebrities. We both laughed at how important Carly's presence must be. Clinton entered the arena, waved to the audience, and then turned around and pointed right at Carly, and waved to the other celebs on the bleachers. He greeted the performers on the stage and went past Carly without seeming to notice her, but then with a sharp turn, he walked to where we were standing, grabbed Carly's hands and pulled her toward him. He held her as long as he could, and then turned toward the deafening cheers of the crowd.

We were back home in New York in time for the eleven o'clock news and, of course, there were Clinton and Carly in that earnest and tender moment. It turns out he probably didn't need anyone's help, but he was clearly very happy that Carly was there. He won New Jersey and the presidency.

As we sat down for lunch that day on the Vineyard, my entire take on him changed. Carly asked, *So, what did you think of last night?*

Last night they had attended a welcoming dinner party at Kay Graham's. This was the President's first exposure to the Vineyard scene. Anyone who was anybody in American political life came to see Kay, who had a sort of summer White House down the road from us. She was the publisher and owner of the *Washington Post* and *Newsweek*, and for a long time, she was the wealthiest woman in America. Many people came to signal their obeisance, even Presidents.

There has been a great deal of praise written about Kay Graham, but I usually left her house feeling both angry with her and sorry for her. There was a poor-little-rich-girl quality that her stuttering, dragon-lady veneer never hid very well. I always thought the men around her were taking advantage of her with inane flattery, which she was easily seduced by. She seemed adrift in the heights of unseemly power and yet completely addicted to it. She could have used a constant bullshit monitor, but no one would ever have the balls to suggest it to her.

At least *I* didn't.

I asked her one night when she was a bit tipsy if she had ever been in love. She said only once in her life, in San Francisco. As she told me, she began to cry, a rare event, and she wondered aloud what her life would have been like if she had followed her heart. I never thought of her the same way after that.

Her house was set on a shallow cove on Vineyard Sound, a part of the island that faces Cape Cod. F. Scott's Fitzgerald's famous description of Daisy Buchanan's home in "The Great Gatsby" captures the ambience of Kay's house. The gentle night breeze blew in from the sea, and woman's skirts rippled softly in the large white living room. More surprising than the number of A-list politicos and celebs in attendance was the U.S. Navy cutter anchored just beyond her lawn. It stood motionless and gray in the calm Vineyard Sound. This was a party trick no one else in this room would ever offer. Only the President of the United States can make one of those appear.

I had my back to the door when the Clintons entered the room. Everything stopped; everything became silent and yet electric. I didn't want to seem the rube, so I continued talking to Henry Kissinger about something entirely banal, like the weather or his golf game. Kissinger also acted completely cool. After all, it certainly wasn't his first President. Finally I turned, and there they were, William and Hillary Clinton.

Bill and Hillary worked the crowd of about forty people. They seemed to know just about everyone. Kissinger and I stood at the far end of the room, and it took Clinton a few minutes to get to us. Not long after being greeted, Kissinger launched into a tutorial for the President on the idiocy of national health care. I thought that Clinton might be overpowered by the gravitas and experience of Henry Kissinger, but Clinton handled him deftly and abruptly ended the discussion with *Henry, you don't have to worry, the American people are still paying for your health insurance.*

The Clintons soon moved the discussion from politics to the children. Throughout the entire time they sat at the table, Bill never let go of Chelsea's hand. I had the feeling that the Clintons' inquisitiveness about Ben and Sally was more than politeness. I thought that one of the important reasons for their visit was to study how to raise really famous kids. Ben and Sally seemed to be doing well in that most difficult of categories: two extremely famous parents. Hillary asked, *Jim how is your son? He's a special child? What's his name?*

I looked around the table. Carly and the Clintons shared something that would always make their lives different from mine—they had beautiful and bright children who were mostly a joy to be near. Eamon was not sitting at *this* table.

I had allowed the most important aspect of my life to be made invisible for the purposes of decorum and ease. I had abandoned the inconvenience of my own life for comfort. My son was a secondary concern, something Alannah would have to deal with as I assumed my place among this elite assembly.

They asked about every detail of his situation, as if they were about to become his unofficial aunt and uncle. If they were faking their concern, they were brilliant at it, and the brilliance never faltered, because they asked about Eamon each time I saw them over the next ten years. I went on about it all, as if Eamon were all I ever thought about, and as if, once again, I should be named father of the year. Little did we know that they had just seen Eamon—all of him.

It turned out that one of Alannah's best friends had a house on the Vineyard, which she rented out in the summer. The house was on State Road, which the Clinton motorcade passed to get to our house. The friend had given it to Alannah for a few weeks of summer vacation. It turned out that Eamon accidentally picked up a Benadryl a previous renter had dropped and swallowed it. He became extremely agitated, ripped off his clothes, and ran outside just as the Clintons were passing on the way to our house. I don't know if they noticed him or not, but there was my sixteen-year-old son, naked for the First Family as they were on the way to see me. It might have been Eamon's dramatic expression of his opinion about power and fame.

The afternoon stretched on; they stayed four or five hours. The conversation ranged over many topics. They wanted to know all about my work with Dr. Coles. They were huge fans and seemed to know as much about him as I did. They had both read a number of his books and were fascinated by his work and my take on it. But mostly they wanted to talk about how they could do a better job.

You've got to stop wearing those Arkansas barbecue clothes, Carly said earnestly. *You know, you need to be wearing Armani, Issey Miyake, at least Ralph Lauren. It's very important. You need to change the image. I can help if you need it.*

He took no offense; he had sincerely wanted her advice. We noticed an almost immediate improvement in his fashion choices when he got back to Washington in September. From that point on, one of the first things he always asked Carly was her opinion of what he was wearing.

The visit ended as the sun was nearly setting over the island. They all gathered by the magical swing set that Carly and James had built for Ben and Sally. It was made out of strong limbs of oak that had been cut on the property. We all took turns pushing each other gently back and forth, a playful opening to a relationship that would include many fun visits and scores of different kinds of conversations. There always seemed to be a yearning for a simple friendship between our two families, but the complexity of the personalities and their positioning in the world would make this all very asymmetrical. Little did I know, as I gave Chelsea a gentle push on the swing, that just a few years later, we would be spending the weekend of the impeachment with them at Camp David. The sunlight on that weekend wouldn't be nearly as lush and privileged as on this first visit to the Vineyard.

After they left, we were sitting in the kitchen reviewing everything about the visit. The phone rang, and it was Jackie wondering how everything went. Carly said, *Well, I still can't believe that the President of the United States just spent five hours in my home.*

Well, Carly, trust me, as they drove out your front gate, Bill turned to Hillary and said, "Can you believe it? We just had lunch with Carly Simon."

———— • ————

CHAPTER NINETEEN

CARLY'S MOTHER DIED ON February 15th, 1994. The last sounds around Andrea Simon's deathbed were supplied by the angelic voices of her daughters. I thought it spoke volumes to how the Simon family conducted themselves around sorrow—they sang. They had a way that was uniquely their own, and singing their mother into eternity was a part of it. They attended to her every need, and when the pain increased, she would whisper for them to sing, and instead of a grimace, a radiant smile would appear as the incestuous harmonies of her daughters' voices surrounded her. Her death was about as peaceful and unhurried as any I had ever seen. She lingered just the right amount of time to say goodbye and avoid too much suffering, and she certainly didn't encourage anyone to pine over her. She felt that she had had a full and rewarding life, and she left without guilt or regret.

Jackie's ending was different. Bill Clinton may have been "just another President," but Jackie was certainly not "just another First Lady." We would soon know that these were the last few months.

She died on May 9th, 1994, at the age of sixty-four. Her battle was more complex and crueler, and she departed just when her life seemed to have shifted a bit. She seemed to be at a new and well-earned threshold, and then it all ended abruptly.

About a month before the end, there had been a final, sad luncheon at our New York apartment. Her ill-fitting wig made her seem like a refugee from some former Soviet country that ended in -*stan*; her kerchief seemed a sign of an ominous and uncharacteristic ending. Her now-lifeless eyes seemed to be struggling to find another source of light. This once-luminescent part of her was waning so quickly, as though the most essential part of her had already said goodbye.

I flashed on so many memories. The night with Mike Nichols and Jackie listening to Placido Domingo and Carly record a duet in the Kaufman Studios in Astoria until late into the early morning hours. Carly had consented to do it if Placido would let her teach him how to sing like a pop singer, no easy task. Or the afternoon on Maurice Tempelsman's yacht, *The Miramar*, when the F-15 National Guard fighters figured out who the passengers were and kept buzzing the boat on the way to Nomans Land to drop their ordnance, and Jackie turned to Carly and said, *Oh, they must have figured out that you're on board.*

And there was the moment escorting her outside on a balcony at Lincoln Center overlooking the main fountain. She turned to me and whispered, *Do you think you could find me a cigarette?* I said, *Sure.* Standing directly in front of us was an older couple in matching green tweed outfits. They were smoking intently. Jackie was blocked from their view by my much larger body. I asked if I could bum a cigarette. They both responded, interrupting one another to tell me in thick English accents, *No, sorry, we never do that sort of thing.* I stepped aside and said, *It's not for me. It's for her.* Cigarettes leapt out of every pocket of their frumpy tweed getups. Jackie and I could barely contain our laughter as the man reverently lit her cigarette.

A long letter arrived for Carly, just a few days before Jackie died. It was on powder blue stationery written in Jackie's school-girly cursive hand. It was over twenty pages long and mostly about how proud Carly's mother must have been of her. It was a very generous thing to do as her own life was slipping away. The letter had the language of finality; she knew something for sure and wanted to share it.

The day of the funeral, we walked across Central Park. It was a brilliant May morning. I had been staring at my invitation: *Caroline Kennedy Schlossberg and John F. Kennedy, Jr. invite Jim Hart to the funeral mass for their mother* JAC-QUELINE KENNEDY ONASSIS. I held it marveling at a strange aspect of my sorrow. It was odd to grieve for someone in two additional categories: death of the most famous person I would ever know, but also the death of the most famous woman of our time.

As we entered St. Ignatius Church on Park Avenue, I saw so many familiar faces of friends and acquaintances, as well as the Kennedy family. I knew all sorts of ways that Jackie felt about so many of the people in attendance. I was often in attendance as Jackie skewered or praised someone, as many of us do, all in the same sentence. She was fulsome in both directions when she got going, and every bit of it sounded a bit like history. (I sometimes wonder what Jackie would have thought of my subsequent adventures. I suspected she might have had some fairly critical things to say.)

St. Ignatius Church was never one of my favorite New York churches. There was something too cold and distant about the multicolored array of marble from around the world that seemed to clash rather than come together harmoniously. Its design robbed it of the grandeur and elegance that I thought Jackie's funeral deserved. It was a mess of baroque architecture. Yet it was certainly appropriate that the Jesuits would be in charge of her sendoff—being America's only royal family. The pastor of the church performed what was a near perfect and elegant job. It turned out that he was a mathematician, and he had the simple and unadorned presence of two plus two.

Mike Nichols was up on the altar reading a familiar passage from Revelation in his reedy baritone.

I will wipe away all tears from their eyes: there will be no more death, and no more mourning or sorrow or pain. The world of the past has gone.

Hearing Mike read this was too hard, and for the first time I began to cry. Carly and I clutched each other closely, and I had the first deep sense of the enormity of our loss. As I looked up at Mike on the Jesuit altar, a smile formed through my tears. There was this little Jewish boy from Berlin reading words that so beautifully said much of what Mike had been able to give Jackie over so many years.

If Jackie and I could have chatted the day after the funeral, she might have admitted what a beautiful service it was, and then would have wanted to know what I thought of the choices. She might have said how touched she was by Ted's eulogy, and asked what I had thought of the simple remarks by the Jesuit pastor. I would inevitably talk about the nature of the Catholic funeral mass, and she would probably humor me as I went on about the beauty of the ritual and its meaning in my life, but at the end of the conversation, she would get to the actual reason for her call. I would have heard her voice get softer and duskier and her intonation would dance with delight as she asked me about her most important concern: *Jim, what did Mike think?*

When I think of those middle years in the 1990s, I marvel at all that we were doing. Carly's career continued to soar. My company had taken off and I seemed to be traveling around the country nonstop. In 1995, Carly went on a countrywide tour for the first time in twenty years, with Hall and Oates as the opening act. Carly chartered a BAC 111. It was a British jet that was originally designed for up to 119 passengers. A Polish billionaire, who now lived in the Bahamas, had elegantly refitted this particular BAC 111 for luxury air travel. The billionaire happened to be a Carly Simon fan and was happy to lend her the plane for the tour. It made for a rather elegant trip around the country. I was on as many flights as I could manage to help with both her flying fear and her stagefright, although it turned out that, for the most part, she handled it better than any of us would have thought possible.

Jake Brackman had married a beautiful and talented singer/songwriter, Mindy Jostyn. Mindy almost immediately became both a great friend of Carly's and musical director of her band. She was a great help to Carly in so many regards, and the added bonus was that Jake often accompanied her to the various gigs and that meant more time spent together with our families. Jake was a great complement to all proceedings. He quickly read the nuances of whatever was going on in the stars' suites, as well as what was transpiring with everyone in between. Mindy played almost every instrument, and she was as good natured as she was talented, so it usually made for a fun group. The tour was magical and music venues around the country were thrilled to see Carly on stage at long last.

Ben and Sally had grown up in the interim; they were now young adults. Their lives were filled with the normal challenges of teenage life, and they benefited and sometimes suffered from their famous parentage. Having a famous mother and father does not always help the process of individuation as a young adult. Yet it seemed to me that Ben and Sally were doing as well as most teenagers I knew. They could be an enormous pain in the ass when they set their minds to it, but they didn't often dig in against us. They mostly wanted to have fun, even with their parents. Also they were both deeply kind to me.

One Saturday in August when Ben was thirteen, the phone rang at three in the morning. He was on the other end. Carly held the phone and after she determined that he was okay, she handed the phone to me.

He won't talk to me, says he needs to talk to you.

Hi Ben, what's up?

Just don't say anything in front of Mom until I tell you.

OK.

First of all. I'm fine.

OK.

But, I've been arrested.

Mmmm—okay.

I've been arrested for running a stop sign in Vineyard Haven.

That would make sense, you're thirteen. Were you high or drunk?

No, completely sober. Just don't let Mom freak out. It won't be helpful.

OK, I got it.

You need a ride home?

No, I'll get a cab when they're finished here.

OK, see you in a while.

I filled Carly in on the conversation. At the age of thirteen, Ben was six-one, and he was hanging out with kids much older. The older kids were all drunk and high, and he decided it would be better if he drove them home than if they got behind the wheel. Ben, however, had really only driven on the dirt roads around the property, so a stop sign was not something he was used to obeying.

Sally also had her share of what seemed to me like pretty normal adolescent exploration and a bit of rebellion. She at times seemed like a sullen teenage girl, but that didn't strike any of us as odd, not even Carly. There was very little that Carly and I had any rules about except their safety. Per James's suggestion, it seemed pretty clear that the job was to try to keep them alive until they were adults. I sometimes acted as an intermediary between them and their mother if they found her unreasonable. Like any teenagers, they took up an enormous amount of focus for Carly and me, but so much of it was just the uproarious fun of watching two independent spirits grow up.

Eamon was not getting easier for Alannah to care for, and there were constant phone calls and difficult trips to Albany to try to figure out what to do. My life seemed an endless challenge of reconfiguration. Carly and I kept trying to sort out our marriage, which still gave us great comfort, yet there was no doubt that there were real problems. Mostly they were still caused by the huge imbalances that we could not realign. Although I was supporting myself quite well by this time, it didn't allow me to make any real financial contribution to our married life. It allowed me to keep a separate apartment in New York, which I was loath to give up, to take care of Eamon, and to participate in Carly's life in a somewhat marginal way, though I was still very much in it. I hoped that time would align us—that in time, the nature of the imbalances would lessen, and the intensity of our love would right the scales.

Somehow I wound up standing next to the President on the almost empty stage of Radio City Music Hall. We were nearly by ourselves; everyone else seemed to have drifted off. We were discussing what a great event Bill's fiftieth birthday bash had been. A cavalcade of stars had performed, including Carly. A Catholic nun was wandering alone pushing a walker in front of her. Bill pulled me toward her.

Jim, come here, I want you to meet someone.

Jim, this is Sister Mary McKee.

Hello Sister, so nice to meet you.

Sister McKee was my third-grade teacher for a few months.

Sister Mary had all the moves and intonations of a grammar school nun. It was as if we were both still her students.

Now you two tell me something. Why do the Republicans get all the rich men, and the Democrats get all the handsome ones?

She posed it not as a joke but as an interrogation of her two star pupils. Bill and I shook with laughter. It seemed an unguarded moment of joy for him.

Jim, I just wanted you to know I once had a real religious education. You know, she's the only teacher who ever gave me a failing grade.

Sister Mary, he wasn't smart enough for Catholic school?

No, no, she gave me a D in deportment.

Without missing a beat, I turned to the President and said, *See you've even turned that into an asset.*

With a strange and sudden change in mood, the President turned toward me, came very close to my face, raised his voice in anger, and said, *What do you mean by that? No, what do you mean by that?*

I gently touched the President's arm and said, *It was a joke, I was just joking.*

The President looked momentarily confused, said, *Oh, OK,* and then strode off the stage into the wings.

A year later I would find myself seated at the big table at the next presidential dinner at Katherine Graham's summer house on the Vineyard in August of 1997. This was the first time this had ever happened. I couldn't figure what I had done to be given this position. At all of the other gatherings, I was relegated to the "children's table" with Rose Styron and Ann Jordan. But on this night, I was seated next to the President. The table included Kay

Graham, Henry Kissinger, Lawrence Eagleburger, and Franklin Raines. The President immediately took charge of the conversation. He wanted to know what the folks around the table thought made a great President. What could he do to insure that his second term would guarantee that he would become one? The others all went on about various wonky issues that would ensure he was thought of as great. Henry Kissinger droned on about how China policy would be the major issue that would determine whether he was considered a great President. When it came to me, only one thought came to mind: *It's about the poetry of the language.*

They all looked at me as though I had said something aberrant. I continued quite sure of myself. *I know none of you will agree, but great Presidents are remembered because of the power and elegance of their language.* I cited Lincoln, Roosevelt, and Kennedy. The table went silent and then the President nodded as if he had some small understanding and agreement.

I then found myself in a fantasy about a call that might come later in the week inviting me to be on the President's speech-writing staff. Sitting there on that glorious summer night, I thought I might have finally found my own path to greatness, as the new Ted Sorensen. Perhaps like Carly's father, who had edited President Eisenhower's famous military-industrial complex speech, I would be called upon all these years later. After all, my life seemed a series of situations that I was completely unprepared for, as far back as Kentucky Street.

The fantasy continued after dinner when Clinton sat next to me on one of the large white couches in Kay's drawing room. As I looked across the room, I saw a sea of prominent faces staring at the President: Diane Sawyer, Barbara Walters, Henry Kissinger, and many other stars in the world of media and journalism. The President of the United States turned to me and said, *Jim, you know the press is not allowed to ask me questions on my vacation. Why don't you do it?*

I was terrified. I fancied myself the resident political expert in the Simon-Hart-Taylor household, but here I was about to become the interviewer in front of the best professional newspeople in the business, as well as every other sort of celebrity.

I began to question the President about the major issues of the day, and when I could think of nothing more to ask, I started to go around the globe for Clinton's assessment of the world. Clinton easily moved from one geographical area to another, providing in-depth analysis and opinions on every part of the world and their leaders. When I asked the President who the most impressive world leaders were, Clinton responded immediately that Boris Yeltsin was the man he was most impressed with, because he had held the Russian people together while telling them that things were going to get worse before they got better. *No American politician would be able to do that. You had to keep telling the American people that things were going to get better or they would never support and elect you.* He also said that Hafez al-Assad, the President of Syria, *was by far the smartest leader he had met—that his grasp of the issues was encyclopedic—very impressive.*

This interview/lecture/chat went on until three in the morning. I felt that a new and more significant bond had been established between the President and me, but that call from the White House never came.

I sat that night in a finely tailored blue Italian-silk suit—two middle-aged men looking across the globe, and for hours into the night, I had the complete attention of the President of the United States.

Not everyone, however, was fascinated; at some point about half way through, Carly drifted away. She often wandered away during a party, sometimes from boredom and sometimes because of her innate shyness. I knew she was very proud of me tonight, but that didn't mean she would be interested in every detail of the situation in Bosnia.

At the end of the evening, the Clintons stood in front of Kay Graham's front door, and Carly was still nowhere to be found. Then, as if they had been summoned out of the thinnest air, Carly and a tall, handsome man stepped out from behind a pillar or a large bush and rejoined the group to say goodnight to the President. The man was an old friend of Carly's whom she hadn't seen in a long time, and they seemed thrilled at the revival of their friendship. Carly and I also seemed revived in some important way; perhaps a new balance was about to be established.

As time passed, we both realized that the "new balance" wasn't going to take place by itself. One evening in the fall of 1996, I sat on the side of our bed in our Central Park West apartment in a tuxedo. I was waiting for Carly to finish dressing for a gala at the Waldorf Astoria. It was an event we weren't much interested in but felt obliged to attend, perhaps a music award dinner for someone like Clive Davis. As I sat there aimlessly channel-surfing, I stopped on C-Span, which was broadcasting a conference at which the Dalai Lama was speaking. The Dalai Lama was comforting as usual. Carly emerged from the bathroom at about the same time a new speaker followed the Dalai

Lama at the lectern. Her name was Sister Marie Jose Hobday. She was a Native-American Catholic Franciscan Nun. She caught my attention when she said, *You know I have great reverence for the Buddhist and Christian traditions, and I have such reverence for his Holiness.*

She made a deep and reverent bow to the Dalai Lama and then continued, *But I want you to know that my tradition precedes both of those great religions by about 30,000 years.*

She was funny, moving, and charismatic, and held master's degrees in theology, literature, architecture, and space engineering. Carly and I sat and watched her entire speech, even though we were already late for the dinner across town. She also said that she told people they had to develop a *gospel skin: a skin that is thin enough to feel, but thick enough to cope with what life brings.* We decided in the limo as we crossed the park that we had to get in touch with her to see if she could help us with our marriage. I immediately thought that anyone who could upstage the Dalai Lama might be able to work miracles for us.

Getting in touch with Sister Hobday was quite simple. We had already met so many different folks in the so-called healing professions: Marianne Williamson, Ram Dass, Caroline Hay, Sylvia Brown; the Queen of England's reflexologist had even worked on our feet. Carly had met just about every crazy healer on the planet already—the stars all loved famous apostles. Carly had just recently met a priest at a record signing at Tower Records, and they had formed the beginning of a friendship. I feared he might be a type I was quite familiar with: a clerical star fucker. He might have been just that, but he seemed sincere and sweet. Anyway, he knew Sister Hobday quite well, and she agreed to conduct a marriage retreat for us in a guesthouse of his religious order in Riverdale, where Carly had grown up. It was only fifteen minutes from Manhattan and quite convenient for us. We spent a long fall weekend with her.

Sister Hobday did not have the demeanor or looks of a pretty Native-American princess; by the time we saw her, she had developed the face of a tribal chief who had seen more than a few battles. We spent the weekend with this exotic Native-American Franciscan. Almost immediately, she began to see who we were. She was quite sure about her insights into human beings. Carly had paid for her first-class flight from California, and that was the only stipend she required for the weekend.

Very quickly, Sister Hobday fell for me, but not for Carly. She was not at

all shy about stating her opinion. I'm not sure if it was my Franciscan background, my life with Eamon, or the nature of my struggle that appealed to
her. Certainly her background was much closer to mine than it was to Carly's. She had grown up in a very poor, large Native-American family. One
of her strange fascinations was that she could not get over how handsome she
felt I was. She kept referring to it in our counseling sessions. Finally, Carly
had heard enough about my physical beauty from Sister Hobday.

Carly pointed to herself and said, *What about me?*

Sister Hobday paused. *Well, he's got the physical beauty in this relationship, but,
well, I would say that you have what I would call* twirl.

Carly took on a look like she had been awarded the booby prize. It felt to
me like Sister Hobday was telling Carly that she should be grateful. Carly and
I almost immediately started to use it as part of our relationship lexicon—that
she had *twirl.*

I supposed that Sister Hobday was observing what almost everyone else
seemed to know, that I needed to be elevated in this relationship if it was
going to work. But it was just too much of a stretch to make my looks the way
to achieve the balance. Sister Hobday had no idea what Carly Simon meant
to her generation as a sex symbol. She certainly did not live in the world of
popular culture or the world of East Coast sophistication.

Nor did she have any idea what Carly could do to a gathering of men
almost anywhere. She should have been with us a few summers earlier on
our trip to Europe, which included a stay at the Villa D'Este on Lake Como.
On one of the evenings of our stay, the owners of the Italian soccer league
overran the majestic villa. Cell phones became popular in Italy much sooner
than in the United States. The owners of the teams were making football
deals by calling each other on their cell phones. Carly had fallen asleep early,
and I had come downstairs to smoke a Cuban cigar. I found these attractive
Italian men in expensive designer suits throughout the public rooms having animated conversations. I went back to the room and insisted that Carly
come and see what was happening. Reluctantly, she said she would join me
downstairs. There must have been thirty or forty men speaking and shouting
into their phones in the main lobby area, when suddenly I heard a gasp, a
sigh, and someone behind me reverently whisper, *bella donna.* In seconds, the
entire lobby was mute. Carly was standing on the main landing barefooted
in a sheer summer dress. As she stood at the bottom of the stairs, there were
smiles and exchanged glances of wonder among the men. They had no idea

who they were looking at. She had appeared out of nowhere, and her beauty had taken their breath away.

Sister Hobday would never see this part of my wife, yet these images were always with me.

So many of them were attached on a subconscious level; obtaining power in this world seemed increasingly impossible. When we had shared the fantasy of my approaching achievement as an artist, it was somewhat easier to keep the teeter-totter even, but as time went by, it became more and more difficult. Carly's fame affected almost every aspect of our relationship, and in a certain eerie way, it mirrored Eamon's reality. It wasn't that the demands of our lives had to be put first, but rather that a unique space had to be constructed within my personality for both my wife and my son, a space within that recognized the profound handicaps of having a special wife and a "special" child. Both of their situations demanded a fluidity of mind and spirit. It would have been impossible to pull off, except both Eamon's and Carly's lives offered so many unusual, exciting, and meaningful places to explore. The most compelling aspect was the intensity of their feelings for me: They both depended on me in a *special* way. They desperately needed to know that one person loved them for exactly who they were. It was such a vast space. Carly lived more in the expression of her emotions than anyone I had ever met, and Eamon's emotional expressions came in very quirky and enigmatic ways. I existed in two upside-down worlds. Staying the right size was the great challenge, and our humor was a necessary salve.

CHAPTER
TWENTY

SHE LIT ONE OF the last cigarettes she would ever smoke and slid into bed next to me. The city was wrapped in a dense, dark fog on this summer night—a perfect setting for the perfect murder. She had just returned from recording a duet with John Travolta called "Two Sleepy People." She seemed enthralled with the night, with John, and with me. She was close to John in some way, and yet she had never introduced us. It didn't matter; she was next to me now. We listened to the new recording a few times and then started to sing along with it.

Our relationship had entered its own film-noir stage: shadowy, distant, and mysterious. Yet we both remained quite sure that we would make it through. Like the sentiment of the song: *We were too much in love.* We just needed a little luck in the dark, or a hidden stranger to light a match and show us the way. We never could have imagined what was just beyond our vision in the shadows.

Around this time, she had started telling me that she hated the way I kissed, and that she was going to have to teach me how to do it properly. We actually had a few sessions where she tried to show me what felt good to her. *No, your lips need to be harder—not so soft.* I tried hard to learn, but I never got it right. I tried to learn how to give her this small pleasure. I wasn't even sure I needed to learn how to kiss, but Carly started to tease me with the pop lyric *It's in his kiss.* I didn't know how she became the expert in this area, but she was convinced she knew better than I.

It was a shimmering October day in 1997. I was leaving for Paris for a meeting with one of my clients. I closed the door to the town car expecting the driver to nod and say *Mr. Hart, Delta, JFK?* Instead, I heard a familiar voice outside screaming my name. Lillian, my unflappable secretary, stood alongside banging on the window. I must have left something essential behind in my office, like my passport.

Carly's on the phone, she's sobbing.

Carly's crying didn't necessarily signify anything: A beautiful picture, a sunrise, a perceived slight, or a fight with her sister, so many things could move her to tears. Yet, she never interrupted me at work with anything frivolous. I ran back into the office and, through her sobs, I heard her say, *They think I have it—breast cancer.*

I rushed home, and we held each other for a long time. The sequence of events is a blur, except for the moment when we stood in a lab at Sloan Kettering and Carly seduced the technician into giving us results so we wouldn't have to wait for the doctor. We stared at the black x-ray trying to decipher the mysterious shapes and shadows. It was another kind of film noir: the one in which love, life, and fate collide in the darkness. Carly should have sung something from her album like "You Won't Forget Me." Our conversation centered on the shadowy teacup shapes in the black film, and we marveled that this awful news came in such a form. We joked about the teacups, as if laughing about them might make them more benign, but it was the tiny teacups that indicated that cancer was present.

Carly immediately donned her super cape and gathered her weapons around her: ray guns, spider webs, unguents, potions, seers, psychics, healing musicians, a priest, a chiropractor, cancer survivors, and every kind of person who could peer into the future or had some expertise in alternative treatments. This problem wasn't in her head; therefore, there must be a path to treatment and recovery. She handled the pre-op phase with courage and humor. Celebrity doesn't do too much to help you with cancer, except it makes getting appointments with the best doctors a bit easier, no small matter in the maze of cancer care.

Fortunately, there are so many practical chores that take up time, such as the search for an oncologist, a surgeon, and a reconstructive specialist. It's a lot to think about when you're scared to death, but it certainly kept us occupied. We quickly made appointments to interview the best oncologists in town. We considered Jackie's doctor, who was supposed to be tops, but that seemed too laden with the specter of her recent death. We interviewed another one who looked like Barbara Streisand playing a physician. She almost immediately told us the names of the famous people she had treated— a complete turn-off. Then there was the visit to Montefiore Hospital in the Bronx where a brilliant oncologist practiced in the midst of the city hospital system. The bleak atmosphere of his small gray office was only outdone by the morose tone of his delivery. He droned on about treatment while barely looking at either of us.

And then there was finally Larry Norton from Sloan Kettering who was unable to see us in his office, but who stopped by at nine at night for a house call. He lectured Carly about how so many celebrities were harmed because doctors treated them differently. I wondered if Larry made house calls at nine to all of his patients. Carly started to give Larry something that sounded like medical advice, and he interrupted her: *I think you are one of the most gifted singers on the planet, but we are not going to listen to your advice when it comes to this. I'm the expert in this room, and you need to know that at all times.*

Carly chose Larry.

Along with the healers, quacks, and seers, there was even a priest who was willing to give her what we used to call Extreme Unction, nowadays known as the Sacrament of the Sick and Dying. The fact that she wasn't Catholic didn't seem to faze anyone. Technically, you're not supposed to receive the sacraments unless you're baptized, but if you're Carly Simon, there's not only immediate restaurant seating, but even a Catholic rite available. Throughout the ritual, she lay on the French provincial day bed in the dining room with large candles glowing all around her. Kneeling before her, I realized that with her eyes closed, she looked as though she had died, but she loved the ceremony, and it gave her a moment of peace.

We petitioned every saint that we thought might be appropriate: Jude, Anthony, Francis, Martin de Porres. We knelt reverently by the bedside and prayed. She was especially interested in the rosary once I explained the theological notion that Mary was the Mediatrix of all Graces; and that in order to get to the son, you had to go through the mother. Given her relationship with Ben, she immediately grasped the truth of this idea. We knelt every night reciting our Aves and held each other close.

Until late into the night before the surgery, she kept talking to people about alternative treatments. There was a healer from Philadelphia who kept her on the phone that night trying to persuade her not to have the surgery and subsequent treatment. He kept screaming at her that *chemo isn't jelly beans, you know.* About every fifteen minutes, Carly would have me listen in on what sounded like the ranting of a madman. If nothing else, it distracted Carly from what was about to happen.

Diane Sawyer, Mike Nichol's wife, greeted us in the doorway as we arrived. She had the most reassuring smile for six in the morning, and she had thought to bring us all breakfast. The surgery took about six hours. As they wheeled Carly toward the operating room, I grasped her hand and all of us kept telling her how much we loved her. In an instant, we were left alone with the sight of the green operating-room doors swinging in final punctuation.

The surgeon, Dr. Jeanne Petreck, was a severely beautiful woman with a sleek, pointy nose and translucent skin that I, for some reason, associated with great healers. Right after the surgery, she drew diagrams for us with circles and other geometric shapes. I didn't know what she said except that the margins were clean, which meant she got all the cancer. The other term we became obsessed with was *blue nodes.* It sounded like a jazz improvisation, or comfy pods circling the earth in outer space. It is actually a test performed to determine whether the cancer has spread from the site of origin in the breast, past the nodes in the armpit; depending on the result, it determines if cancer has spread throughout the body.

We were told it would take forty-eight hours to get the results of the blue-node test. I left Carly to grab a cup of coffee, and as I walked up the block, I noticed there was a Catholic church on the opposite side of the street. I crossed and read the plaque on its front: The National Shrine of St. Jude. Since I didn't believe in this anymore, it took a pull from some very frightened inner voice to get me to go in and get down on my knees. The voice softly gave me orders and insisted that I pray, that I beg and plead without any mediation from my rational self. I needed to connect my heart to this God through St. Jude. The church itself was called St. Catherine of Siena, and the shrine to St. Jude was in a side altar. I was drawn to an odd symmetry: St. Catherine was the most brilliant and powerful Italian woman of the fifteenth century. Legend claimed that she had persuaded the decadent popes to move back to Rome from Avignon. Many people had begged them to abandon the hedonistic orgy of the Church's Babylonian captivity, but Catherine had somehow gotten the job done. She had been able to place a mirror in front of the most powerful men of her time and change history.

Also, what a coincidence, I had attended Siena College. I built a universe of connection to plead for the survival of my wife.

At first, I tried to make a negotiator's argument, reminding the saints, Mary, and God about all the truly good things I had done in my life. Perhaps I could barter that there was more owed to me than I owed to God. I went through a litany of the selfless deeds I had performed, as well as the crosses that God had already given me to bear, and presented the plea that I had been Job-like in my attitudes. I especially emphasized the hardship of Eamon. I tried to convince God that this was the one break he had to give me. Also, I thought I might have an unused inside track, because he had spoken to me all those years ago and called me to the priesthood. I especially called out once again to Jim and tried to imagine if he had lived long enough to fall in love with a woman. Finally, I just stared up at the statue and begged for God's mercy to please give me this: *The Miracle of the Blue Nodes.*

After an hour or so on my knees, I crossed the street back to the hospital. As I entered the room, I could see that in spite of her drugged post-op state, Carly was nearly jumping out of her bed with excitement.

The blue nodes are negative.

I didn't understand what she was saying. Her sister Joey explained that we had received a special favor from the lab and had the results a day early. I fell into the chair and cried, and Carly and I and Joey cried together.

Theodora Dance was Carly's alias in the hospital so that the news wouldn't leak to the press. The name came from a game that we started to play one Thanksgiving. The Hart-Nichols-Simon-Taylor-Sawyer clans spent a number of Thanksgivings together. At a recent one, I was intrigued by a college friend of Jenny Nichols who had changed her name from Mary Ellen to Lexington. We began to wonder how all our lives would have been different if we all had different names: ones that fit our adult personalities. At the end of each meal over the long weekend, we renamed each other, and Carly, we all decided, should have been named Theodora Dance.

Our next Thanksgiving was shortly after the surgery, and I wrote a long poem, which I read at dinner that year at Mike and Diane's. It was the story of the miracle of the blue nodes and it was entitled "Thanksgiving Theodora." The poem ended with the good news, and its aftermath.

And like hardened sinners everywhere
we reel at the thought of forgiveness.

The earth had shifted and, as much as we loved each other, we couldn't make things right. *It takes a really big man to love a really big scar* was the new lyric she had written. She never really believed that I was not bothered by the scar. Too bad we didn't have a prenup for breast cancer, so we could have agreed beforehand on how we would act. It might have been a more valuable document than the one we did have.

Carly thought that I was turned off by the imperfection of her maimed body, and nothing I could say would convince her otherwise. The truth is, I wouldn't fully understand what was happening for a very long time. It had nothing to do with her scars, but rather with a new set of feelings that would take years for me to understand.

Somehow, our not touching became acceptable. *A woman needs a man like a fish needs a bicycle*, I thought. I was more deluded about it than Carly. I kept telling her we would find a way, but she wanted something more concrete than my promises, so she dug into tangible solutions.

It had been eleven years since we had met on that train ride along the Hudson and, with a strange optimism and sense of hope, we renewed our wedding vows the following April of 1998 with Mike and Diane, and Bill and Rose Styron at the Federated Church in Edgartown.

Carly retreated to the Vineyard and began working on a new album that she wound up calling *The Bedroom Tapes*. She recorded most of it in a tiny studio that she had set up in Sally's old bedroom, hence the title. We were increasingly cut off from each other, but still somehow trying to be together. My business had continued to grow, and I was constantly on a plane going to yet another hotel in another city. We often spoke three or four times a day and, oddly, had mostly stopped arguing about our relationship. Within these distances and barriers, a new tenderness took hold. We became even more aware and sympathetic toward one another, and we didn't want to spend our limited time together arguing or even discussing what was wrong. Our romance became a tricky dance in which we were convinced that only the two of us could really comprehend the strange nature of our lives. When we were together now, we would often end our day propped up on our pillows reading poetry to each other. The sound of Dylan Thomas's words filling the silence of a Vineyard night was our favorite. And it was in these moments that we were still sure that we wanted the journey to continue.

Good-bye, good luck, struck the sun and moon,
To the fisherman lost on the land.
He stands alone at the door of his home
With his long-legged heart in his hand.

One of the strange highlights of 1999 was spending the weekend of the Senate vote on impeachment at Camp David with Bill and Hillary. Carly thought that they should not spend this weekend alone, that they should have friends around them. We arrived on a bleak midwinter Friday in February. We were somewhat surprised by the drab quality of Camp David. Carly could immediately see why Jackie had spent only one weekend there during her time as First Lady. It was rustic and rather unattractive. The idea that heads of state from all over the world came to visit the President here was a little surprising. We couldn't imagine the King of Spain or the Russian President spending a weekend here with what looked like imitation Ethan Allen furniture and, at least in the winter time, a sparse and unattractive stand of scraggly gray trees. Carly immediately thought that she would get in touch with Ralph Lauren and ask him to redecorate the cabins as a service to our country. In a conversation over the weekend, she asked Bill who had decorated the cabins, and he said that Hillary had just done a lot of work on them. Carly figured it would be too insulting to suggest a makeover. The most amazing part of the weekend was the equanimity of Bill and Hillary. They actually translated the impeachment as a final victory. Bill had come bounding into the meeting hall on Friday night and began to talk about how it was finally over, that the bastards couldn't do anything to him anymore. He said that they had been after him for thirty years and now it was over. We huddled together all weekend like old friends. Saturday night we watched a new movie called *Happy, Texas* about two escaped convicts from a chain gang who wind up in the town of Happy, Texas, where they are mistaken for a gay couple that is supposed to run the town's teen beauty pageant. It seemed an odd choice given what President Clinton had just escaped from and survived. We finished our stay with a moving chapel service on Sunday morning. I wasn't sure if they thought they had the help of God, but they seemed to be able to reconstruct their marriage in the most difficult of circumstances. Carly and I found it inspirational: our issues were nothing in comparison.

★ ★ ★

The Fairmont was one of my favorite hotels; it recalled a certain part of old San Francisco chic sitting atop Nob Hill overlooking the bay. The antique-styled flocked red wallpaper summoned images of other times—ghosts of dance hall girls surviving earthquake and fire. The tech boom of the nineties brought me here often for my clients. Like New York, San Francisco has its own oxygen and ether: seedy and elegant all together. New York is the other city that has its elements jumbled: an expensive brownstone next to a porn store, so familiar and comforting. The haphazard zoning silently whispered "anonymous," and it liberated me from the part of my life that was intrusively public. Yet on this warm spring night in 1999, I was quite alone in a struggle with a vague but powerful melancholy.

I had no idea about how or why to tell Carly about the new and powerful pull I felt—that was still in the future. This night on the phone, she climbed into my loneliness and feelings of failure. She felt guilt for her part in the way we had become distant, and she blamed the breast cancer treatment: the lack of estrogen in her body that left her without desire. This was true, but we both suspected that there was more going on. She would later realize that she was no longer physically attracted to me, and yet, like me, she so wanted to be.

She arrived at a quirky and definitive solution.

Darling, you need to get laid.

What?

You have to—it's been way too long. You have to go to a whorehouse.

I can't.

You must, really you must.

I need to take a nap. I'll talk to you later.

OK, but you have to do this for us, for both of us.

It was a risky idea, but there was something about it that seemed right. It was radical enough perhaps to interrupt and restore us. After a short nap, I called her back. She was bursting with delight and mischief.

Are you ready?

I hesitated.

A diffuse glow shrouded the city from the thick fog rolling off the bay. I listened to her on my cell phone; she kept encouraging me as I made my way down the hill toward Chinatown. I noticed the quote by Sun Yat Sen over the entranceway to the neighborhood: *All under heaven is for the good of the people.* Here I was the ex-choirboy, former priestly aspirant, sober man in recovery, and dutiful and loving husband who had sincerely promised *with this ring I thee wed and pledge to thee my fidelity,* being led by my wife to betrayal. It was odd, but we were desperate. Perhaps the quote I most needed wasn't Sun Yat Sen's but St. Augustine's, the one I had learned all those years ago at Graymoor, *Love God and do what you will.*

The massage parlor was located on the second floor, and Carly was still on the phone as I climbed the stairs. When I opened the door, an aggressive Chinese madame greeted me from behind the desk.

Mister, what you want tonight? I have many girls.

I was trying to speak to the madame and Carly at the same time.

You have to. Please do it. What are the girls like? Are there any pretty ones? Remember, this is my treat.

I don't think I can do this.

You have to, for both of us.

Sir, what you like?

Well, I can't do it with you on the phone. I just can't.

OK, call me after.

OK, I love you.

Oh, I love you, Jimmy Hart.

I hung up and the madame pointed to the girls who sat on an L-shaped couch in an area behind the desk.

Which one you like?

As I looked at the selection, I realized that nothing about this attracted me. I was about to betray my marriage vows without an ounce of desire. This was completely off the mark; the last thing I wanted tonight was an Asian prostitute in a seedy massage parlor. I couldn't. I ran down the stairs out onto the street and hurried back to the Fairmont.

When I got back to my room, I called Carly.

That was quick, what happened?

I couldn't do it.

Why?

I don't know, maybe you on the phone and the girls.

But you're horny—aren't you?

Yes, but I love you so much.

I know that, but this was just about sex.

I know, I just couldn't, let's not talk about it anymore.

OK darling, but I really wish you had. Goodnight.

Goodnight. I love you so much.

It was still early on a Saturday night, so I watched a pay-per-view movie and thought I would just fall asleep, but some other part of me had known what I was going to do all day. At about midnight, I left the hotel in a kind of frenzy. I walked two blocks down a steep hill to the Nob Hill Theatre, famous for its male strippers. I sat in the back of the tiny theatre watching handsome young men take off their clothes, and somehow, in spite of the seedy atmosphere and the other rather creepy-looking patrons, I felt at home. Some part of me felt a solace that I had never known, a kind of fellowship I had never truly explored, and I sat late into the night watching one boy after another disrobe and dance, and with each piece of discarded clothing something within me felt restored.

I wondered if I could share this with Carly, and then I buried it and realized I never would. How could I explain it to her? I had little understanding of it myself, but it certainly didn't feel like infidelity. This part of me felt similar to the narrow auditorium with its tiny stage, like a small, dark, detached room that I could visit occasionally. It felt so divorced from my actual life as not to be real, as if I had fallen into a strange rabbit hole that only opened when I was in cities like San Francisco or Vancouver.

I had left the theatre after three in the morning. The damp air of the San Francisco summer night surrounded me, and I felt young. I was nearly fifty years old, yet something about this night assured me that I would have a long time to explore these feelings. Somehow, spending those hours staring at naked men made the years expand before me, and the moist, bracing air of the San Francisco night made the hours in a sleazy porno theatre feel restorative. I had solved the problem of fidelity: I knew I would never betray Carly with another woman.

CHAPTER
TWENTY-ONE

———◆———

I THINK YOU MIGHT be gay.

I was barely awake, yet I jumped as I heard that word. At first, it felt like the final reduction of my life. Over the past year, she had been steadily making my space smaller and smaller. On every trip I made to the Vineyard, I would find yet another drawer that was once mine reclaimed by her for another purpose. And now the final insult: She was even reclaiming my heterosexuality. I protested loudly, and then within a few hours, I accepted the terrifying fact that she might have a point. At first, I thought she had this feeling because of her remarkable feminine and artistic insight. That's what she let me think, but that wasn't the story.

On a recent business trip to Palm Springs, I had searched for some remaining trace of an old seminary friend named John Konesky. I had been told he had contracted AIDS in the late eighties, and when he became terribly ill a few years later, ended his life there. I felt compelled to know the details. Was there someone he had loved at the end? Had he left a final message? John and I had remained in contact for a long time; then toward the end, I had lost touch with him. I wanted to see if I could find anyone who knew what had happened. I called every gay organization in Palm Springs to try to find out. Carly had noticed my hotel bill when I got home, and she called all the numbers. *I think you might be gay* wasn't an insight into my new sexual preference, but a result of her sleuthing. Yet within a short time, I admitted to her that something was happening, and that perhaps my depression might be related to this growing sexual confusion. I promised her that I would see a shrink as soon as I got back to New York.

Carly's psychiatrist on the Vineyard had given her three recommendations for me. I wasn't sure why I chose the one I did, but his last name did rhyme with "Say-Hey," Willie Mays's nickname in the fifties. His office was on the ground floor of a nondescript yellow brick building on East End Avenue. The river was just a few steps away, and I wondered as I stared across at the Manhattan Psychiatric Center on Wards Island if a place like that might be in my future. Whenever we had passed it in my childhood, my father would announce its real name: "The Cracker Factory." The river reflected my state of mind—muddy and gray without a chance of changing course. The only feeling I had inside connected directly to a deep reservoir of sorrow. I was mostly just lethargic and depressed. The idea of "being" anything particular didn't feel very urgent. My entire life seemed bedeviled by something I thought I had handled long ago. Now it seemed like it was the only thing I could talk about. It was clear that I needed help. I didn't understand what was happening, and both Carly and I needed some explanations. She was much clearer about her needs, and she was getting more and more frustrated by them.

It's not fair, what you're doing isn't fair.

What am I doing?

You don't want me, but you don't want anyone else to want me.

That's not true, I do want you.

Show me, do something, sweep me off my feet like a man.

How do I do that?

See, you don't understand. I need you to want me, to not care about the consequences.

Why don't you sweep me off my feet? Why is it up to me?

Jim, that's just the way it has to be.

Is that so?

Yes, why don't you just admit you don't want me anymore?

Because that's not how I feel.

Well, then you have to get help. I know you're depressed, but you have to get help with that too.

OK, I'll call one of the shrinks, I promise.

If you're gay, we have to face it.

I had struggled in various ways my entire life to try to "face it," and I had no real answers. Perhaps an expert would be able to help. I doubted it, but it was worth a try.

Dr. "Say-Hey" was a tall man with skin folds and an Adam's apple reminiscent of Ichabod Crane. He had a big head, bushy black eyebrows, and was at least my height if not taller. The tempo of his speech was laconic, which was heightened by the bland decor of his office. Perhaps we were just too big for the small space. I was the more masculine, something I sensed the doctor immediately disliked.

Dr. "Say-Hey" had written numerous books and was a celebrity gay shrink himself. Most of what I remembered feeling throughout was sorrow for him; he just didn't seem smart enough to help me. When I finally told him that I had to leave his care because he was the most depressed person I knew, he didn't take it well. I also believed he confused me more about my sexual identity: He kept telling me that I wasn't gay. I would call Carly right after each session to discuss what had happened, and I was rarely optimistic because the confusion just seemed to be getting deeper.

For the next two and a half years, my depression deepened. My life seemed to be a series of challenging and entertaining exteriors, like a sprawling Potemkin Village of responsibility. Each façade fronted onto someone else's life, but in truth, there was no room built just for me. Each time I tried to look deeper within, I would discover pools of sorrow that seemed too amorphous and confused to plumb. Lately, the façades weren't holding up very well, and everyone seemed to want so much more than I could give. The only truthful way to respond to almost anything seemed to be to shrug my shoulders.

By the end of 1999, I had made the decision to leave IPC Enterprises, the company I had co-founded and helped to build over the last nine years. My partner and I just could not to see eye to eye on the future of the organization, and I had no interest in fighting with him over it. I would shortly just leave it all to him. At the same time, I was being courted to be the chairman of a dot.com startup in Seattle.

We brought in the millennium on New Year's Eve at Bill and Rose Styron's house on the Vineyard. We sang various renditions of songs from the twentieth century. Diane Sawyer and I seemed to enjoy it most. We both loved to sing. I especially remembered doing a rendition of Legs Diamond's favorite tune. Bill Kennedy had discovered it when he was writing his novel about him. It was called "Happy Days and Lonely Nights" and might have served as an anthem for what was really happening to Carly and me as the new millennium approached. The lyrics reflect the happiness of love and how each lover teaches the other so many things, and yet when it fades, only one thing remains: "Lonely Nights."

For the next few years, we would often be alone and lonely, she on the Vineyard and me in New York. We tried hard to make the times we were together seem like a marriage.

In the spring of the new year, Dr. Coles called from Cambridge and asked if I would become the publisher of *DoubleTake* magazine. This was a literary and photographic magazine that Coles had founded in 1995 with a ten million-dollar grant from the Lyndhurst Foundation. The publication had been housed at Duke University, but they had jettisoned the project once the money ran out, and Dr. Coles had brought it up north on his own. A few months before this, I had a long visit with Coles and essentially told him that the business model he had been using was unsustainable. The conversation was brief but memorable.

Jim, I'd like to you to be the publisher of DoubleTake *magazine.*

Bob, there's nothing I'd rather do, but I am leaving my marketing and advertising company and I am committed to helping with that transition, which is going to be complicated. This afternoon I'm on my way to Seattle. I have just taken a job as the chairman of an Internet startup there. So, I just won't have the time.

Bob was undeterred.

Jim, you know I am a psychiatrist.

I laughed.

Yes, a world-famous one.

Well, I think you need to listen to what you said. "There's nothing I'd rather do."

Yes, but . . .

I think we're going to have to make this happen.

Bob, let me think about it for a couple of days. I'll get back to you.

So, in the first six months of 2000, I was involved in the running of three different corporations. I was wrapping things up as the CEO of IPC; I was the chairman of a new company in Seattle; and now, in spite of my own reluctance, I became the publisher and CEO of *DoubleTake* magazine. I wondered why I thought I could handle all this. Carly interrupted all of it by giving me a ten-day trip to Rome as a fiftieth birthday present. At first, I thought we were going together, but it turned out that I would be going on my own and staying at the luxurious Hassler Hotel above the Spanish Steps.

★ ★ ★

Adam's arm stretched above me, and I considered the beauty of his musculature, imagining him as a lover. The bend of his neck, the long extended bicep, and the perfect mesomorph physique were triumphantly crowned by the beauty of his understated manhood. It made me think of the elegance of my desire: to be loved by the most exquisite being ever created, the father of original sin.

I was alone on the floor of the Sistine Chapel all by myself, with not another soul around. Someone had arranged for me to be there alone for two hours in the early morning. This first man, floating directly above me, had traded pure life for a secret: God's secret. It may have been the very secret that God was ashamed of, one that he couldn't control, and now, because of Adam, it had to be shared with everyone.

And still, I knew so little about the dimensions of my desire that I did not know the proper answer to *attivo or passivo*, the question that I had been asked the night before while on a massage table at "Europa," a gay bathhouse off the Via Veneto. The beautiful young Italian man massaged me and wanted to know if I wanted more. I didn't. I just wanted to be near men who did. I wanted to hope that there was a possibility. I remembered another feeling that had happened one afternoon in my junior year of high school when a beautiful blonde boy lifted his naked body out of the swimming pool, and I saw him and felt something within myself for the first time. I realized that I had wanted to stare at him the same way I was staring up at Adam now: full on, without any judgment. I never could. I would never allow myself to do that. It wasn't allowed. There above me was the most astounding depiction of our failed selves. Michelangelo had captured the great beauty of God's first imperfect man, and it touched me, not unlike my night with the boys dancing in San Francisco.

It felt as if these vague, ancient feelings had taken over: What had been peripheral and manageable had become central and powerful. I was betraying the person I loved most in the world with my subconscious and somewhat unconscious self. How had this happened? I suppose it happened all along the way. How could Carly and I ever imagine this amorphous spirit that was now guiding me to places that would ask *attivo or passivo?*

Are you sitting down?

I was in my room at the Holiday Inn in Little Rock, Arkansas, on a Thursday afternoon at the end of August 2000. I was on a business trip for my new company. At first, I thought it must be something about her health or maybe with the kids, because I could tell from her tone that this was serious, or rather that it was significant. Her tone had the ring of humility, something out of her control.

Baby, we will get through this, no matter what, we will get through this together.

I presumed we would get through it more or less together. That's how we had lived so far.

OK.

She didn't pause or stammer; she launched directly into the explanation. *There is going to be a gossip item in the* Daily News *tomorrow that Andrew and I are having an affair and that we are in love.*

The Little Rock late summer invaded every corner of the room. The Holiday Inn's green-striped towels got wetter on the racks, and the faux stucco walls sweated with the heat. Andrew was the handsome old friend that Carly had been with at the dinner for President Clinton on the Vineyard some months earlier.

Is it true?

Just remember, we are going to get through this together.

Barely present, I listened to the rest of the plan. Andrew's powerful father was going to call the *Daily News* and ask them to squelch the piece. Carly was hoping it wouldn't appear, but I really wasn't listening. I looked out at the bright sun in Little Rock and stared at the flat, dry, uninteresting city and wondered how the Clintons had lived here for so long.

I hung up, closed the curtains, and fell asleep. I awoke hours later and looked out into the flat landscape in the darkness. The bleak scene made me want to go into the bathroom, lie down on the cool tiles, and hold my face against the floor. I wished that I used after-shave, something that would sting me back to life, some little sensation that would brace me for the nights and days to come.

I imagined Carly with him on our bed naked. I saw him as a man, something different from dancing boys or portraits on ceilings. He was sweating next to my wife. His hairy, muscular body was summoning the urgency of her desire. How could it be otherwise? When I asked her whether or not it was true, she said, *I think I'm in love with him, I have to tell you the truth.*

Silence. After all I had been through, this was my reward. This was it. So I got up from my deep stupor and drove downtown, not far away, and found the only gay bar in town, The Backstreet.

I would have loved to get drunk, but I hadn't had a drink in years, so instead I imagined picking up a guy and bringing him back to the Little Rock Holiday Inn.

That was probably as far as I was willing to go, but that night in that strange southern capital, I traveled far away.

Andrew is not the problem. There was a place for his entrance like a weakened body that is more prone to a virus. I'm tired of hearing how brilliantly upstanding you have been. How you have fought off all temptation and would never think of it. Talk a little about your weaknesses and what you're willing to do to change.

I had no weapons left to fight for her. Andrew was a multimillionaire who was promising to fly her to appointments at Sloan Kettering in his private plane. All I had left was my private, unrevealed self, and she was so very tired of not having access to *that*. In the same letter, she went on to tell me that she was going to go on another vacation without me.

I'll think about you—about your darling face with its left upward slant. That smile—it's beguiling and it's the one I love. I love your bisexuality. You think I don't. I'm envious of it even. I'm a little scared of it too. I wish for you to let yourself out of whatever cage you have forced yourself into.

The cage felt as though it just kept getting stronger and more permanent. After San Francisco and Little Rock, there was no longer any doubt in my mind about my attraction to men. It had become obsessive, partially because it was so forbidden.

I went to see my father during this period, but his Alzheimer's had progressed so rapidly, he no longer knew me. He had a vague sense that I was someone close to him, but he couldn't quite get that I was his son. My parents were living with my sister and her family in an apartment in their home in Long Beach. I took him to St. Ignatius, the church of my childhood, one Saturday afternoon for mass, and I sang the hymns with great brio to get my father engaged, hoping it might trigger his memory. My father didn't remember the words, but he was mesmerized by my performance. He couldn't wait for each hymn to start. I sang the recessional as loudly as I could, and my father stood next to me transfixed. As the organ music stopped, my father flung down the booklet of hymns he was holding.

You're a pisser. You should have been a priest.

My father was forgetting his life, as I was being begged by the woman I loved to honestly discover mine.

I'm not begging for you to understand me as much as I am for you to understand yourself enough to be more delineated about your needs. If, if, if, if, well—what if? There's always that miracle of us having the same new unstuck needs that mingle and twine in the near future. It's so intoxicating. I won't project.

For now, I just say thank you for so much time and patience and sharing of time, love and joy and sadness and much too much of my Barnum and Bailey world. Sweetest one, bye bye for tonight.

I was hoping that my favorite line of Carly's letter would prove to be true.

Jim Hart, you are a creative of such uniqueness that you should be proud and surprised and digging for the weeds to get out of the way so you can sprout.

Yet, when I thought of real freedom in my life, I thought of Eamon bounding toward me on his way to college. I thought of him being finally able to tell me something about how he felt. If he could just once tell me how he felt about being alive, if he could just tell me about his being in love with someone or something, then I could get free, but he never could. He just kept repeating the same question.

What time is it?

Fathering Eamon was only getting more difficult. Alannah called many times a week often screaming or crying or both about how impossible Eamon was becoming. He often just wouldn't get dressed for her, or he would punch and kick her and his sister Siobhan. The question she would ask me was: *What was I going to do?*

Dr. Coles began most of his conversations with a deep sigh, and then, *Oh hello, Jim.* He still didn't seem to understand that the magazine *DoubleTake* was unsustainable as it was then constituted, and he only wanted to operate the magazine in ways that were in harmony with his vision. This was a lofty and worthwhile goal, but he expected me to operate the day-to-day publishing needs of the magazine while raising millions of dollars to keep the business afloat. Most of my conversations with Bob ended with the same question from him: *What was I going to do?*

Carly's brief affair with Andrew did not last, and she was once again tired of us living apart so much of the time. It seemed there was always a new, urgent tragedy that I had to be a participant in, which often meant taking sides with Carly against another family member or close friend over a slight, real or imagined. Lately, they seemed to be more imagined than real. I had moved to Cambridge and that had not made things better. After Cambridge, I moved back to my New York apartment to cut expenses and be closer to potential funding sources for the magazine. Carly had so many needs that were not being met, and her question, not surprisingly, was: *What was I going to do?*

Just a few months earlier, on a sunny Friday afternoon on Massachusetts Avenue between the magazine's office in Somerville and my apartment in Cambridge, I considered suicide for the first and only time in my life. *What was I going to do?*

My only tangible solutions were to begin treatment with Effexor and start smoking cigarettes again after eighteen years of abstinence. In addition to the nicotine, the rituals of cigarette-smoking and the oral satisfaction seemed to calm some part of me, and the wreaths of smoke seemed to call to other-worldly spirits. Yet that question remained and attacked from all sides. It even took on a physical component, terrible back pain.

What was I going to do?

A small light-blue pill suddenly appeared to set me free. Moments before, I had been on the floor of our Vineyard bedroom writhing with back pain. It was early spring of 2002, and my life felt like it was coming apart. Also, I had been diagnosed as anhedonic: *lacking the ability to experience pleasure from activities usually found enjoyable.*

When Carly asked, *Would you like a Fioricet?* I just said yes.

The back pain lifted within minutes. The combination of drugs in the pill (acetaminophen, butalbital, and caffeine) provided a sudden and much-needed magic. Soon the late summer breeze turned into a gentle zephyr, and all of my problems, including my physical pain and anhedonia, seemed to vanish. I had barely taken an aspirin in twenty-one years, but in an instant, this little blue pill treated every single thing that was wrong. I had the sense that I was, for a moment at least, on the same white clouds as Adam, surrounded by the eternal sky-blue safety of a loving creator. I left the Vineyard and returned to New York with new buoyancy and confidence. As soon as I returned to New York, I went to see my GP, who recommended a back specialist at Beth Israel Hospital and gave me a prescription for Fioricet. Although it was not indicated as a medication for back pain, he thought that since it was working, I should continue it. Oddly, when I saw the back specialist a few days later, he said the same thing.

Wavelike, like its blue color, Fioricet washed over and through me. The confidence of my old self returned. I didn't have to second-guess my decisions about anything. I was instantly restored. I had listened to far too many people, from Dr. "Say-Hey" to Dr. Coles to Carly, and to my own frightened selves. Now I was back in my original voice in the choir loft with notes soaring through the wooden rafters, and the world below was being healed. It was now within me, that tender voice soothing all pain. I once again knew the innocent wonder of perfection.

I took Fioricet as prescribed for a number of weeks and maybe months four times a day. Then I stopped taking them in the morning and afternoon and doubled up later in the day. Soon I was taking four, six, and perhaps eight at once.

After swallowing a number of little blue pills, I found myself talking to a guy named Roberto on a hook-up line. Even though it was after one in the morning on a Sunday night, he invited me to a party at his place. He had a thick Spanish accent, and he stood next to me completely naked, as were the other eight or nine guys in the room. His apartment was off Columbus Avenue on 74th Street. I was astonished at what I saw. Roberto pulled me aside after a short time and said, *Want a hit of rock?* I sensed my head nodding up and down before I really understood the question. I had no clear idea what *a hit of rock* was, but I could tell, given the look of the glass tube he was holding, that it was something I should be afraid of.

Have you done it before?

No, never.

He smiled and his deep brown eyes lit up with delight.

Here. I will show you.

He took a small yellow pebble off a plate on the coffee table in front of him. He placed it in the glass cylinder, which had a metal screen on one end. He held the tube at about a seventy-five degree angle and lit it. Most of the smoke gathered in the pipe and he sucked it in, and then suddenly he exhaled an enormous cloud of acrid yellow smoke into the room.

Here try it.

He tried to hold the pipe for me the first time.

You have to turn it.

As he lit the pipe, he moved it in circles, and the whole operation became quite clumsy. I inhaled as I would a cigarette. I held the smoke for as long as I could. I repeated it a couple of times with no real effect.

I'm gonna shotgun. I blow the smoke into your mouth. You inhale with your lungs—not your mouth—watch me.

Roberto inhaled deeply; his chest rose and he held his breath for twenty seconds or so, then he put his lips on mine and blew as hard as he could. I felt the cloud of smoke from Roberto fill my lungs. I held it in for about the same amount of time that Roberto had, and then released a large yellow plume of smoke. In that moment, almost everything was altered. The effect was immediate. All pain was washed away.

I have blotted out, as a thick cloud thy transgressions, and as a cloud thy sins; return unto me, for I have redeemed thee. Sing ye heavens, for the Lord hath done it: Shout, ye lower parts of the earth.

From the lower parts of the earth, I could feel my salvation. For perhaps the first time in my life, I no longer regretted any part of myself. I was as whole as I would be at the day of the Last Judgment. I tried to light the pipe a few more times by myself, but the shotgun method worked much better.

Shortly after the sun rose, I returned home, high and as happy as I had ever been. By noon the next day, I had called Roberto's dealer for my first delivery. Spike arrived about twenty minutes after I placed the call. I gave him $200 in twenties and he gave me three small Ziploc bags filled with the tiny off-white pebbles. This first time he also brought me ready-to-use glassware, so all I had to do was tilt the pipe upward for the first hit and begin my day. I was thrilled that I wasn't a drug addict. I was only an alcoholic, and therefore the drugs were going to be fine. Most of the people in the program had a different opinion, but I didn't believe they had attained my level of recovery, and I had never had a problem with drugs. I had no desire to drink, and I was certain that crack wouldn't be a problem. I would only use this substance occasionally—socially—and remain a sober alcoholic.

CHAPTER
TWENTY-TWO

———————————•———————————

I SLOWLY OPENED MY apartment door and listened as Spike climbed the stairs to the second floor. I heard the soft, rhythmic ting of the glassware gently touching in his pocket. As he hit the turn, I poked my head out. His body filled the narrow hallway, and his eyes darted from side to side. He was dressed in dark nylon gym pants, a Yankee baseball cap, and a hooded cotton parka. Some days he looked the essence of a New York City drug dealer, but today, with his hood up over his head like a cowl, he might have been chanting a Te Deum: *Oh God I Praise Thee*, which is what my heart sang whenever he arrived. His presence was the glorious, breathing answer to my greatest fear, and the final plea of that ancient prayer: *Lord, let me never be confounded*.

He burst into a large smile as he entered and then spread out the morning delivery on the stone coffee table. I needed my first hit. It was almost eleven; I was in trouble. My heart was beating as if it might dart out of my rib cage and escape from my body. My brain jammed against my skull, firing with random electrical jolts. The sweats and tremors were frightening yet somewhat familiar from the old boozing days. It was the sudden onset of bouts of extreme sorrow that made it so harrowing. The feelings weren't connected to any recognizable stimulus; they felt lodged so deep within me that only a massive hit of crack could reach them.

The longer I crashed, the more frightened I became. It wasn't the physical torture alone, which was exquisite, but the emotional and psychological dialogue that fought to destroy me. It triggered a choppy rage in which I could only feel the peaks of my anger. I would see an image, and a spike of fury would overtake me. Moments later, I would blank to a mental white noise and, when that ended, spike again. Then, when I was at the far edge of the ride, before the new uptake, my darkest thoughts would emerge.

Soon the drugs would course through my body. I adored the swing of the pendulum: from the darkest shades to near perfection in less than a minute. My mood would shift that quickly from deep despair to nirvana—what a ride! In a moment I would feel an explosion in and around my dick; as a part of the perfect promise, it would always infuse me with explosive desire. The once-submerged sexual urges caromed like silver balls hitting the stanchions in an old pinball machine. The boys and men came toward me unzipping and dropping their clothes with untamed, noisy, and vividly lit sex. It was all I had left: the only dependable signal in my brain. My father and God had relieved me of my childhood and adolescence, and Eamon had stolen my fatherhood. The program had failed, and my marriage to Carly had strangled essential parts of my manhood. It was no wonder I had become this. In an ultimate mind-fuck, I had become that awful thing that my father had screamed all those years ago: *You little fuckin' cocksucker.*

I could see the *Enquirer* headline: "Carly's Crack-Addict Husband and His Secret Gay Life." I spiraled downward, which was why Spike's honesty and competence were so important. When I needed another hit, I needed another hit. Every pore would be polluted by my sins, so I needed a powerful drug to drag me through it.

Did you bring the glassware?

Yeah.

Spike produced two thin glass tubes. He grabbed the hammer and a sawed-off number two pencil; then he squeezed the thin mesh screens into the ends of the glass cylinders. The screens needed to be just the right thickness to create proper tension against the inside of the tube. He did this using the hammer and pencil with carefully calibrated force and near-perfect aim. He packed the screen at one end, placed the pencil inside the tube, and struck it just enough to compress the mesh against the floor, making it snug without breaking the glass. My results were never as satisfying as Spike's. There was always a better draw when he fixed the glassware.

After a couple more hits, I traveled from the universe of my pain to a doorway of hazy bliss. It was as if Our Lady of Atonement, the woman who had first inspired my childhood dreams, had finally appeared to me in her raiment of burgundy and blue. Her golden tiara glistened through a cloud of yellow smoke. My father beat me, but there was no pain, and when he used that terrible phrase, we laughed knowingly together. My long-forgotten novel became a bestseller and, most importantly, Eamon never had his first seizure.

There was a twinge in my right thumb from striking the wheel of the lighter. I had smoked about eight hundred dollars' worth of crack in the past two days. I didn't smoke it by myself, I was a generous host, and there was never a shortage of visitors once they heard the phrase *I've got enough.*

I felt especially generous since I had learned how to shotgun using a condom. I would take a hit, hold it as long as possible, hold the rubber ring tight against my mouth and exhale into it. The condom expanded like a balloon, and I would then squeeze the opening shut to capture the smoke. Then take a breath or two, pause, put the condom to my lips again, and drag the smoke back into my lungs to get a double hit from one drag. In the last few months, most of my hits were double hits. Sometimes, I could get a third with the same cloud of smoke.

The first time Spike used my bathroom, his assessment of me changed.

Hey man, you teach at Harvard?

One of my awards for *Excellence in Teaching* hung on the bathroom wall over the toilet.

Yes, I did.

Cool.

I wanted Spike's admiration, perhaps to be his only almost-famous addict. I wanted the kind of special treatment I had so often seen given to those around me: a look in his eyes of unwarranted admiration. Yet he was not about to cross any normal boundaries. Early on, I offered him a hit from my pipe, and he let me know, *I don't play that way.* He said he had never smoked crack in his life. As I thought about that odd fact, I took another hit, held it as long as I could, and blew another large, acrid yellow cloud above him toward the ceiling. The smoke filled my apartment night and day, and I never understood why the people on my floor didn't notice it. It had a distinctly sweet and pungent aroma, like a burning plastic bag filled with sugar. The odor lingered for days.

What do I owe you?

Four hundred.

There were four bags over the usual amount, so it was going to be a good couple of days. I didn't know that this was going to be my last run. I handed

Spike the thick wad of twenties, hoping he would leave quickly. I wanted to get fucked up right away, before too much paranoia set in, and I knew I didn't have too wide a window. The space between perfection and extreme paranoia was getting smaller and smaller.

He checked his pockets one more time and then left. I located a non-lubricated condom and in no time I was flying. I would need to pull back a bit. It was too early in the day to be this torqued. So I stopped and pulled all my cleaning supplies from under the kitchen sink. I was going to expunge the filth, make the wood sparkle like in an old Mr. Clean commercial. I had tried just about every kind of cleanser I could find. In the end, I decided that I would have to scrape each piece of dirt out by hand. I used paint scrapers, Brillo pads, screwdrivers, knives, and coat hangers to dig into the wood's filthy cracks. I never tired of trying new implements. The stains had to go. I saw it as my most urgent and perhaps final task, a quest that I had to complete before the end of things, and while I scraped, the hours flew by.

Night descended over 97th Street and I found myself crouched in the darkness, no longer scrubbing, but hiding beneath the windowsill so *they* couldn't see me. *They* wouldn't be able to detect my movements if I stayed low. I peeked between the slats and noticed that the streetlights on West 97th Street were surrounded by undulating halos. I had noticed many strange events over the past months, but these glowing, pulsating lights made a strong impression. It made me think I might have a chance, that *they* might not get me. I became distracted as I noticed men and women, friends of mine, dancing in midair outside my second-floor window. I knew it wasn't likely, yet there they were, laughing, gyrating, and waving. A flapper stood in the alley outside the window on the back stairway. Every time I went down the stairs, she waited leaning against a small tree. She waved to me and always softly sang the same Edith Piaf song (*"Non, Je Ne Regrette Rien"*). I always hummed along and waved back. Tonight though, there was a new voice, and I fell to the ground as I heard it. He stood just outside my door asking, *Where's Dad? Where's Dad?*

This wasn't possible. Eamon lived hours away outside Albany. He couldn't possibly be outside my door. Given his many handicaps, the people dancing in midair were more likely to be there than he was, yet I kept hearing him wondering loudly, *Where's Dad? Where's Dad?*

I ran into the bathroom where I had another pipe and locked the door behind me. I placed a gorilla hit onto the wire screen; it crackled as the flame melted it against the wire. As I exhaled, I felt a rush of relief, and then a spurt of familiar pleasure, and the sound of his voice went away. The bathroom was the safest place. It had no windows, so I couldn't be seen; also, it had a vent, so the pungent smell was more difficult to detect. I could break the crack pipe and flush it before the police knocked down the door to my apartment. I stacked furniture against the front door whenever I was in the apartment and leveraged it against the opposite wall. This would give me time to get rid of everything before the SWAT team broke in. Why hadn't they busted me? They just kept lurking in the hallway, and I heard every word they said. Their walkie-talkies blasted; their voices intermingled with the piercing static. A man urgently whispered, *Get him, get him now*, then a female voice with a Bronx or Brooklyn accent, who had the ultimate authority, responded, *No, don't fuck this up like the last time. Don't move. Nobody moves until I say so.*

I returned to my couch and took a few more hits. I was delighted by the motion as the flame of my Bic performed its dance against the front of the pipe. It kissed the screen gently as I inhaled from the other end. I felt safe again: *Lord, let me never be confounded.*

I was safe on the subway, but walking the short distance from 97th to 96th Street was a challenge. After I made it through the turnstiles at the 96th Street station, I could relax. I felt invulnerable there. I carried my drugs and glassware in the six pockets of my cargo pants. I didn't stay underground long. I usually surfaced in Chelsea and quickly faced the bricks of one old factory building or another. I would light up, take a massive hit, blow out a huge cloud of smoke and presume that no one knew what I was doing. I thought I couldn't be seen. The narcs from the Upper West Side wouldn't know where I'd gone. After an hour, I'd head back uptown, passing them as they sped downtown in the opposite direction.

The subway was my first conscious memory: my father and I riding on an elevated train above the city. The buildings below were tiny and insignificant; my father's delight was infectious. He wore a long blue winter dress coat and fedora and held me tightly in his arms. He carefully placed me on the rattan seat and then roared with laughter. Other people on the car were dressed in pastel shades. They never spoke; they just smiled and gestured. The elevated car would suddenly jerk, then soar upward and without warning plummet. Minutes later, he picked me up and held me close to him. Surely, I would never come to harm.

As I waited for the uptown train, I remembered how he looked standing on the platform, his body draped over the Chiclet machine. It was hard to tell whether he was about to dance or start a fight. He leaned against the metal columns, which displayed his taut, muscular body and then stretched his arms high above him, a celebrant in an esoteric ritual only performed in this subterranean world. He looked like the high priest of the IRT. How I wished he could caress me now and give me his blessing, but he was deep in the throes of late-stage Alzheimer's. He knew less about where he was than I did.

As I emerged from my reverie, it struck me without warning that I had to stop, as if the vision of my father's compelling masculinity was reaching out and telling me that if I didn't stop now, I might never get another chance. When I arrived home, I dropped the dime on myself. I called a close friend in recovery. As soon as he answered, I told him I had been on crack for months. There was a long silence.

Really?

Really.

Who's gonna tell Carly, you or me?

I will.

OK, call me right back.

I opened the blinds on one of the front windows, inhaled deeply, and let the smoke fill the room. The halos still flickered around the streetlights, and I took this to be a sign of rescue. I sat on the floor awhile and tried to figure out what I was going to say. I dialed, and she picked up on the first ring. As I heard her voice, I knew everything would be okay. Her deep, rich alto soothed me. The sound of it always affirmed me, made me feel safer and closer to her than anyone I had ever known. She intoned my name *Jimmy Hart* as if it were a hosanna, an exultation, as if she were naming me for the very first time, each and every time. In that moment, I had no doubt about her love for me. So my dear friend Carl and my wife Carly decided that I should go to McLean's psychiatric hospital. I agreed, took a couple of Xanax, and was soon filled with a rapturous joy, knowing that no matter what happened, I had a wife and a friend who loved me.

I had done it again: so filled with the arrogance of one who had risked everything and survived, I felt engulfed by the god-like wisdom of my experience. I had thrown it all up in the air and now it fell. No one could assail my courage in the line of fire. I had survived a second time, reengaged in a battle that kills so many. Perhaps I was even more daring than my father.

Maybe that's all I had needed to prove, that I could be as reckless and brave as he had been.

As the Xanax took over, I contemplated the wonder of what I had seen, what I had become. I threw the leftover pieces of rock into the toilet and flushed them away. I was glad that my father didn't know what had happened, because it would have broken his heart—a small gift of Alzheimer's.

In no time, I was off to McLean's in Belmont, Massachusetts. The material my new shrink wanted to talk about surprised me. It wasn't my father, Eamon, Carly, fame, failure, addiction, or sex. He wanted to spend most of our time investigating my many secret lives and their origins. Little did I know how long ago the secrets had begun, or how deeply some of them were buried.

TWENTY-THREE

ARE YOU KIDDING ME?

The large black security guard grunted.

Two days ago, I was smoking crack around the clock. I don't need you to watch me have a cigarette.

Sir, those are the rules.

When I finished, he walked me back down a screened-in corridor and into the lock-down at McLean. It seemed important that I tell everyone I met in the hallway that I was capable of having a cigarette on my own. It made me even angrier that neither the staff nor the other patients were the least bit concerned.

Due to my program work, I had visited a number of psychiatric facilities over the years, and I didn't recall any of them having little screened-in cages for smoking. I found it demeaning. I remembered a song that we sometimes sang in the Albany/Troy days—"A Bird in a Gilded Cage."

You may think she's happy and free from care.
She's not, though she seems to be.

As I remembered the lyrics, I felt a deep, pervasive sorrow.

'Tis sad when you think of a wasted life.
For youth cannot mate with age.

It all felt wasted. I stared down at the blue Styrofoam slippers and realized that I was behind a locked door. How could I have let so much be taken from me? It didn't dawn on me for a long time what I might have stolen from her. I wasn't ready to face that side of things. My denial, disassociation, repression, and all of the other psychological dodges of a drug addict were in place. I was deeply sorry, but not yet ready to face the real consequences of my actions. Instead, especially in those early days, I wanted to focus on my grievances against her. For example, at some point, she had insisted that I not sing in the house *because it interrupted her creative process.* Everyone else could sing in our house but me. I sang softly as I walked back toward my room.

And her beauty was sold for an old man's gold.
She's a bird in a gilded cage.

I wandered into the game room, and sitting there was a tall, young man with flowing brown hair and soft blue eyes. He had the look of a folk musician from the seventies. He sat at a table in the middle of the room staring at a chessboard.

Hey man, wanna play?

I didn't want to. I knew it would take more concentration than I had. Detoxing from a year of crack wasn't the right time to play chess.

I'm not very good.

Me either.

I realized I didn't have anything else to do, so I sat and he quickly set up the board for both of us. He had a wisp of a mustache, and he stared at me a bit too long. It bordered on the flirtatious, but in this place, it may have been his medication. As he reached to move his knight, I saw the bandages just above both of his wrists.

Tried to kill yourself?

Yeah man.

First time?

No, second.

I'm sorry.

Yeah, love sucks for me.

I stared at him, but really didn't know what to say, so I just repeated myself.

I'm really sorry.

Then he switched the questioning.

You?

Oh me, well, I'm here for crack.

Wow!

Toward the end of the game, my cell phone rang. Carly started all of our conversations the same way. She would say my name with a loving kind of mock enthusiasm. Said by her, in her low alto tone, it made every part of me feel covered, as if just her voice alone was enough to see me through.

Jimmy Hart!

I always responded the same way.

Carly Simon!

The call only took a minute. She had just wanted to say goodnight and tell me how much she loved me.

Shortly after I hung up, I was checkmated, a perfect ending. I was ready for sleep. My meds were beginning to take effect, and it had been quite a journey to get here. However, it turned out that my new friend Tom wanted to talk some more. He wanted to know all about me, so I quickly told him my story, as if I were speaking at a twelve-step meeting. He kept asking more and more personal questions. Finally, I told him I had to get some sleep, and that I'd see him in the morning. It was a long night on the thin hospital mattress.

Early the next day, I shuffled out in my slippers and robe to get my meds at the nurses' station. The other inmates were assembled, and they stared at me with a certain fascination. I assumed it was my status as the new guy on the floor. I sat next to a large pasty-skinned man with waist-length blonde hair. It was tangled, poorly bleached, and unkempt. He told me his name was George, and he immediately launched into his story. He was a pre-op transsexual suffering from depression. He spoke in an affected manner with a certain tone and body language that implied an intimacy between us. He spoke loudly so that everyone sitting in the corridor could hear him.

So honey, you're from the Vineyard, huh?

My look of surprise did not faze him.

Oh, I know about island life; I lived on Nantucket a few years.

How did you know I was from the Vineyard?

Listen, Mary! I know who you are. Your name is Jim, right?

He winked at me as I started to say yes. I started to speak, but he interrupted me.

Honey, you can't fool me.

I suddenly realized what had happened. It was from the call last night. He thought I was James Taylor.

I'm not who you think I am.

Oh, don't worry, I won't tell anyone.

You've been here before, haven't you?

As I looked around the waiting area, I realized that he wouldn't have to keep his promise, because everyone else already knew. They were studying me and smiling somewhat eerily, as if they had all been given an extra dose of meds. A guy opposite me reached under his gown and pulled out a James Taylor CD. It was his *New Moonshine* album. James was dressed in a black turtleneck surrounded by shafts of white light. There was no question that I could have been a double for this photo—even the pose looked familiar.

Listen, can you sign this for me? It's my favorite album. I had it snuck in this morning. I can't believe you're here.

I tried to tell them the truth, but the more I denied it, the more I could see them believing it. Of course they thought James Taylor would deny who he was if he was in the cracker factory. I quickly took the CD and scrawled, *With love, James.* I then had to sign six or seven more scraps of paper for the other inmates. I signed them all *James Hart*, which they seemed quite happy with: They assumed this was James's alias, which might be even better than the real signature. They could tell people that they had been in the loony bin with James Taylor, and he had signed their scrap of paper with a fake name. One day, one of those scraps might appear on eBay, under the title *James Taylor's alias signature while in the psych ward in 2003.*

Standing there in McLean's on the second day of my detox, the last person I wanted to be confused with was James Taylor. In my hypersensitive, highly sexualized crack jones, I didn't need to fantasize and wonder if James's body felt like mine when Carly and I made love. If we looked so much alike, did we feel alike? This was when I most needed a self to fall back on, and instead I was signing my name over a picture of James. I had lost my identity to a man I barely knew.

After another day, I was transferred to the Pavilion. This was the name of the high-end evaluation program at McLean. They would spend the next two weeks evaluating my situation and eventually recommend continuing treatment in another, longer-term program. Within the first couple of days, I received a number of phone calls. Mike Nichols, Carl Bernstein, Alec Baldwin, and numerous other noted folks reached me on my cell phone. Yet it wasn't until I heard Michael J. Fox's voice that something else started to break, something that reached beyond my ego. We had spent time working on our recovery together a few years before. As I heard him say his name, I started to cry—something about his inherent goodness touched me.

I can't believe you called me.

We hadn't seen much of each other in the past few years.

Really?

Really, I mean I'm so, so . . .

I sobbed as the sincerity of his concern washed over me

Jim, of course. You helped save my fucking life. Man, just hang in there.

It was a brief chat that gave me some much-needed hope, but I couldn't yet delineate the meaning. I had been a bit of a magician in the lives of many people, and yet I had lost the magic myself. I had delivered the deep belief I had in recovery to them, and they had watched me deal with my own addiction, my son's handicap, my losses, and my unusual life around fame, and now, in spite of my best efforts, I had lost the battle.

I hadn't forgotten the power and truth of this message, but didn't know how to reach it amid my current problems. It felt like the stars no longer hung there for me. How could my life with Carly continue? How could we be one again? Could this team of shrinks and physicians really show me a way—way to be at one? I recalled the prayer we said at the end of every chapel service in the seminary.

That they all may be one,
as thou Father in me and I in thee.

I just couldn't figure out why I had been sent this latest set of impenetrable woes, especially the one concerning boys and men.

As soon as he opened the door, I knew he was gay. Dr. Sam's office was suffused with the smell of potpourri, and the aroma seemed to match his look, a bit too sweet. He was going to be my personal psychiatrist for the two weeks I was at McLean. The other psychiatrists, psychologists, and psychopharmacologists kept testing me and adjusting my medications, but this one was going to talk with me. He was small, and I wondered if he would be able to handle me. He had on an expensive dress shirt patterned with blue checkered boxes. His silk tie was tasteful. I figured he probably shopped at Louis in Boston, a high-end designer store on Newbury Street.

Hi, Jim.

Hello, Doctor.

He spent some time explaining the purpose of our next ten visits together. I would be seeing him every day. He would be a critical part of my evaluation to see where they would send me for further treatment.

It turned out that he wasn't easily upended at all, His manner of inquiry seemed too meek, yet it made me want to help him; there was something fragile in him that I didn't want to disturb. As I sat in a remote attic room in an ugly red-brick building, I realized for probably the first time that I was desperate for a solution. After brief pleasantries, we began. I launched into the story of my father: the tale of his violence, alcoholism, and criminal past, and his remarkable recovery. I told him of the unbearable pain of seeing my father in the late stages of Alzheimer's, and then of the pain and suffering of having Eamon as my son. Then he said something that stunned me.

So, you have lost both your past and your future.

I just stared at him, silenced by this insight. Finally I spoke again.

Yes, I guess it feels that way.

I wandered through my life story. I told him about the seminary and the death of Jim. I could hear my voice break as I spoke. I could again feel the pain and confusion that I felt all those years ago standing atop the frozen canal staring down at his wool watch cap.

Then I talked about how much Carly and I loved each other. It was the only salve left. It was all that made my life bearable, and it had something to do with the force of her feelings. Somehow, she could still intervene in my struggle. It was how she held me in every imaginable and creative way that made each breath possible. It was clear that we were still in love with each other in spite of all I had done. He wasn't that interested in talking about my father or Carly. He wanted to focus on Jim. He wanted me to stay with my feelings at the moment when I lost my first love. He wanted me to try to identify what had been taken away so many years ago. My initial prejudice was erased by his insight and tenderness, and I think he may have been the first person to touch the essential core of my problems and give it context and understanding. He was the first therapist I ever felt any transference for, and I experienced some strange form of psychiatric puppy love for this man I would see for only ten days. I thought about him all the time and wanted to be with him every minute of my stay. He proved to be more than man enough for my complex problems and opened me up in a way that I found miraculous.

At the end of my first week of confinement at McLean, I saw Carly for the first time. We were meeting with a couples' counselor, and I knew I was going to have to confront some of the truth of my behaviors in the past year, and admit it to Carly. Her body slumped and her beautiful blue eyes ran from me. She just wanted to escape from the small visitor's room as fast as she could; she didn't want me to see the horror of how this was going to hurt her. I started to cry as we approached the topic of my sexual behavior. I finally just blurted it out.

Yes, I was unfaithful to you. I've been having sex with men.

She kept patting me on the head after I told her.

I never slept with a woman, not once.

She didn't want me to feel any more guilt than I already did. How could my intense attraction to her end in this state? It was a state that demanded she love me perfectly, and I had completely subverted her ability to do it. I presented her with the most remarkable challenge: find a way to love me while I destroy our lives with an impossible construct.

The most powerful sexual feelings of my life had been formed with her, and I had found one of the only imaginable paths to extinguish it. It vanished in a cloud of smoke, and it felt as though the effects of this drug had forever switched my wiring. Women would never turn me on again; something had rerouted the pleasure centers in my brain and permanently altered me. The attraction to soft curves and her perfect slope had now been replaced by a passion for hard muscles and all things male, from the touch of a beard to a whole new set of smells.

I never thought I would tell anyone about something that happened the final days of my run, but I found myself telling it all to my new psychiatrist. As I told him, I realized that I didn't know how much of this had actually happened or how much I had hallucinated. I told him everything I remembered, and somehow I recalled many details. But I had been smoking crack for more than two days without any sleep, so it was hard to trust the truth of my report.

I remembered chatting with someone at the end of the dark bar at the Eagle, a leather bar in Chelsea. He introduced himself as *Master Rick*. He invited me back to his place, and I found myself in a taxi with him headed across town. Soon I found myself suspended from the ceiling, and he switched from hitting me with a whip to using a thick black belt. This implement had resonance in the memory of my physical abuse.

He insisted on my calling him *Daddy*. I had never called anyone else but my father *Daddy*. Actually, I don't remember anyone ever asking me to do this, but Master Rick was quite insistent, and while I was thinking it over, he kept hitting me harder and screaming, *What's my name?*

My defenses were pretty much gone, and he was filling me with an array of additional drugs. I had no particular objection to calling him *Daddy*. My real daddy was deep in the end of his battle with Alzheimer's, so he wouldn't be terribly offended.

After I said, *Yes, Daddy*, it wasn't long before he was saying eerie but soothing things like *That's a good boy*. It was eerie because, after all, I was over fifty.

Did your Daddy beat you?

I let out a guffaw between the strokes of the belt, which was answer enough.

But you loved him, didn't you?

I hesitated with my answer. He repeated the question as he hit me with the hardest stroke so far. It prompted a response, *Oh, yes.*

So, you loved your daddy.

His emphasis on the word *love* was both sinister and intimate. It seemed to please him, and he began to kiss and caress the parts of my body that he had been torturing. It was not unlike my real father, who had tried so hard to heal the wounds he had caused. It had been a valiant effort, but nothing could ever quite fix it.

Somewhere in my reverie about my father, *Master Rick* appeared again, just his voice, asking me what my limits were. I remember proudly replying, *None*. My memories about my father were hardly precise, but I kept swinging back and forth, between now and then. It was a most unexpected form of therapy. However, as I moved from my present torturer to memories of my father, something seemed to break, some part of what I had long repressed broke open. *Master Rick* began to be concerned about my not being grateful enough. I remember hearing him yelling and hitting me very hard. He was screaming, *Say thank you, Sir.*

I said, *Thank you, Sir*, immediately, and once again the beating stopped. He gave me a few more big hits on the pipe, had me snort a few more lines, and then I heard him say to someone else who had come into the room, *Let's give him some smack.*

I don't quite remember much except that I felt very proud when I heard Master Rick saying, *Oh, you don't know, man, this guy can take a ton of fucking drugs.*

I was high, happy, and vague. My mind was comfortably far away, while my body kept racing and pulsing. In this detached, amorphous, and suspended state, I had been able to adapt quickly to the dramatic emotional swings of my father. I could shift with improvisation and speed.

I floated away, high above the ground as sonorous music swelled beneath, above, and within me, the fulsome strings of the *Pearl Fisher's Duet* above, the brass of the *Berlioz Requiem* below, and the tight female harmonies of Mozart in the distance. All pain vanished with my body strung across the room; I traveled through a series of blue-eyed women who had saved my life, from Sister Leona to Carly. They all had blue eyes. This torture was my final penance before my Last Judgment, and I had finally atoned.

I just don't know if all of this actually happened. Isn't that odd?

That's all we have time for today. We'll pick this up from here tomorrow.

At my final meeting at McLean, my team concluded that I should be sent to the Betty Ford Center for further treatment. As I flew across country from Boston to Palm Springs, I read Dr. Sam's notes. The left corner of the stationery said *Harvard Medical School,* and the Harvard logo was in the center of the page.

For the last year Jim has been in flight, trying to escape his pain. A twelve-step program guru with twenty-one years of sobriety, Jim turned to crack and sex to combat anhedonia and to achieve a physical and psychological anesthesia.

Yes, I had been in flight: soaring, gaining altitude, unfettered, totally alone, and completely safe. Crack had opened the long-sealed doors to the darkest corners of the self and made them all acceptable. Yet something about this was way too ponderous. Perhaps it was just an overwhelming desire for unimpeded fun. How about that for a diagnosis? I found a path to more fun than I had ever imagined knowing.

He frequently said that drugs and sex do exactly what he wants them to do. In this way, relapse is paired with a narcissistic infantile wish to be perfectly loved. In a sadomasochistic reenactment, he relived the beatings of his childhood and had the desire to repeat this experience as it activated the intense bond that he formed with his father.

It struck me that this was very smart, but was it accurate? After all, the only sure thing I knew is that I relapsed because I picked up a drug. The doctor's explanation continued and was much more complex.

Sexual acting-out was maintained via intellectualization, and rationalization as exploration of his bisexuality. Anger, shame, and guilt would regularly overwhelm the repression barrier and would be managed by isolation of affect and passive-aggressive behavior. As he became deeply entrenched in this lifestyle, he relied on interjection and schizoid fantasy to cope with separation and loss.

In this way, it is possible to understand Jim's difficulties as bereavement for the loss of a variety of loves: the innocent love of his friend Jim, the intense, stimulated, and conflicted love of his father, and the intellectual and passionate partnership with his wife Carly Simon. Drugs and sex illusively obviated the need for grief and indeed for love itself. In spite of the inevitability of catastrophic consequences if he continues, Jim is not clear that he wants to change or stop this pattern. As such, Eros and Thanatos exist as inseparable twins within him.

I wondered how a place called the Betty Ford Center could possibly help me if I had found a way to "obviate grief and love itself." How could I now change the unchangeable or, as my old pal James Joyce put it: the ineluctable.

I noticed the last line of his appraisal.

None of Jim's behavior is easy to relinquish for the stark simplicity of being sober and monogamous.

CHAPTER

TWENTY-FOUR

───────────◆───────────

AS I STEPPED OFF the plane, the desert sun seared through me. I tried to be hopeful; I tried to think that this would be the beginning of a new and meaningful existence. I just didn't know how it could be done; perhaps the intense heat would be part of it and seep through me in some cleansing and cauterizing way.

Carly just kept working. She was coming to Los Angeles to record something or receive another award, but I didn't really know how she was doing. Most of our conversation was about Sally's upcoming wedding and Carly's anger over it taking place at James's house on the Vineyard rather than ours. She just couldn't understand how Sally could do that to her. She could barely talk about anything else. She was obsessed with her hurt, and I was injured by her obsession with it. She never wanted to talk about us; perhaps she couldn't.

I immediately disliked "The Betty." It was filled with prison-like rules and attitudes while assuming the language of the enlightened. I was in a room with three other inmates, and I found their personalities in early recovery mostly irritating. But it was the staff that I found most disturbing: They were laced with a sort of cruelty that did not really reflect the disease model; they treated us as though we were bad, selfish, and spoiled children who needed to be punished for delinquent behavior.

After the first few weeks, I felt I couldn't take any more. After being sober and very active in my recovery for twenty-one years, I felt I knew a lot more about this then most of the people running the institution.

I think it began to turn as I watched former President Gerald Ford flip a hamburger on my plate at the Memorial Day picnic. He stood in front of me in a tall chef's hat and stared off into another world. I said, *Thank you, Mr. President.* The President seemed to have already slipped into his last forgetfulness, and he stared over my head toward the blue sky at something far away. It was a perverse cartoon, and I couldn't imagine how I was appearing in it. It felt like everything had tilted in this simple exchange, and that my appetites had once again trumped my beliefs. In the act of accepting the burger, I had surrendered to my lifelong enemy. After this event, I began to notice everything that the staff did, and it seemed like a kind of cruelty that was intentional, that they thought we deserved to be mistreated. And then there was the incident that put me way over the top.

I screamed as loudly as I could; tears flowed.

That's it. I'm out of here. That fucking asshole . . .

Liz, my counselor, interrupted.

Do you know who that "fucking asshole" is?

No, but that's it. I'm out of here.

He's the CEO of Betty Ford.

I couldn't respond. I just kept pounding my clenched fists against my thighs over and over.

Jim, there's something else you need to know.

What?

He IS an asshole, if that helps at all.

When I entered the lecture hall that morning I was ready to be enraged, and the CEO of the Betty was the perfect provocateur. I arrived late, so I didn't catch the speaker's name. He was tall and somewhat handsome with wavy hair that had been trained into submission. I had a bad feeling about him as soon as I set eyes on him. He talked about a meeting with this senator and that governor and how Mrs. Ford had told him this or that, and how President Ford had told him something else. Somehow he was going to overwhelm the sick addicts in the room with his self-importance. After much more shameless name-dropping, he switched tactics, and I heard him say something that touched a deep place within me.

If I lined up a hundred priests and ministers in front of this room, I can assure you that ninety percent of them would know nothing about the disease of alcoholism.

My arm shot up in the air at the end of the statement. My voice wavered as I struggled with the intensity of my anger.

Why would you say such a thing to these people? It's complete bullshit.

I gave him and the hundred or so people in the hall a quick inflamed tutorial on the origins of the twelve steps of recovery and their religious basis—coming mostly out of Protestant and Catholic thought. I asked him if he knew that Bill Wilson's sponsor had been a Jesuit priest, and finally I said, *What the fuck are you talking about? If it weren't for church basements, we wouldn't have a place to meet.*

I knew I had won the argument when he screamed: *Listen, I have over twenty years of sobriety.*

I responded immediately with *So do I* and ran out of the auditorium to find my counselor and get out of this place.

Jim, there's something else you need to know.

What else?

We were so impressed with your psychiatrist at McLean that he's been in charge of your care for the last month, even though he's not on our staff.

I had tried to call Dr. Sam at McLean numerous times in the past month, and he never answered. He picked up Liz's call on the second ring. She quickly told him what had transpired and how I wanted to leave.

As I heard his voice, I screamed into the speakerphone.

I should sue you for malpractice. Why did you send me to this right-wing prison?

Jim, do you know that your treatment plan only had one word on it?

No, I don't know anything. No one will talk to me, including you.

Jim, the word is "Containment." We all felt strongly that you needed to be locked up for your own protection.

It just seemed another form of prison, but it kept me sober for the time I was there. Yet there were other voices that could always help me—one in particular who called from all over the world while he was shooting his latest film.

It's Mike!

His voice was a soothing contrast—a touch of aloe against the desert sun.

How's my boy?

I always found myself searching the sky whenever Mike Nichols called, as though I might find him in a cloud or a star above the desert. His tone and diction seemed to come from so far away: a place where people actually knew things; a person filled with proper answers to human problems.

Hangin' in, I guess.

The shade from a nearby strip mall felt ominous as it crept toward me.

I don't know. I have the feeling that I've fucked everything up beyond repair.

You have, but that's what always happens.

I had expected him to disagree with me, to say I wasn't so bad.

I just feel so sad. I sighed to let him know.

In what way?

That I've wound up with the booby prize—some sort of leftover life.

Oh that. That's how we all feel—no matter how it turns out.

I wondered how Mike could feel this way.

Really?

The great joke is that it's usually more than enough.

Even mine?

Yes, especially yours.

Really, why do you say that?

Because it will be your own.

That's what I'm afraid of.

It's the only way in the end.

The only way?

You will be happy and unhappy as before, but in different proportions. Nothing is better than owning your own life.

Well, I guess I need to trust you.

Don't you know, we all will love you with or without her?

Mike had once jokingly said that I may have been his Gerasim—the Russian peasant who in Tolstoy's story *The Death of Ivan Ilych* holds Ivan Ilych's legs in a position that comforts him as he approaches death. He had given me so much in our time together that I hoped I might do something important for him during his final act, but from the start, he never seemed to need anyone's help. His artistic achievements looked like something ten incredibly talented people might have been able to do if they never slept. His social life was nonstop, and his care for numerous people throughout the years was stunning. He was a committed husband and father, and he even had time to talk to his recovering crack addict friend in the desert as he worked on one of his most challenging projects—*Angels in America*. I sometimes couldn't get over his concern for me. After all, what had I ever done except taken the right train, and yet he always assured me that there was more to come. I was now on an endless seesaw between recovery and relapse. In the world of rehabilitation, it was often hard to tell what was helping and what was making things worse. Mike's reassurances were different. They always made me feel better. I had much less trust in the Betty Ford Center. During my last week as an inpatient, I went to a private session on grief, which I had avoided until the last possible moment.

Jim, when did you lose your dreams?

The question came from a counselor who hadn't had an ounce of insight in three months; but as I heard it, I knew it went to the heart of the matter. I flashed back to the image of my mother all those years ago, and wondered about the lyrics of her favorite song, "Young at Heart." Would I be able to laugh as my dreams fell apart? I certainly wasn't laughing, nor had I really pursued my own dreams in a long time.

Carly didn't make it to family week at the Betty. I had been encouraging her not to make the trip, because I thought that the endlessly self-congratulatory staff might do more harm than good. It seemed to me that they were overly interested in her attendance, not because she was my wife, but because she was Carly Simon. Also, I felt I had already unloaded enough truth on her at our day-long session back at McLean. Many people involved in my case were surprised at her not appearing, and they began to have a different perspective on our relationship. They began to tell me with more certainty that I had to leave her, but I was sure they were too dim to understand the nature of our relationship and its remarkable strength. I had accepted the fact that I was not invited to Sally's wedding. Carly had told me not to come. She felt that my presence would be too much for her to handle, and I guess I needed to respect that. That I was to be exiled at such an important moment seemed wrong, but the rights of a gay crack-addict stepfather are limited at best.

When did I lose my dreams?

I designed the last phase of my aftercare at the Betty pretty much on my own. The formal part of the program was over, and they thought my suggestion of staying in the desert a few more weeks had merit. I would participate in a couple of outpatient visits every week and attend twelve-step meetings in Palm Springs, especially gay meetings, to try to figure out this new part of myself.

After five months of treatment, I may have needed to find my dreams again, but instead I found myself crouched in terror staring across the motel courtyard. The Palm Springs police and the California State Troopers had amassed outside the gate beyond the pool. They had been waiting there for hours, and my panic had finally gotten the better of me. Evening had turned to night, and I could no longer hide beneath the lounge chairs or control my fear. I started to scream at them to come and get me. There I stood in my speedo with the white drawstring dangling untied in front to me, yelling like the lead character from an old James Cagney movie: *Come and get me. I see you. Come and get me; I'm right here. Come and get me.*

I was sure they would rush me, yelling into a megaphone: *Put your hands in the air. Hands in the air!* Instead, the next thing that happened was the motel manager, who had just recently started referring to me as the *International Man of Mystery*, was asking me if there was a problem. I told him there wasn't and that he should mind his own business. My only problem was that I had snorted too much crystal meth and had been in a paranoid break for the last six hours.

Instead of following my treatment plan, I found myself mostly at a casino downtown. Somehow, in spite of months of treatment, the desire to escape was more powerful than the cure. Within two weeks of my release from the inpatient program of Betty Ford, I had relapsed. This last phase of my "treatment" for alcohol and drug abuse consisted mostly of being in a hypnotic trance induced by the sights and sounds of slot machines blinking, clanging, and whirring while high on crystal meth. I went for crystal because I couldn't locate any crack in Palm Springs. Hours went by quickly, and I cut off all the repressed emotions. I had once again confused recovery with the relief of pain.

A few days later, I experienced another impediment. I stared across the motel room at a handsome young man in a skintight white speedo as he tied up and quickly found a vein. He jabbed his arm; his head jolted back, eyes closed, and he went limp. Then his eyes reopened and his face was suffused with a slow, deep smile. I knew that he was in far too deep, and as he passed the used syringe to me, a fleeting thought crossed my mind: *I might be as well.*

I had never gone so far away. I awoke in the middle of the following afternoon. I thought I heard a familiar voice beckoning to me. As I looked out the sliding glass door of the motel, I saw a beautiful but curious sight. There was a long sloping lawn that ended in a clear blue Adirondack lake. It looked like a scene from upstate New York. My Albany writer friends Bill Kennedy and Joe Gagen were combing the lawn searching for me. I could hear Bill's voice.

Jimbo, you okay? Where are you man?

This vision seemed to last forever. I tried, for what seemed like hours, to open the door for Bill and Joe, but I just couldn't get off the mattress. Finally, when I did get up, there was the same boy standing on the other side of the white door in his tight white speedo ready to do some more drugs.

He was a different kind of vision, in a dream I was now living that I didn't understand. I had seen him just a few days ago on a faux rock by one of the many swimming pools in the Warm Sands section of Palm Springs. He was a vision of lithe male beauty, and he had attached himself to me. He had smooth tanned skin and deep brown eyes—brown eyes not unlike my own, but in his I could already see the ending. I was afraid he would never survive his addiction. He was much too committed to riding it all the way. I had a ringside seat at the end of his life. I had never been so sure of an ending as I was with Alex.

We took a cab to the casino where we played the slot machines for hours into the next day. The various spinning wizards, burning kon-tiki huts, cackling witches, magical sphinxes, and Cleopatra herself all spoke to us as we rapidly won and lost money. I could see in his soft, open expressions the excitement of every bell, clang, and whirr of the machines that seemed to spur him on. He often passed out in my lap and I would hold him gently until he came to. Then I would help him feel better one more time with some crystal and a syringe. While I had many people trying to help me, I seemed to be the only person left in his life.

I needed something way beyond myself. After an audience that Mike had with Pope Paul VI, the valet asked Mike if he would like to take a look at the pope's private quarters. It turned out that the valet was a huge Mike Nichols fan. Mike, of course, said yes. As they stood in the Pope's bedroom, the valet opened one of the top drawers of the dresser and lifted out a hunk of wood.

Would you like a piece of the True Cross?

Mike knew it wasn't exactly right to say yes, but he did. I wanted to beg him for a sliver, so I could hold it against Alex's body and save him from the ending. Perhaps I could press the wood against the track marks on his arms and he would be healed. I so wanted this young boy to survive. I never knew for sure what happened to him, but if he did live, I would have loved to report back to Mike that this miracle had occurred because of him. I sensed that no one had ever cared for Alex, and I wanted to care for him the way Carly had cared for me. There had been weekends during the past year when I returned to the Vineyard. I would take off my shirt and reveal a long, ghastly sore that stretched across my back from all the crack use. She would spend hours bathing and caring for my body, terrified about what was happening. I somehow convinced her it had something to do with my back problems and tension. She had never known me any way other than sober, so the idea that I had been gone on crack-cocaine never entered her mind. I wouldn't give her any information. I would just shrug: *Probably just stress.*

Hello!

It's Mike.

Oh, hi Mike.

How's the boy today?

I guess okay. Sort of feeling the cloud lift a bit.

He laughed not missing the reference.

It's an awful drug.

Yes, but it sure does eliminate depression.

He constantly tried to keep my spirits up.

Believe me, it will all work out. It is what you are about.

I hope so, sometimes I get so depressed.

Something that helps me through these times is when I realize it's just life— that's all.

Yes, so don't make such a big deal about it?

Exactly.

Don't forget our friend Auden.

What did he say?

One of the great things about Mike is that his voice would fill with mischief before he told a punch line. He knew he was about to tell you something so funny that he couldn't stop laughing. He was already enjoying the thought of it.

He recited a limerick by W. H. Auden. It reminded everyone that death can come to the young, the rich, the funny, and much to our delight, even the very well hung.

I detoxed on my own once again the day before I returned east, and I arrived home pretending that I had been sober and watchful for the last five months, ready to resume my life. I think I had the best of intentions, and I still hadn't touched a drop of alcohol, so in some odd way I considered myself technically sober. I went to meetings for a while, and then I didn't. I was "chipping" a bit but really not doing very much. Taking drugs again had started when I accidentally found a loaded crack pipe in the inside pocket of a suit jacket. Once again, I thought if I just did a little, my life would become manageable.

TWENTY-FIVE

HERE'S A PIECE!

The naked blonde boy held a small piece of crack between his thumb and forefinger. The black kid next to him grunted but kept searching through the fibers of the Oriental rug. They were completely obsessed. I finally screamed.

Stop this. Stop it now. I hate this.

I was just coming down from my high of the last couple of days. I hated when other addicts who were jonesing did this carpet-search thing. It was too desperate, and it made our despair way too graphic. Here we were: low-life crack addicts scrounging around the floor looking for tiny bits of rock to keep us from detoxing. They couldn't help themselves; they kept searching.

I said to stop it now. I kicked the black boy on his ass. *Stop it now or you'll be leaving.*

He stopped. As frantic as he felt, he didn't want to be shown the door.

I'll call Spike. He'll be here in an hour.

Of course, they were wondering how we would survive until then. They didn't know about the five pipes from the last week that I had saved and put in one of the kitchen drawers. These were completely clogged, but they could be used for stove hits—one of my favorite things to do toward the end of a run.

I don't remember the blonde's name, but he was a Scot. I could see him in kilts with his gorgeous long legs and the handsome face of a Viking heritage. His name was something like John MacGregor or Patrick McGowan, one of those names that permitted him to wear a tartan. As he held the glass pipe, I imagined it was a bagpipe chanter, and he was beautifully playing "Scotland the Brave." There was so much that I could imagine when I was on a long run. We had been at it a few days, and no doubt we were in some form of disassembly, but I really don't remember what happened. Often, more and more people would arrive during a long bender, and more things would happen in which I didn't always participate. Sometimes there was sex, or the pretension of sex, and sometimes there was the endless search for sex; but most often with serious users, we just smoked crack in various stages of undress. Also, more people dropping in meant more and different kinds of drugs. In no time, we might be smoking or shooting crystal, snorting or shooting coke, taking a hit of Special K, or drinking orange juice or Kool Aid with GBH. The combinations were endless, but I still had not had a sip of alcohol. As I often told the other players, I was an alcoholic and I didn't drink. I was only a few months out of Betty Ford in January of 2004, yet in spite of all that time in rehab, I was still trying "social" crack use.

Alannah had called sometime during the middle of this run, and I had oddly taken the call. She insisted that I come to Albany to see Eamon. I hadn't seen him for almost three months, and she was furious. After all these years, she knew how to get my attention. She knew that was ninety percent of the battle. If she could do that, she usually got her way.

Listen you mother-fucker, you've got a son here.

Hi.

I'm not even talking to you anymore, but your son, your only child in the universe keeps asking, "Where's Dad?" You better get your ass up here now.

I'll be up tomorrow.

You better be or I'm just gonna come down there and drop him off.

Eamon at a crack party: It was an image I had never thought of, but it terrified me. I had one day to straighten out, which wasn't going to be easy because the party was just building up steam. In fact, John, or Patrick, or Angus, or whatever his name was held up one of the blackened pipes I had given him. It was filled with gunky residue.

A stove hit?

After a few days of smoking, the residue in the pipes would build up, rendering them useless. The aficionados, who were also the ones always scouring the carpet for lost pieces of crack, also tended to be stove-hit experts. You wanted to jam enough gunk into the end of the pipe to get the best possible result. You needed more intense heat than you could get from a lighter to melt the residue. It tasted awful, but it produced a very powerful hit.

I always said yes to this. A few times they were so powerful that I found myself coming to on the floor in front of the stove. Today, Angus took the black ring off the first burner and turned up the flame. The trick was to heat the pipe without cracking it. We had four or five pipes, so we expected to be high for a long time.

Jim, you ready?

I stood right in front of the stove next to him, but he forgot to twirl the first pipe in a circular motion over the flame. I saw a billowing cloud of smoke, and then there was an explosion. Hot glass filled with heated specs of tar flew everywhere.

What the fuck?

I jumped back screaming as pieces of tarred glass struck my face and chest. The flying glass burnt my torso and the left side of my face, but it was minor. We quickly checked each other out, and then I grabbed the next pipe.

I'll do the next one, before you kill us.

I held the pipe over the flame. I soon was inhaling a thick acrid cloud, which caused sudden spinning and hysterical laughter. After forty-eight hours, it felt like the party was just starting. I had to summon all my will-power to even think about making it to Albany by tomorrow afternoon.

As the evening turned to night, I realized that the only possible way to do it was to smoke straight through to the train ride on Sunday morning. At nine o'clock Sunday morning, I began to worry because I couldn't get the people to leave. There was plenty of stuff still left, and no one ever left a crack party with chunks of rock unsmoked. I lured them out the door with doggie bags, and most of them departed reluctantly. Angus was the last to leave, and he kept trying to persuade me to stay. He wanted another couple of days. Who could blame him? I was a great drug companion; it seemed I had always been so, even when the drug was just alcohol. I packed my glass pipes carefully and put a couple of bags of crack into my luggage.

Somehow I made it to the train station, bought a ticket, and climbed aboard. I probably had ingested enough cocaine to power the entire train. As soon as my head hit the seat, I was sound asleep. I have no recall of anything until the train conductor was shaking me awake, screaming at me: *Hurry up, you're going to miss your connection.*

I had no idea where we were. I just got up and ran to the train across the track. I desperately wanted to get a hit, but I knew it was too dangerous. I figured I could make it another couple of hours to Albany.

Alannah must have been enmeshed in her own problems, or needed a break so badly that she didn't care; I must have looked pretty scary, but she didn't seem to notice. Eamon didn't care at all. The fact that I was twenty pounds thinner didn't bother him in the least. He just kept gleefully repeating, *Mom, Jim Hart's here. Jim Hart's here.*

Of course, Jim Hart was barely there. Alannah had a spare car for me to use, and as soon as I could get away from the house with Eamon, I pulled over, dug out a pipe, placed a large piece of rock on the screen and inhaled deeply. As I exhaled the huge yellow cloud into the car, Eamon pantomimed my actions of inhaling and blowing out the smoke. Then he said, *Cigarettes.*

When the effects of the crack took over, I began to believe I might survive the weekend. The first thing I needed was a room. I drove carefully down the hill into downtown Troy. Just as we passed RPI, Eamon said, *Carly Simon.* He pointed toward the CD player and said, *Carly Simon play. Jim Hart, play it.* I knew he wanted me to turn on the CD player, which probably had a Carly Simon disc already in it.

In his boy soprano, he would sing the lyrics over and over until I was so sick of Carly that I would beg him to listen to something else. Sometimes, I think, when he felt particularly insecure, he wanted Carly. Needless to say, I did not want to hear Carly on this day, but he wouldn't relent. It was particularly bizarre to hear him sing some of her racier lyrics like *All I want is you, and the sexy hurricane that we share.* Carly and I hadn't shared a sexy hurricane in some time, and my guilt over my behavior was all-consuming. I got us to the Holiday Inn in downtown Troy as soon as I could. I would be able to smoke all I wanted without interruption. I was careful with my intake. I didn't want to endanger my ability to watch him. It was a thin line I was trying to walk: being just the right kind of high in order to watch a severely handicapped boy. Somehow I got through the next couple of days, and once again, no one seemed to notice.

Eamon and I spent the weekend in this tattered Holiday Inn in downtown Troy, New York, a city I knew all too well. Most of his time was spent spinning tops, each time gleefully yelling, *Look what I did.* All I remember is lighting the crack pipe about every half-hour or so to get enough drug to let me watch most of "March Madness" on TV. Luckily, he didn't have a seizure while we were there. I called Carly a couple of times during my stay, and each time she seemed preoccupied with other things, though she did sing for Eamon. Her voice from afar may have been the only security he felt that weekend, and he beamed when she started to sing to him. Often when he felt himself slipping into some trouble at school, or if he felt frightened at a new situation, he would just say, *Carly Simon*. Somehow he knew that invoking her name would get him out of trouble. I think I felt very much the same way. In spite of crack, I would always have Carly.

Proving that I could be an equally irresponsible step-parent as parent, in February of 2004, I traveled to South East Asia with Sally and her new husband Dean. Carly somehow thought this journey to a foreign and exotic world might give me a place to breathe and gain new perspective: a sort of pilgrimage or spiritual search. In spite of all my drugging over the past few years, I hadn't drunk any alcohol. I crossed that barrier as I sat at the bar at Kennedy Airport and ordered my first drink in twenty-two years. I remember holding the sparkling tumbler up in the air and capturing a rising plane in the reflection of the glass. I was up and flying once again.

My behavior for nearly two months would be a strange recipe for any spiritual search. There was my excessive daily drugging and drinking. My behavior reflected the complete opposite of any intention to save my marriage. In so many ways, I was completely out of control. Through it all, I kept writing to Carly about how we might be able to work things out together.

Dearest,

Another sunset swirls down around us. It releases the day here in a way that it does not in any other place I have ever been. It doesn't happen; it appears more like a vision, something shimmering across the Mekong. . . .

It is hard to write this without crying, but it is your soul the world needs and it is your endless, loving stretch that I so long to have around me. I feel I have destroyed my life with you and don't know how to get it back. And yet I feel this sort of thought and feeling entraps you in a place you shouldn't have to be, that you deserve so much better than I have been able to give. . . .

I guess somehow I must let you go, for that is constantly the message that I get from you, and I just can't find my way to that place. I'm sorry, I'm so sorry; somehow I can't find a way to stop carrying you around. It is unfair of me to tell you this stuff, but I feel so without my compass so without my north Carly star.

I cry today and thank you in the approaching sunset that I have been here and have witnessed your love now setting so beautifully, and as with the sun, I don't know how to bring even one fucking ray back, but perhaps there will be new days for us. I will let you know from this part of the struggling world. . . .

Upon my return, she would learn the true story, and it would break her heart. I think we both knew that our life together was coming to a close; we just didn't know how to shut the various doors.

What do you mean? Jake says it's a book party—that Bill Kennedy is giving you a book party.

I was squeezing the phone as hard as I could. She had insisted throughout the summer that we were going to publish a book of my poetry. I think it was part of her last efforts to make us work, or perhaps a parting gift if we couldn't. She was also looking at apartments to buy in New York, so that we could be together in a way we hadn't in a long time. I was once again on a train from New York to Albany, and the light seemed to be bleeding through me.

It's just a small party.

Somehow, I became convinced she wouldn't find out about it. I told her I was going to see Eamon for the weekend, but Jake Brackman had told her about it because he was going to attend. I don't know how I thought she *wouldn't* find out. It was some very deep and odd part of my denial.

Jake says the whole Albany crowd will be there.

Well, I guess so.

How could you do this to me?

I was sure you wouldn't want to come.

Now she was screaming at me.

How could you not invite me? I am your wife. I published the book! How could you not have invited me?

I never thought you would come.

It was true; only once in all these years had she come to Albany with me, and that was just after we had first met. I did think she would find an excuse not to make the trip from the Vineyard, but the real reason was that I wanted to be able to drink. I would have to pretend to be sober and behave like a dutiful husband if she came; I just didn't feel like it.

She had not only published it, but it had been her idea: she designed it, took the picture, pretty much wrote the introduction, and helped me choose the poems. It was a last-ditch effort by her to bring us somehow closer together and recognize my talents as a writer. There was another reason I didn't want her there: I didn't want to share my night with her celebrity. I wanted this to be just mine.

A number of people read my poems that night from my newly published volume *Milding*.

I remember the last poem I read that evening, inspired by the Rubaiyat of Omar Khayyam—"The Bird is on the Wing."

I think the last lines may have captured what I truly wanted.

To know the final blessed breath alone
and chew the heart of love into its bone.

CHAPTER TWENTY-SIX

CARLY SAT NEXT TO me trembling in the darkness. I thought she might
not make it this time, that this might be the crisis from which she wouldn't
return. I had brought her to the Easter Vigil service at St. Luke's because
it was around the corner from our new apartment on Commerce Street in
Greenwich Village. This was Carly's final attempt to try to integrate our lives
again. We were now living in the place of her early childhood.

The Easter Vigil service is about hope and the miracle of the Resurrection. The "new fire" was lit in the vestibule, and the Episcopal priest intoned
the *Lumen Christi* (*Light of Christ*) and then began to light the tapers from the
Paschal candle. He proceeded up the aisle singing. He intoned it three times
before he reached the front of the church. Slowly we emerged out of the
darkness, as all the tapers we were holding were lit.

The story of Christ's triumph over sin, death, and darkness seemed to lift
her spirits as she squeezed my hand tightly for the first time in days. So much
had happened in the last few years, but the final straw seemed to be Mindy's
death. Mindy Jostyn was Jake's wife and Carly's musical director and close
friend. It wasn't just that Mindy had died so young and tragically, but from
Carly's perspective, everyone seemed to be handling it too well. No one
seemed to be in a state of deep, unremitting grief that Carly found herself in.
It just was too much for her to withstand.

My father died just a few days after Mindy, so it was an odd season of
mourning. His funeral mass was at St. Ignatius Church in Long Beach, and
the church choir I had been a member of since boyhood had agreed to sing

for the service, as long as I sang with them. Carly was being driven in a limo to the church, and she was late and lost. She didn't think she could make it because of her anxiety. I knew she wanted me to let her off the hook, to tell her it wasn't that important to me, but that would not have been the truth. I desperately needed her to be with me. We had spent little time with my family during our marriage, and I needed her now, and I told her so.

A veil had come down, so that when she met my family, whom she actually liked, she could barely speak to them. She arrived at the choir loft with our brown poodle Molly in her arms. The choir director Dr. Nicholson immediately shouted, *If the dog can sing, he stays.* I thought my father would have loved this at his funeral. He and my mother had a poodle for many years.

They pointed Carly toward the alto section and handed her a piece of music. She said, *I can't read music.* "Peachie," one of the mainstays of the alto section since I joined as a kid, and also the local librarian, pointed to the music as though she were dealing with a child in the children's section of the library and gruffly said, *Of course you can, the notes go up, and the notes go down—sing.* Carly obeyed and added her voice to the choir.

I was so worried; she seemed almost comatose as my family gathered to say hello. We needed to do something as soon as possible. I completed my father's burial service at the cemetery, which was out on the eastern tip of Long Island. The next day, we decided that Carly needed medical attention. We drove through a rainstorm to Boston to see a team of specialists. They adjusted her medications and recommended a long rest. The onslaught of recent truths and the cascade of deaths were more than she could handle. I tried hard to take care of her. In some important ways, I was the helper and comforter, and in other ways I was the very agent of her afflictions. I was still blind to it. I hadn't yet made the connection that I was central in her unbearable sorrow.

T W E N T Y - S E V E N

SNOWFLAKES FELL AROUND ME: specs of white in the lengthening afternoon shadows. The rush of uptown traffic slowed, and the harsh sounds of the pavement softened. The snow wrapped the afternoon in a sullen white bunting, and I was protecting myself with large amounts of John Jameson and Sons.

Standing outside the White Horse Tavern, just off Hudson on West 11th, I realized my marriage had ended. I stared across at Annie Leibovitz's apartment, just steps away from a well-known Village celeb restaurant called The Spotted Pig.

No, I'm spending Christmas with Richard.

There are no gratuitous absolutes, yet it struck me that this might mean it was over. Carly had been carrying on an affair with Richard since the middle of June. For months, our phone calls had included some form of the same exchange.

We have to do it!

I can't, let's talk about this tomorrow.

Okay, tomorrow.

The same conversation would take place the next day. We kept switching roles. We never were both ready at the same time, but over the last few weeks, Carly had engaged a lawyer and the initial drafts of the documents were finally being prepared.

Oh sweetheart, it's not like with you. I will never feel that way with him.

But you love him.

Yes, of course, but in a different way.

What kind of different way?

Oh baby, I don't know, it's just different. You should understand. You always said that you could love two people at the same time. I never thought I could, but here I am.

So you love him?

Yes, in some way.

She had already told me the way. She had come alive with him physically, something she thought she would never feel again. She loved him in that way that changed everything: the same way I had touched her on that train ride all those years ago. I started to cry, as I understood it once again in the falling snow. I finished a cigarette, pulled myself together, and went back inside.

I often sat and stared at the black-and-white painting of Dylan Thomas in the back room. I sat on the exact spot, on the same barstool that he was sitting on in the painting. He had been with me when I left my first love and my God all those years ago, and here he was again.

This room was a tavern masterpiece of whimsy: little white horse heads everywhere, including the strange horse-head chandeliers over the bar. It felt as if nothing had changed. It felt the same as I remembered it the first time I stepped inside the door in 1973 with Ron Vawter. There was a different clientele back then, much more of a workingman's crowd. A Dylan Thomas fan would occasionally interrupt that ambiance. They would enter, usually stare around the room, and often ask a question like *Do you know where Dylan sat?*

After a couple of these visits, I noticed that the bartender pointed to a table in the corner the first time, and a stool at the end of the bar the next. When I pointed out his inconsistency, he explained the obvious: *How the fuck should I know? That was thirty-eight years ago.*

How the fuck should I know?

The anger and truth of it seared through me. At fifty-six years of age, I was still asking the same questions. Shouldn't I have found the answers by now? I had been to two of the best rehabs in the country. Yet Dylan stared down at this late-blooming conflicted faggot, married to a famous woman whom he still loved. I was also still the father of a severely handicapped son and unable to find a career to suit my life.

I told myself that she didn't have the right to leave me. She had the right to have an affair after twenty years of marriage, but I had the final rights as her husband after all I had been through with her. I had been there for all her challenges. I never shirked a one, I thought, not one, and this was my reward: a barstool on West 11th and Hudson Street.

It turns out that drunks don't have many rights; they mostly have excuses. I was trying to figure out how I was going to tell myself, and those around me, what had happened. I could tell them the part about meeting her. The other drunks at the bar were always asking me to tell a new drunk, a friend, or a family member the story of our meeting. After a short time, whenever a famous name would come up, my crowd of about a dozen folks turned to me to find out if I knew them, and what I thought of them. They took my judgment as gospel. Whenever these names came up in the future, they would say, *Yeah, Jim knows him; says he's a fucking asshole,* or *Jim knows him; says he's a great guy.*

After the resolve from a few more drinks, I went outside and called her again. I heard myself scream into the phone, *I don't want a fucking thing from you, just divorce me.* I hung up and returned once again to the bar and drank as long as I could into the wee hours of Sunday morning. She called me sometime early in the next week as we approached our nineteenth wedding anniversary and said: *I've decided on how this divorce will be.*

She presented a group of figures to me: a settlement that she and her people had worked out. I had no idea if it was fair or not, but I said, *Whatever you think is fair is fair. That's the way it will be. I love you, and I will never discuss this again.* We never have.

We cried together briefly, and I quickly planned a drunken and drugged holiday in the Dominican Republic. I spent the week in a stupor trying to blot out everything one more time by retreating into the darkest recesses of the Caribbean night. I was without the world I had built for the last twenty years, and on my return, I was going to be living in the darkness of a tenement apartment on West 97th Street. After all I had tried to be, I would be left alone, yet it did seem to be the only way.

The endless days of Bill Styron's suffering had ceased. He had battled bravely in so many ways against so much. As we entered St. Bartholomew's Church, the sounds of Vivaldi reverberated against the stone and intertwined with the words and glances of the mostly famous who were shuffling in and warmly greeting each other. I stood there wondering about his past and my future. It was February 2nd, 2007. Bill and I were both leaving our worlds at the same time, his with a memorial remembering the great shadows that his life and work had cast, and mine with memories of shadows surrounding everything. I remembered Bill's warning after one of our first long evenings together; he took me aside in his kitchen.

Listen to me, don't ever be a walker. Make sure you have a life of your own—no matter what it is. Just don't become a walker. It will kill you.

He couldn't have been more emphatic or certain. I had to ask him what a walker was—a man who just escorted a famous woman around town. A walker had no life of his own, and he wanted me to be sure to have my own life. Even the crackle and pop of the crack pipe seemed to be a life of my own. I think Bill Styron would have understood the nature of my pain—perhaps it was that awareness that made us so comfortable with one another from the beginning. Perhaps we knew what we shared: In my case, deep unutterable sorrows. In his, secret visions of demons yet to be unleashed, but already deeply feared. Carly and I had spent a lifetime with Bill and Rose over these past years. Little did any of us know what was in store.

Carly arrived just as the memorial started. She sat a few pews ahead of me. She seemed fragile and adrift. This was the first time we had ever been apart at a public event. We were in the midst of reviewing and signing all the divorce documents, so it was a hard time for us to be with each other. Our lives were not going to be shared today, nor any of the days ahead. I grasped that this was the start of my new, unwanted life; so much that was ours would have to be abandoned.

I wondered if Carly and I were having our views obscured by what lay ahead, or if our new lives would be something like we both vaguely imagined. It is impossible to know the way to our own endings, but Bill's memorial gave me a most surprising and simple clue about how to handle that dilemma. I listened to the thoughtful, clever, funny, and moving things said by so many of Bill's renowned friends. President Clinton claimed that reading *The Confessions of Nat Turner* influenced his decision to go into politics. Mike Nichols recalled their long nights together where they recklessly squandered time, and then with a humorous twist said that Bill had the best clothes sense because he never seemed to know what he was wearing. Peter Matthiessen said of Bill that he had a delicate and undefended sensibility, which explained why everyone sheltered him. I sat in the great expanse of St. Bart's and listened to Bill's words intertwine with the quartet now playing Mozart, and it all struck me as way too vast to lose.

Then, finally, the priest rose and stood in the middle of the sanctuary. He had been silent throughout the service. He stood baldheaded in a cinctured white alb and a plain clerical stole. The modest hesitation in his delivery emphasized the simplicity of his message: *So, I think what this afternoon has clearly reminded us is that life is short. Life is short, so be quick to be kind.*

In an unpredictable moment of kindness and clarity, I found myself a few weeks later on my way to a recovery meeting at 60th and Park Avenue. Something within me finally broke open, and I knew I was going to get sober again. When they asked for people with sobrieties under ninety days to raise their hands, I did, and sobbing like a melodramatic drunk I said, *I have one day.* In usual fashion, they applauded for a very long time, and many people who knew me from all the previous years gathered around me afterward and seemed thrilled to see me give it another try.

CHAPTER
TWENTY-EIGHT

THE WALMART PARKING LOT was a dirty gray snowscape. It was Saturday, and Eamon was having trouble staying put in the hotel room. I didn't have any tops for him to spin, so he kept pacing back and forth and asking me, *What are we going to do today?*

There wasn't any answer that would satisfy him, so I thought getting him into the car would be a good idea. He often calmed down as soon as the radio was turned on. For years, I thought he only liked top-forty songs, but I recently discovered that he was often just as happy humming along to classical music while air-conducting the orchestra. A Beethoven symphony was on the radio, and he busily began humming along and gesturing like a maestro.

In March of 2007, the Albany store was the largest Walmart in the country. I bet that fact changes every couple of hours, but the store was enormous even by their standards. It was a vast duplex crammed with every item that daily living in Middle America could possibly require. Eamon and I wandered around the store, and finally he started to say, *Hi, how ya doin'?* to everyone we passed. Some folks didn't get it, but the ones who did usually gave him a big greeting back. He wasn't that interested in their responses. Like a seasoned politician working a line, he acted as if his greeting itself had the real value. He would have to hurry on to the next voter.

Carly was now living with her new man on Martha's Vineyard, and I was trying to find one in New York. I was often stunned by this new setup, dazed whenever I thought of it.

Eamon was pulling on my arm now saying, *Let's go.* I noticed the shape he was in for the first time. His face was dirty; he wore filthy white sneakers with Velcro clasps that kept them closed. His jeans were too big; he kept pulling them up as they fell around his ass, and there was black dirt underneath his fingernails. It was difficult to keep someone like Eamon clean all the time, especially in the winter.

I didn't know where to go, so I stood staring at the miles of frozen foods before me. I was unable to move with Eamon insisting, *Let's go.* As I stared at him, I became as frozen as the rows of vegetables in the cooler. I couldn't believe that my life had come to this: Eamon and I in a huge shopping warehouse, and then blaring over the sound system came Carly's voice singing the introduction to *Coming Around Again.* Eamon started to happily sing along,

> *Baby sneezes,*
> *Mommy pleases,*
> *Daddy breezes in.*
> *So good on paper,*
> *So romantic,*
> *So bewildering.*

I just stared ahead at the rows of frozen vegetables. Then I grabbed Eamon close to me and started to sob.

I had wandered the streets of New York for the past few months trying to survive my newfound sobriety. My shrink and gay recovery group helped me embrace a new life. I would now be able to attend to Eamon in a new way. We had finally placed him in a group home. His behavior had become so unruly that Alannah was having increasing problems managing him. She had also taken a job at St. Lawrence University, which was located very near the Canadian border, so it was impossible for her to continue to care for him. Many people had told us to place him in a home, but no one had convinced us. We thought he should remain at home as long as possible. Eamon's long- and short-term needs finally shouted at us: he needed to be somewhere safe when we were gone.

As we visited the group home that first day, we were faced with another issue: The other people seemed so damaged. They all seemed to be part of a terrifying collection of truly handicapped people. One boy shook my hand and refused to let go, and when I tried to disengage, he gripped even harder, and when I tried to pull away, he made a frightening sound. Another large and hairy man sat in a lounger and moaned loudly the entire time we were there. The people who ran the group home and the staff could not have been more attentive or understanding. We had to face an admission that we had somehow avoided for all these years—that he might be that damaged too. There were so many feelings around it: mainly our guilt at abandoning our child to strangers.

Somehow, the more we saw him in this setting, the more we wanted him back. I thought I might be able to figure out a new arrangement whereby I could care for him in a better way. I had left the whirligigs of fame and privilege, and perhaps now I could attend to my first and most important responsibility.

I also found myself in a completely new world. From my life as an assumed heterosexual, I had jumped into an almost completely gay world, and it lacked so much of the allure and texture of the life I was leaving. I often felt myself lost within the confines of 97th Street. The slanting gray light seemed laden with fear and trembling, like the frightening color of a storm on the North Atlantic. I was in completely uncharted waters. All I really knew was that I had to stay sober—there were many days I dragged myself through, but I had to stay sober for Eamon, if nothing else. I also actually owed everyone some sort of explanation, and if I didn't stay sober, I feared I would never find one.

I enter my apartment and the room is always waiting. I notice that the blinds are still filthy, coated with the smoke of crack and cigarettes. Now I am without drugs, and the pull of the anticipated high is absent. At the age of fifty-seven, I am going to have to face it all at last. How could I stay sober? I didn't know how, but I would just have to do what they told me and hope for the best. Hope that in some way, I might break open and live my life, but it didn't seem possible. Carly told me that one member of our extended family had said, *Be prepared, he might kill himself.*

The voice of my father grew larger. I so wished he was still around to hold me and remind me, once again, that I needed to be healed by the love of strangers. I wondered, if he were still alive, how he would have processed the gay news about his son.

I suspect he would have had a similar response to Eamon's on a snowy midwinter's day in January of the prior year. I had gone to see Eamon for a few days. Along with his sister Siobhan, a classmate from the Emma Willard School, and Alannah, we found ourselves watching *Brokeback Mountain* in a packed theatre in Albany. The entire audience sat breathless as Heath Ledger began to violently mount Jake Gyllenhaal for the first time. You could almost hear the theatre gasp and then go silent. Inside the silence of the auditorium,

Eamon's loud, high-pitched voice shouted the unasked question on everyone's mind: *Where's the girl?* The audience roared with laughter. I had the
same question on my mind. For the first time in over thirty years, I lived
every day not so much in the presence of men, but rather in the absence of
women, so Eamon's question loomed large: *Where's the girl?*

Every cripple has his own way of dancing, was one of my father's favorite say-
ings, and now I would have to learn how to be without a woman by my side.
There were so many things to know, and I knew so little in many ways.

I listened harder than I ever had before. I went to gay recovery meetings daily. I listened to story after story of childhood sexual abuse, continual
admissions of low self-esteem from bullying and internalized homophobia,
and the exciting adventures of the wild drug-and-sex world of New York
gay life. I was in the middle of a search, one of many broken gay men, each
trying to find himself anew. And in the real time of my life, it was confirmed
again: a power greater than myself would be necessary to restore me to sanity.
It was still the same, the very same. The journey looked and sounded a bit
different, but the essential ingredients really didn't change. I was once again
being forced to accept a new and surprising life as quickly as I could. I knew
it would be the only way.

It was a brisk, early November night when I opened the door to a nearby
French restaurant, Alouette (The Lark.) I was on the first blind date of my
life, and there waiting at the bar for me was a man named Robert with a
sweet and real smile, a flash of blue eyes, and the sexiest head of white curly
hair. Something within me burst a little for him, something that had been
long contained and repressed. In the beauty of his kind and luminescent eyes,
there seemed to be a light that shined just for me. I could feel that, for the
first time ever, I was going to be able to reach across to him in a way that I
had yearned to do from the very beginning, and that he would return my
embrace. I was falling in love at the moment with something that I had so
secretly feared all these years, and the deepest piece of my own deception
melted away from me forever. Nothing so startling—I had to fall in love to
finally face this part of myself, *so romantic, so bewildering.*

A little more than a month or so later on Christmas day, Robert had
the day off from his usual work with drug addicts. He was, of all things, an
addiction specialist. We sat in a local well-named diner, The Metro, to have
a late breakfast. My cell phone rang and I recognized Alannah's number,
and as I answered, I heard screaming and crying. I could also hear Eamon

cursing abusively in the background. He was having a meltdown on Christmas day, and Alannah couldn't bear the fact that the boy she had loved so dearly had now entered a new phase of wild abuse. She kept hanging up. She was so hysterical that she couldn't continue her conversation with me. I looked across from Robert and sighed.

I'm so sorry, I know this is your only day off, but I have to go to Albany now. Eamon is in rough shape. I have to help.

Robert looked stunned, and I assumed that he was angry about having our Christmas plans disrupted.

I'm so sorry. I have to go right away.

Then he said something that I was completely unprepared for.

What do you mean? I'm not going with you?

What?

I couldn't speak. My voice was caught in my throat. I began to softly cry.

I'm sorry. No one has ever gone with me.

Three hours later, Eamon, Robert, and I were in our car happily singing Christmas carols all the way back to New York. Eamon spent Christmas week with me spinning his tops, overeating pasta, singing along to song after song, and constantly laughing and smiling without ever leaving a five-foot radius in my living room. Every couple of hours or so, he would say *Carly Simon*, my cue to play yet another Carly medley. He would clap his hands with delight as her voice began. Eamon didn't know about such things as divorce and separation, and Carly would always be his stepmother. Nothing could ever change the feeling he had when her deep alto tone washed over him and called to some joyous and secret place within him.

CHAPTER
TWENTY-NINE

IT WAS ALANNAH'S NIECE on the phone. She was sobbing as she tried to tell me, and then, unable to say it any other way, she just blurted out, *Eamon's dead.*

I stared at the floor as the early morning light spread across the living room. I stared at the cable box under the television—it was 7:28 on Sunday, September 27th, 2009. When I had picked up the phone, I knew it would not be good news at this time of the morning, but not this.

Finally, I got Alannah on the phone. She was sobbing so intensely that she couldn't really speak.

I'll be there as soon as I can.

The next few days were to contain many surprising moments: Eamon's two school bus drivers turning away from the casket with tears streaming down their young faces; Eamon's brothers Chris and Shane taking care of all details; Sally Taylor making it to the funeral mass just as it was about to begin, looping her arm around my waist and leaning her head on my shoulder; and Carly arriving at the beginning of the wake, and frantically trying to figure out how to say the rosary as she knelt beside me, not as a star or ex-wife, but as my dearest friend and my son's stepmother. I knelt between Carly and Alannah, and the prayer I had said so many times since childhood had a new meaning: *Blessed art thou among women.* Our various romances had created the world that surrounded him at the end. I only wished Carly could sing "My Romance" to him one last time and raise him from this sleep just as the song had done so long ago.

He had just been with my boyfriend Robert and me the weekend before. He had lost some weight, but I thought it was a sign of health. We will never know. He couldn't seem to get enough of us. He was up early on that Sunday morning between the two beds in a motel in Williamstown, Massachusetts. As I awoke, he spun his two tops at once and softly said with a tone of certainty, *I did it. Look, Dad, I did it.*

On the drive upstate, I was mostly on the phone talking to everyone to let them know. I had driven from New York to Albany so many times that I knew every hill, valley, and straightaway. I could predict the vistas by the sound of the road and the slant of light. I barely had to look. I just stared out into space.

Alannah's mother wanted an open casket in the old Irish tradition. I would never fight her over it; she had been far too great with Eamon to deny her. I imagined Eamon in the casket: I knew when I touched his face, it would feel like cement. I remembered my first body way back when I was seven years old. Then there was Jim. Father Damascene took me to see him the night before the public wake for the school. He was in his black cassock. His face was a bit bloated, but what struck me was a pair of black-corduroy slippers. They looked so elegant on him. He wasn't yet in the coffin. He was on a marble ledge with his arms folded over his chest in his cassock and black slippers. I would have loved a pair of black slippers on Eamon. How crazy; he was going to be cremated. What difference would it make?

I kept thinking about Eamon's younger sister Siobhan and how she would handle it. She had been so close to her brother, and together with Alannah's mother and sister, she had seen him through all these years. And how would Alannah ever deal with this? She had sacrificed her entire life for him. She had thrown herself under him for his survival. He had died just a few feet from her in the next bedroom, and there was nothing she could do. She had saved him so many times, and finally he slipped away from her. She kept talking about how she had made a deal with God: that she would take care of him no matter what, as long as He didn't take him away from her.

We held each other for a long time and sobbed, and then finally realized we had to get on with it. Father Juniper had died less than two weeks before, and my mother had just been admitted to the hospital on the day of Eamon's burial. She would die just a month later, but as I stood in the odd and overwhelming warmth of the funeral home, I remembered the wonderful lilt of her laughter. I could feel the warmth of her stretching all the way back to

Kentucky Street. Something about her permeated the event, and as I looked out at the church the next morning, I could feel her there. I could hear her singing "Young at Heart" in her bare feet all those years ago.

The willow stood on the opposite bank of the river; its leaves still shaded the place where Jim had fallen. A soft breeze blew through its branches. It had been more than forty-four years since that brutal night. I had just left the June 2010 reunion for the class of 1968.

I stared into the water at the spot where he had fallen. There was no one around, so I stripped off my shorts and t-shirt and waded into the water. The coldness reminded me of our nighttime swims as students. This was the spot where the main tributary of Queen Catherine's Creek joined the Seneca Canal. The depth was over my head by a couple of feet. I dove down and touched the bottom, hoping to put my hand on the exact spot where his body was all those years ago.

I was freezing, but I didn't want to get out. I wanted to be with him now again, somehow, under this same willow. I finally climbed out, dried myself off with my t-shirt and sat beside the creek, and I felt the memories of those days flooding through me. It felt as if the river itself were carrying each image in it: buttoning my cassock for the first time; seeing myself as a priest, blessing, forgiving, and healing everyone I met. Then I heard the sound of men and boys singing the "Kyrie Eleison" from the Missa De Angelis.

There were Jim and I wrestling on one of the beds in his dormitory, and then standing next to each other on the stage with our singing group "The Chancellors," smiling as we hit the right notes and harmonized on the Beach Boys' hit "In My Room."

The breeze subsided and the sun beat down, warming me after my swim. I thought of the night Jim appeared to me after his death. As I stared out at the water, I began to sob.

I glanced at the water one last time, and I heard Carly's voice.
We, the great and small
Stand on a star and blaze a trail of desire . . .
Let the river run.

I thought about my desires from the very beginning until this moment. I tried to find some meaning, a way to frame it all. I would need the providence of things outside myself, to reach out again and be near the strum of another soul. All my loves were one on this June day, and perhaps for the first time, I could feel the dimensions of my grief, that the sorrows of my life were way too much for me, or perhaps for anyone. And yet, feeling them all together somehow made it easier, as though the voices of each one were comforting the other.

I got back into the rental car and drove up the west side of Seneca Lake. The afternoon sun sparkled over the water, and the lakeside vineyards dazzled in reflection. I drove in a trance induced by a sure feeling that no one else would ever possess all of this. It was a powerful and yet kindly light, and I sighed at the beauty of my way north.

ACKNOWLEDGMENTS

———————◆———————

I'd like to thank:

Alannah Fitzgerald and Carly Simon.

Larry and Betty Hart—the original storytellers.

Larry (Danny) and Marie—my brother and sister. For living this story with wit, warmth and understanding.

Ben, Sally, Chris, Shane, and Siobhan—my other kind and generous children.

Traci Kachidurian, Robert Weeden—for the gift of first love.

Ellen Boyle: No words—just endless gratitude.

Peter and Joyce Parcher—for their friendship, support and guidance.

Honor Moore—for her generosity, guidance and friendship.

The Graymoor Friars, all my St. John's Brothers, and the Royer Family.

Joe and Vera Gagen for the hearth of the family we choose. Barry and Claire Callaghan, Bill and Dana Kennedy, Bill and Jeanette Herrick, Tom Smith and Barbara Weiner and the entire Albany "Hard Core." "You know who you are."

Henry Shapiro and Marijo Newman—my friends and companions at daybreak.

Mike Nichols, Ned Slattery, and Father Juniper Alwell—for their wit, tenderness and love.

To the gifted writers and readers who contributed their time and talent: Honor Moore, Victoria Redel, William Kennedy, Edna O'Brien, Edmundo Desnoes, Felicia Rosshandler, Christopher Kennedy Lawford,

Carl Bernstein, James Hatch, Henry Shapiro, Joseph Gagen, Barry Callaghan, Judy Collins, Marianna Vieira, and Sheila Weller.

My editors—Lorna Owen, Adam Korn, and Bonnie Kelsey

For my writer's group, especially Sue Mellins, Joanne Lyman, Anne Bayer and Felicia Rosshandler.

Exile Quarterly—for its support to me and so many writers.

Peter Simon—for his generosity and talent.

The team at Cleis Press—Jarred Weisfield, Megan Kilduff, Stephanie Lippitt, Josephine Mellon, and Emi Battaglia.

Kevin O'Connor—my tireless, talented and generous agent.

Jacob Brackman—the essence of a pal.

Melissa Bellinelli Tereshchuk—for her stunning friendship to the end.

George Finegan, Roy Mitchell, Web Francis, Frank Mauser—for what they so freely gave.

Lambda—for all the mystical Wednesday and Saturday nights.